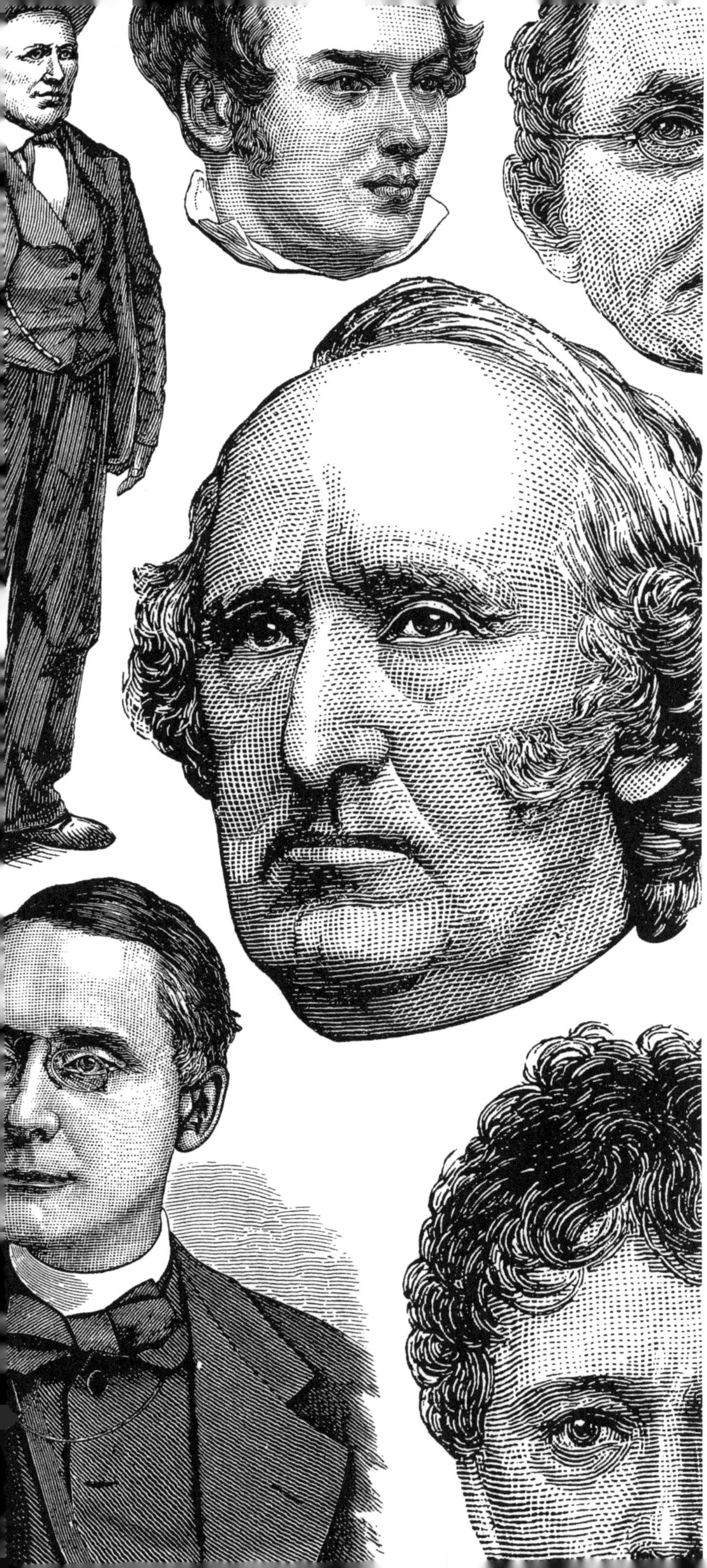

PORTRAITS OF MEN

AN IMAGE ARCHIVE FOR
ARTISTS *And* DESIGNERS

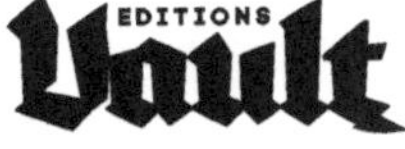

INTRODUCTION

Men: A Pictorial Archive for Artists and Designers by Vault Editions is a remarkable exploration of 19th-century engravings, a treasure trove of inspiration for artists and designers alike. This meticulously curated artist reference book opens the door to a world of captivating characters and expressions. It's an essential resource for those seeking to infuse their creative projects with timeless character. Within the pages of this archive, you'll find a rich collection of images that capture the essence of masculinity through the centuries, allowing you to delve into the past and draw inspiration from an array of striking and enigmatic figures. Whether you're a fine artist aiming to imbue your creations with a rich sense of historical authenticity, a graphic designer on the hunt for distinctive figures to elevate your designs, a collage artist eager to craft surreal and whimsically absurd imagery, or a tattoo artist in need of the perfect reference material for a gentlemen tattoo, this book stands as your indispensable resource.

Dive into this exceptional collection, and let the engravings within *Men: A Pictorial Archive for Artists and Designers* spark your imagination, enrich your artistic endeavours, and transport your work into a world of timeless allure.

Disclaimer:

Vault Editions Ltd. believes that the images in this book are no longer protected by copyright and are in the public domain after taking reasonable steps to determine their copyright status. However, please note that Vault Editions Ltd. cannot guarantee that your use of the images will not infringe the rights of third parties. It is your responsibility to conduct your own analysis and satisfy any copyright or other conditions for your proposed use of the images.

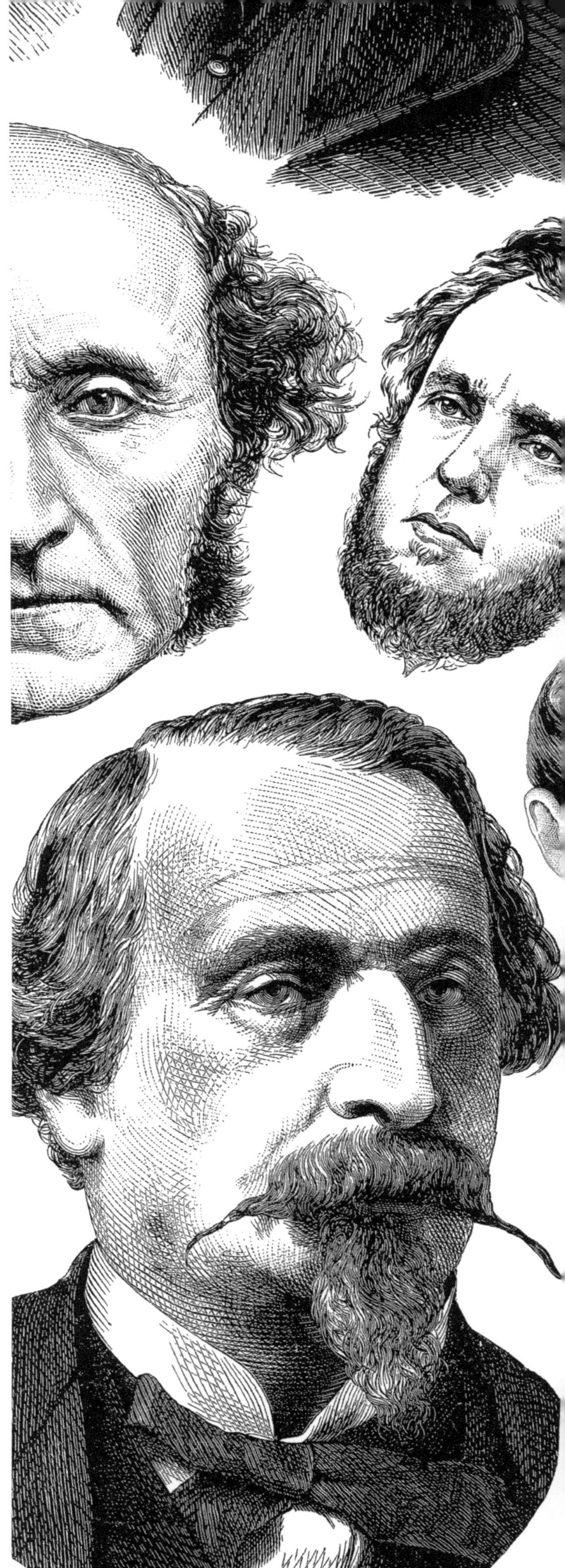

DISCLAIMER

In *Men: A Pictorial Archive for Artists and Designers*, it is essential to acknowledge the historical realities of the 18th and 19th centuries when these images were created. During that era, racial biases were prevalent, leading to a significant lack of portraits and representations of ethnic minorities. The absence of such representation within this book does not stem from a curatorial decision made by the publisher; rather, it is a stark reflection of the biases that prevailed during that time. We, the publisher, would like to underscore that the absence of ethnic minority representation in this book is a direct consequence of the historical context and should not be construed as a reflection of our contemporary values or intentions.

This book contains images of historical figures. We, the publisher, want to underscore and emphasise that we do not endorse the past actions or ideologies of these figures. The purpose of this book is solely to provide artists and designers with a varied resource of male figures, expressions and poses for creative inspiration.

DOWNLOAD YOUR FILES

Downloading your files is simple. To access your digital files, please go to the last page of this book and follow the instructions.

For technical assistance, please email:
info@vaulteditions.com

Bibliographical Note

This book is a new work created by Vault Editions Ltd.

ISBN: 978-1-922966-24-7

MEN: AN IMAGE ARCHIVE

VAULT EDITIONS

01

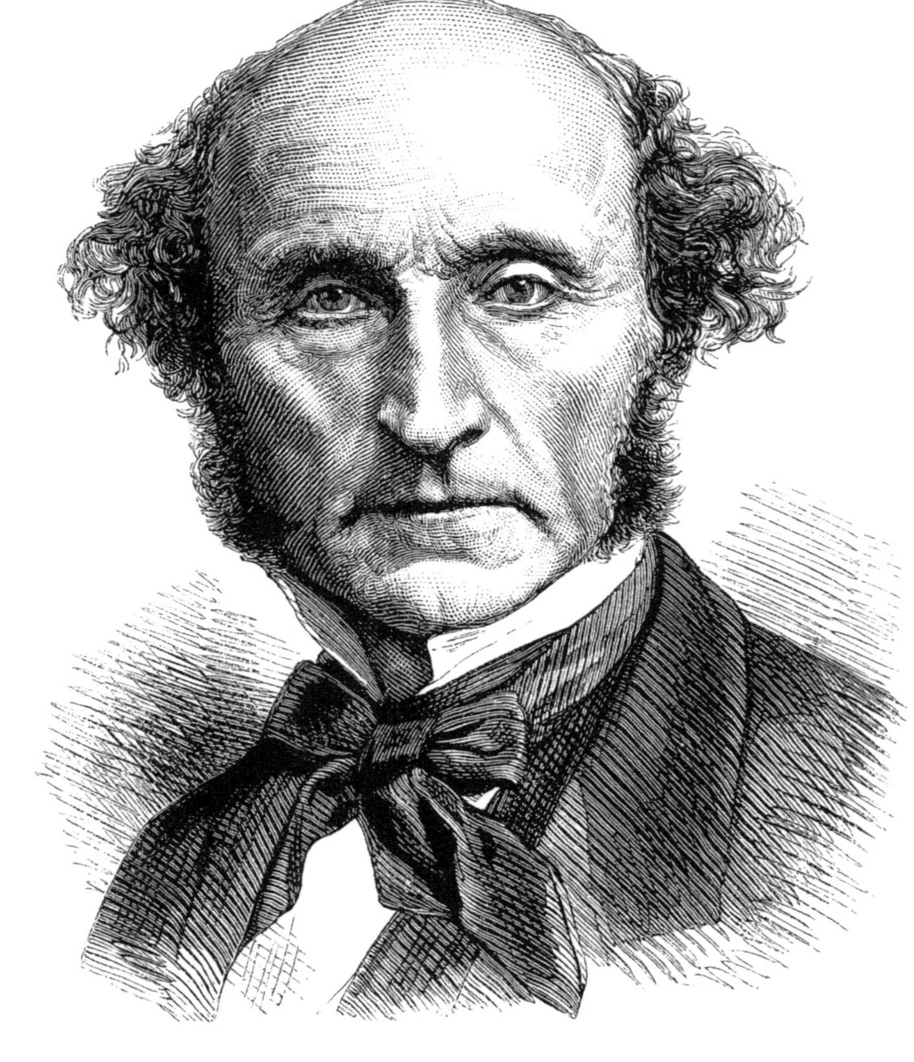

02   03

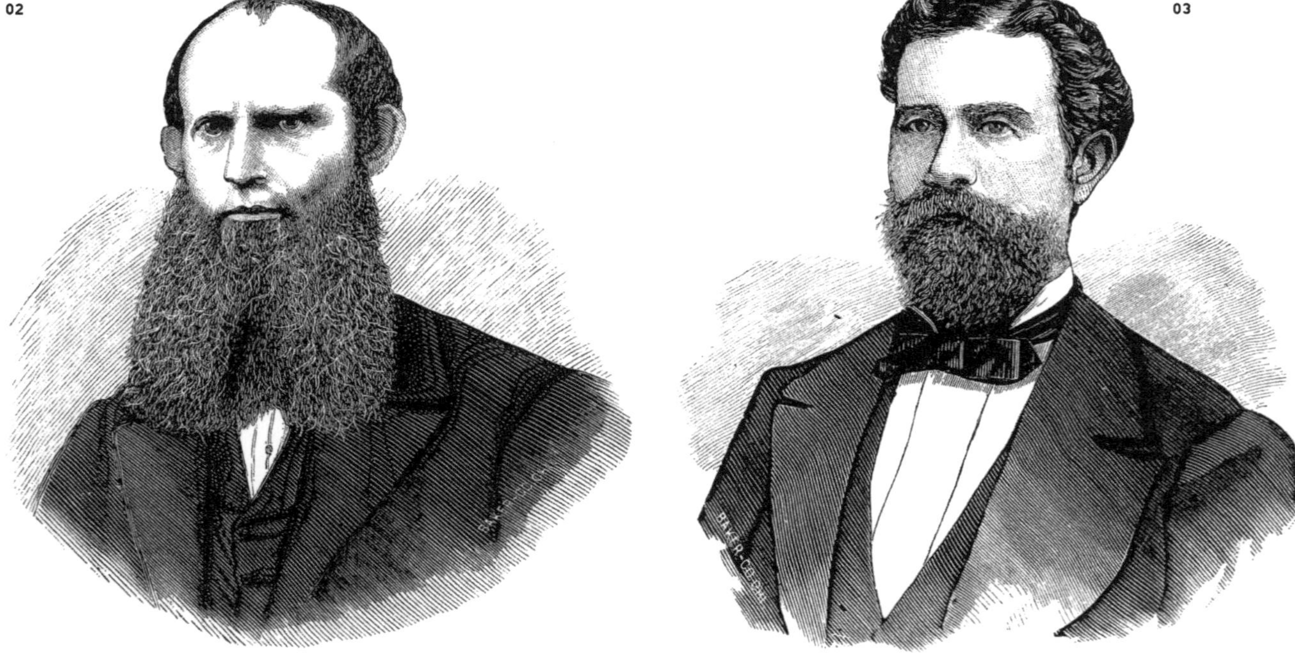

04

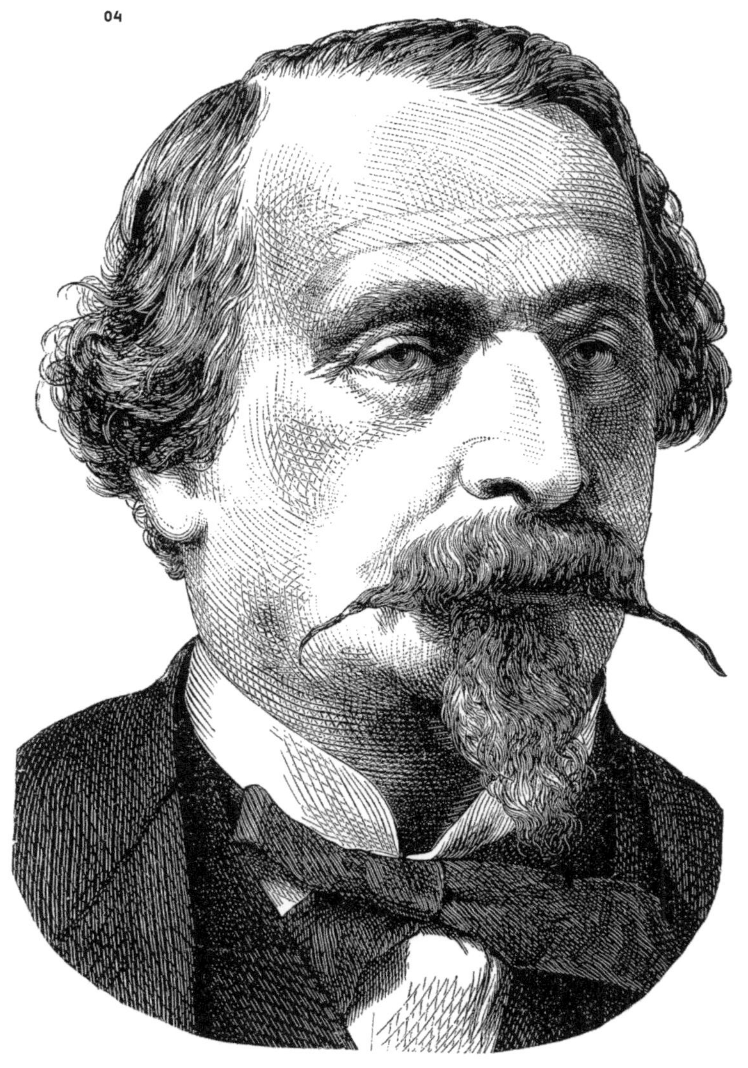

05 06

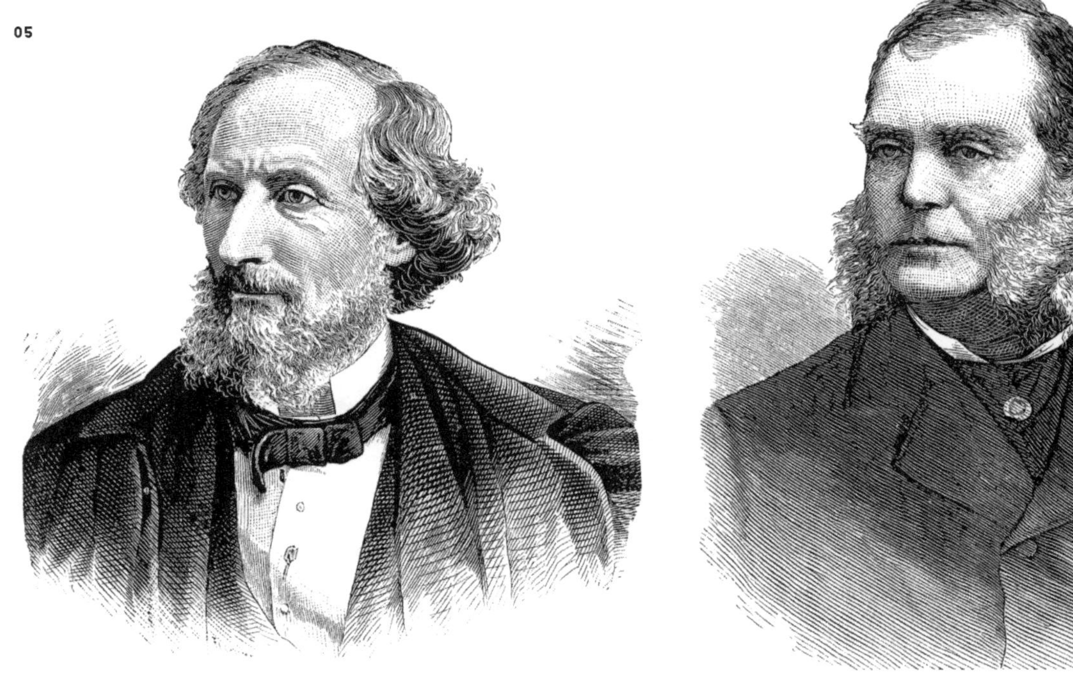

07

08

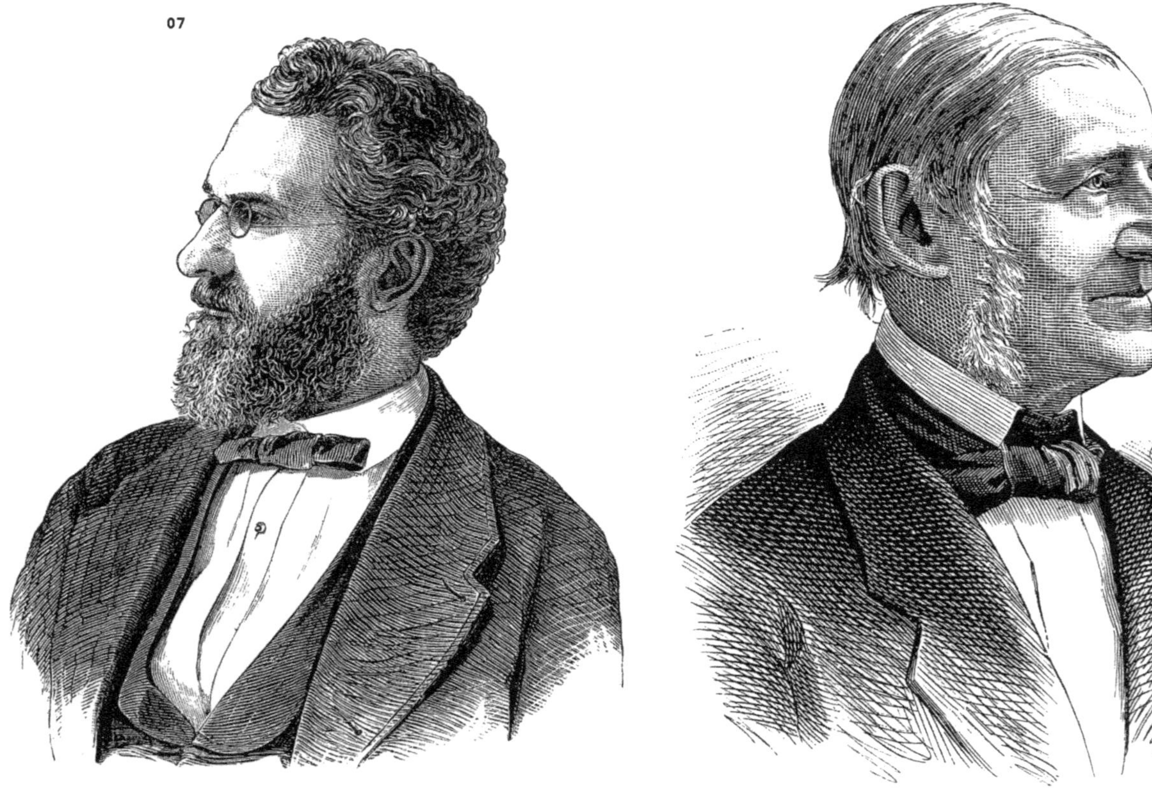

MEN

09

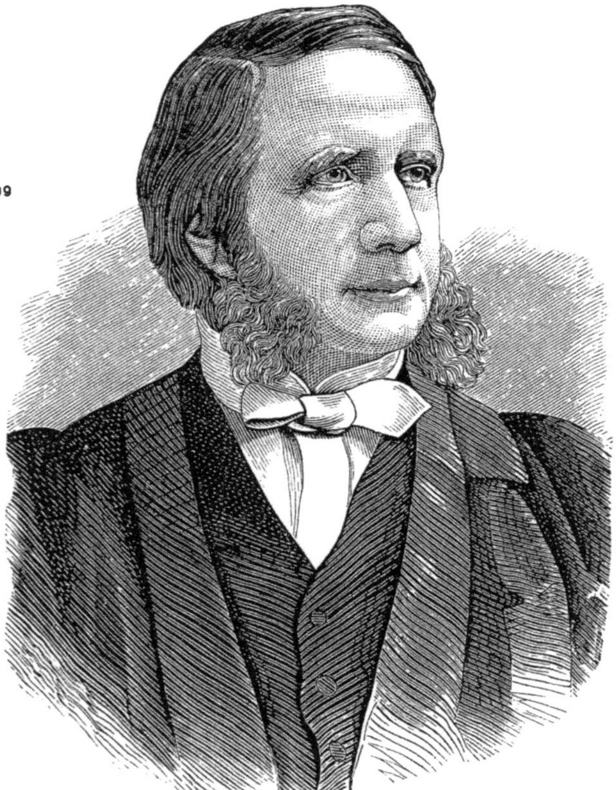

10

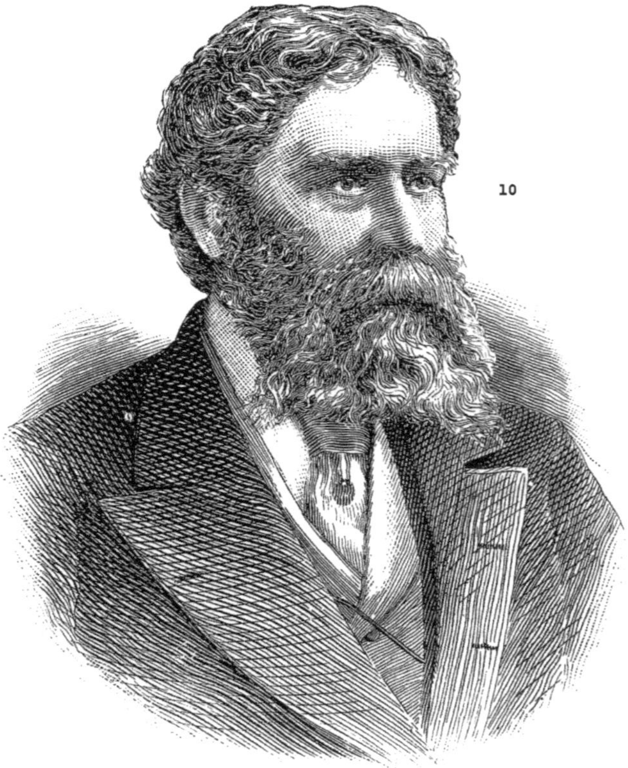

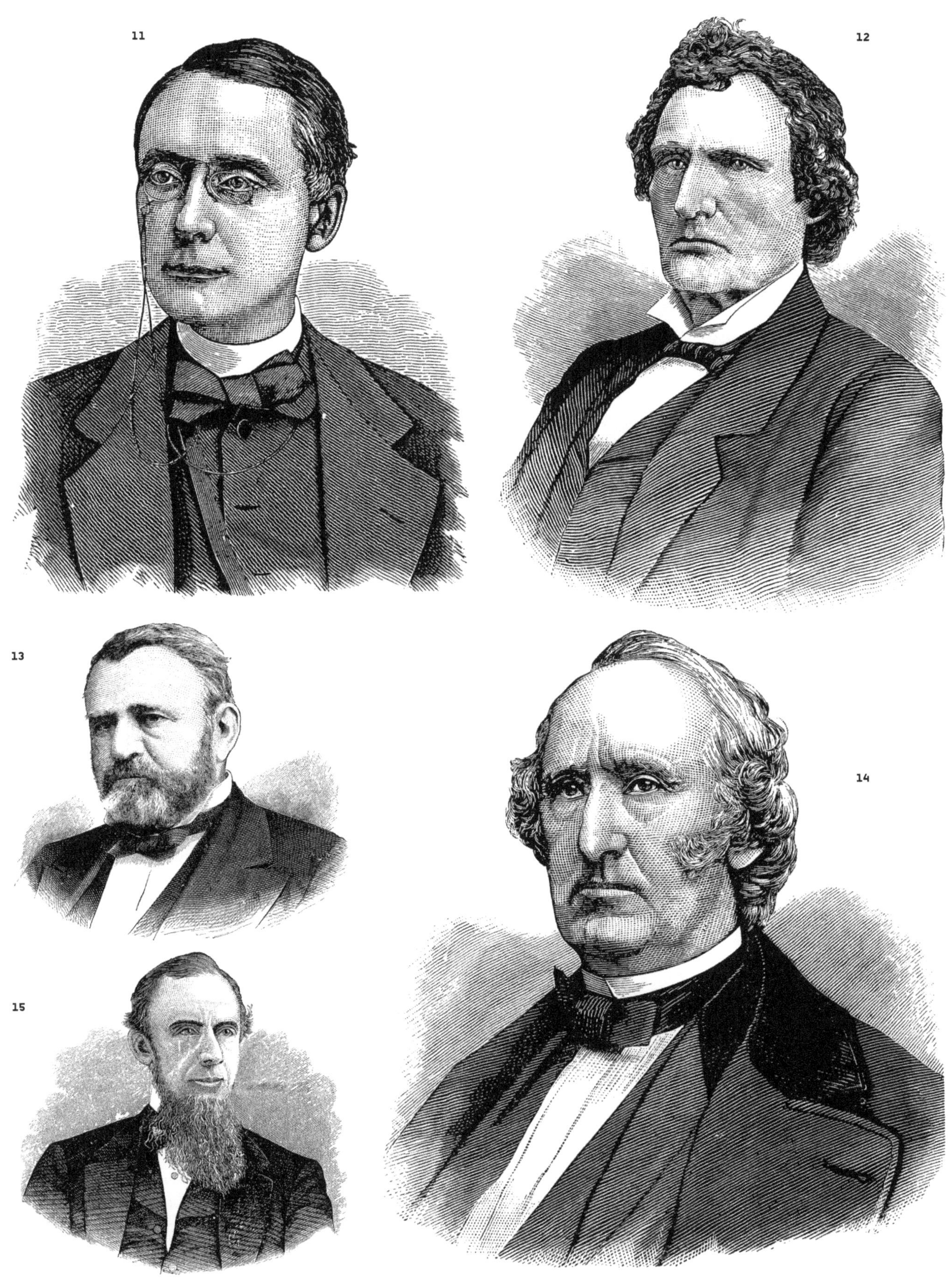
11
12
13
14
15
MEN

16

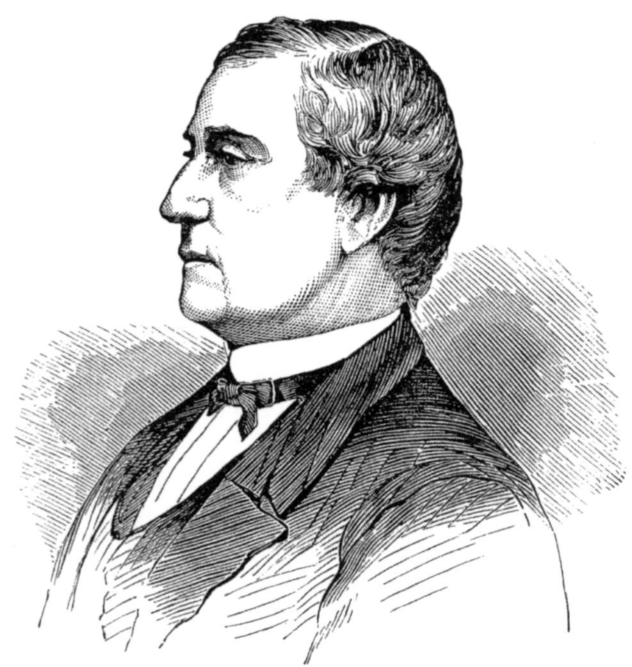

17

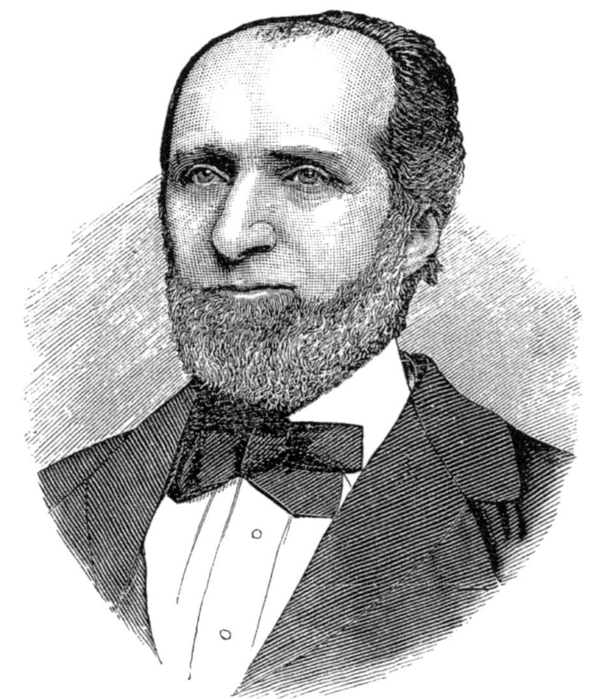

MEN

18

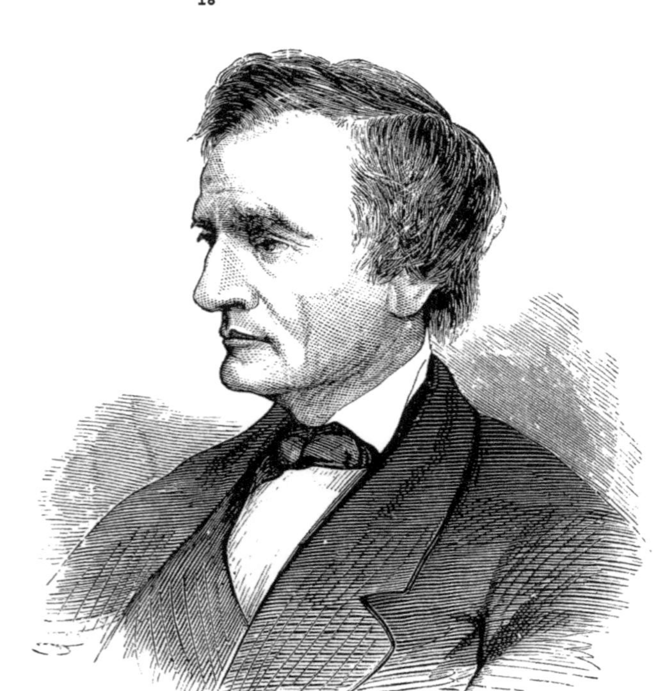

19

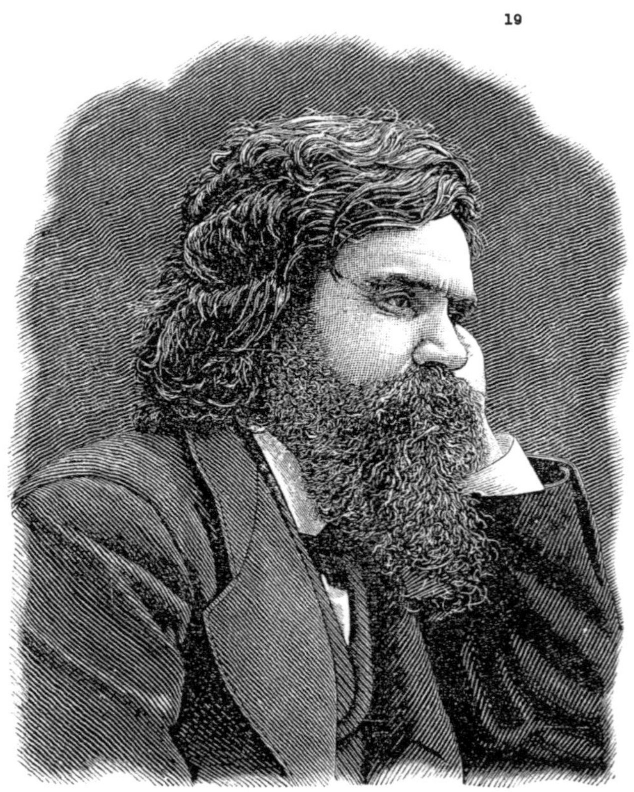

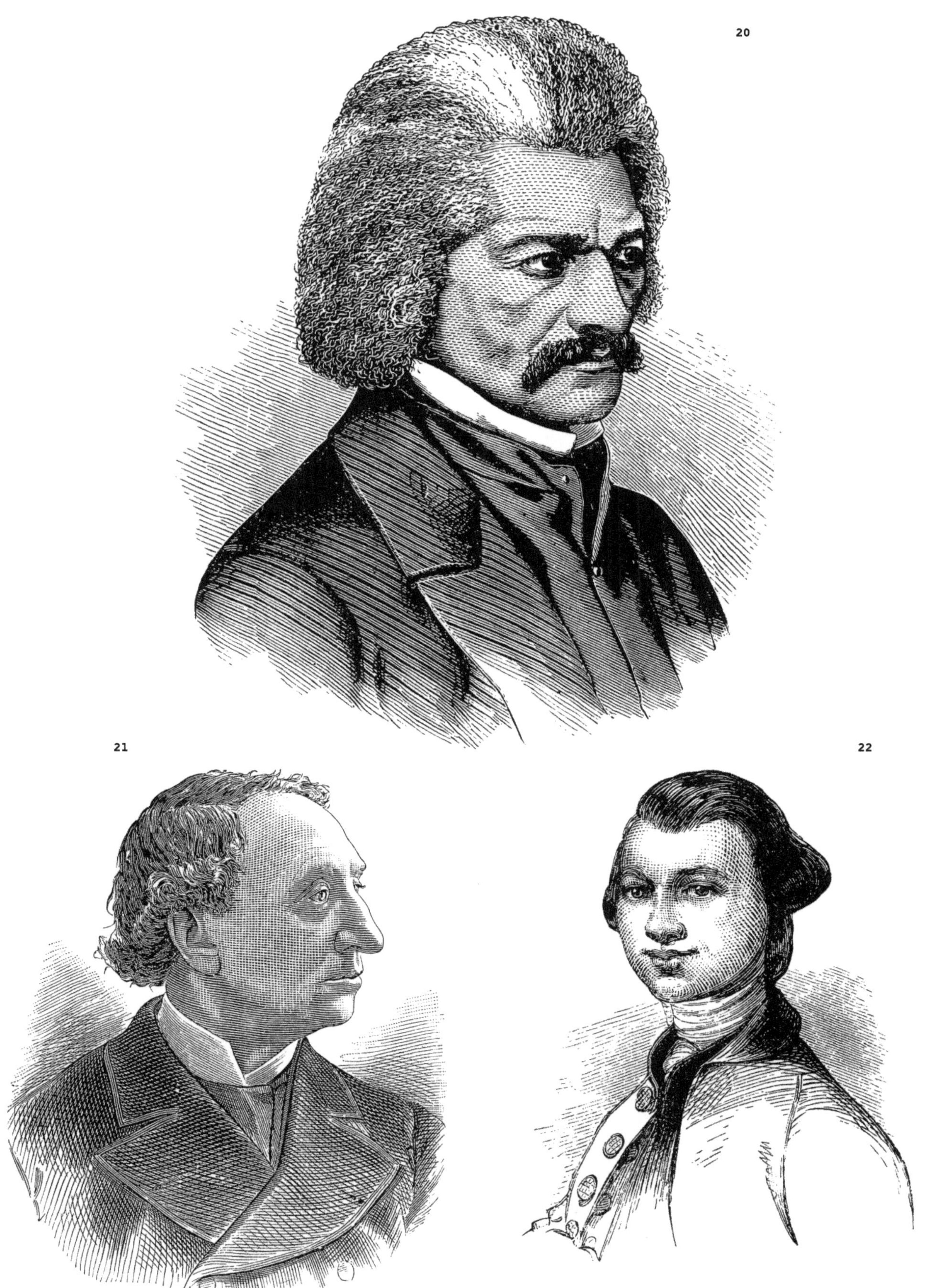
20
21
22
MEN

23

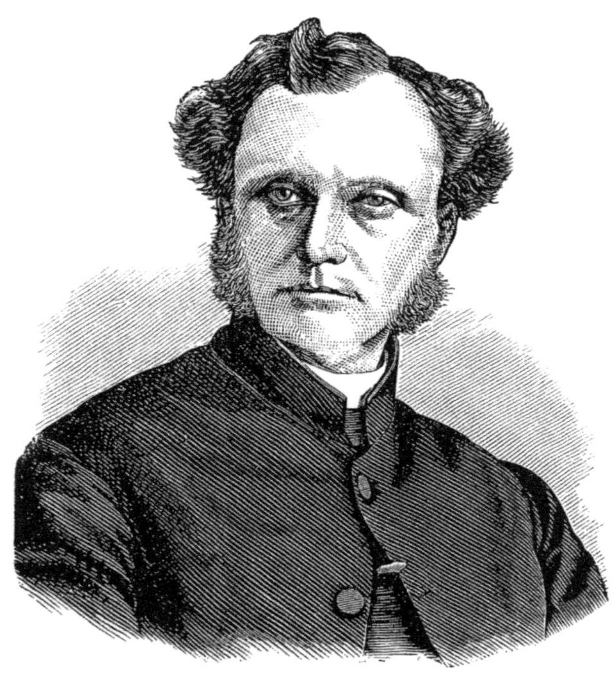

24

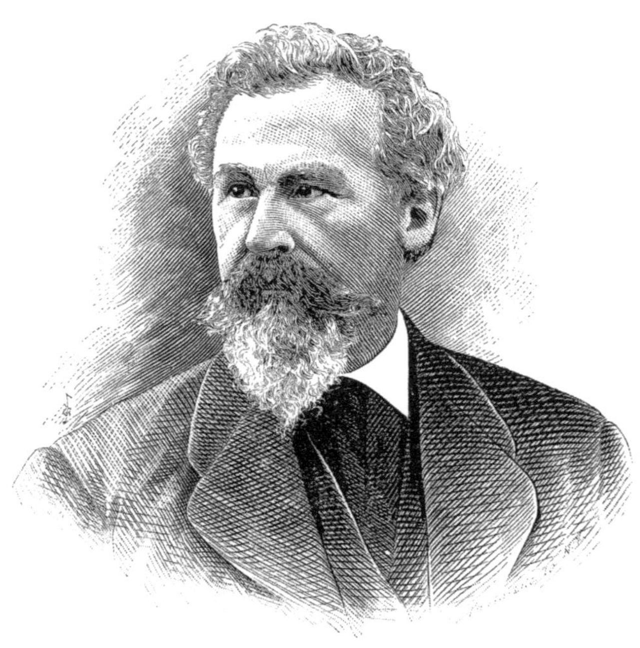

MEN

25

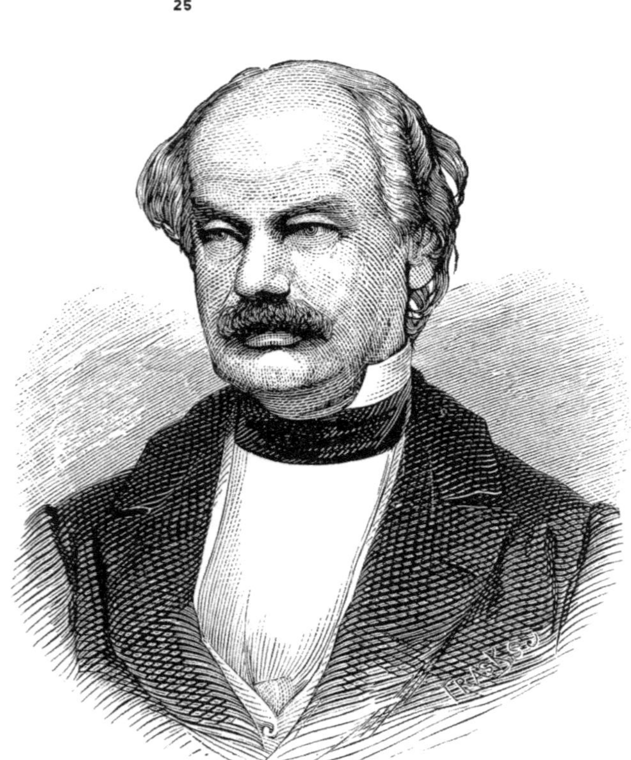

26

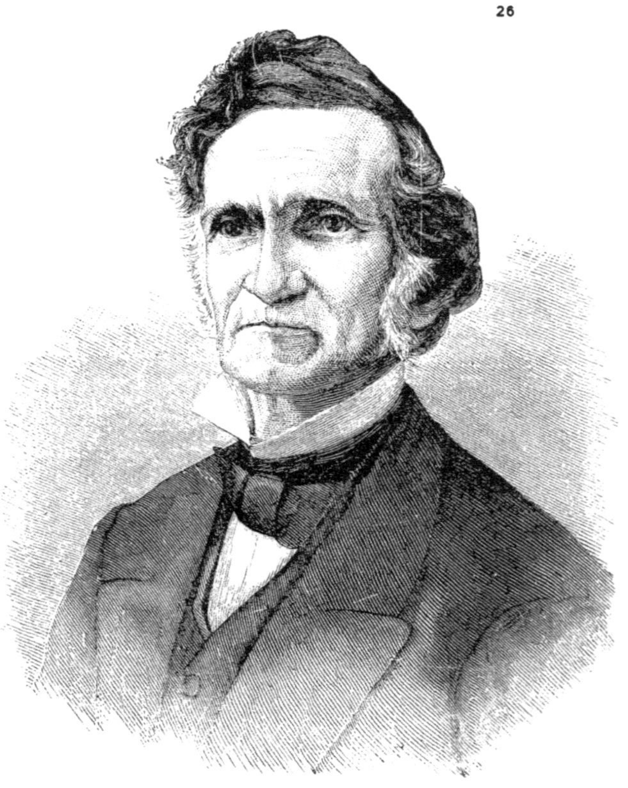

27

28

29

MEN

30

31

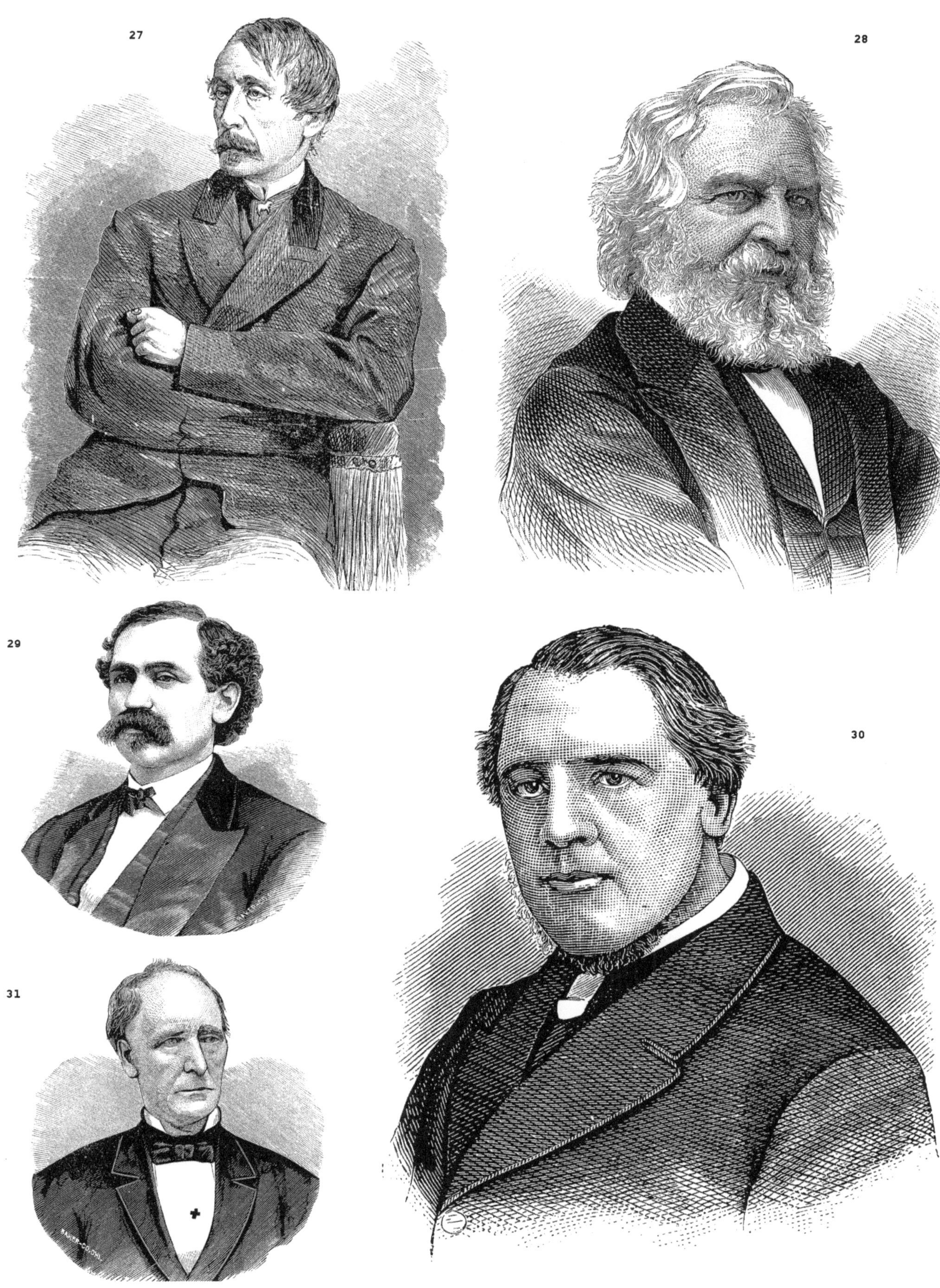

32

33

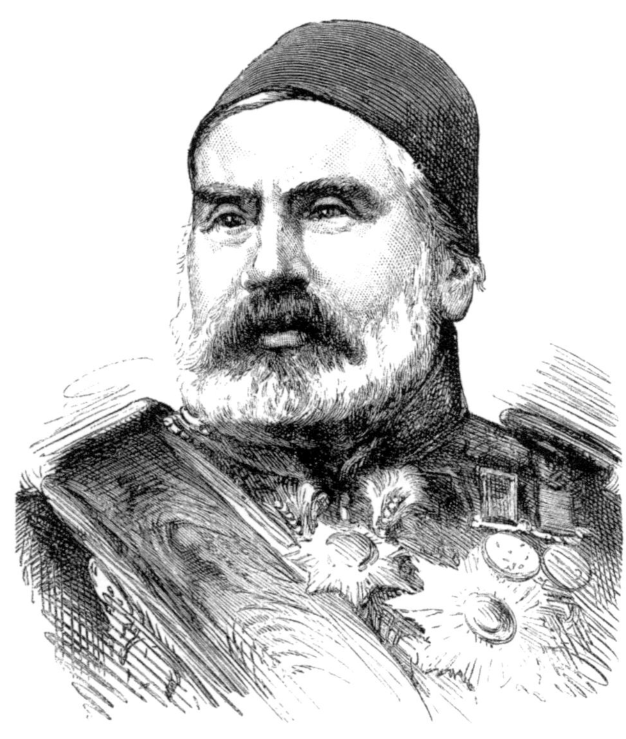

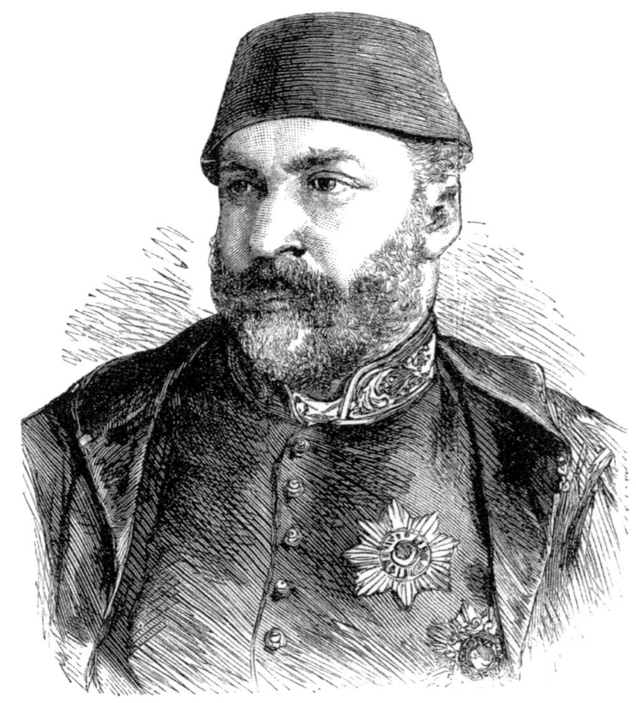

34

35

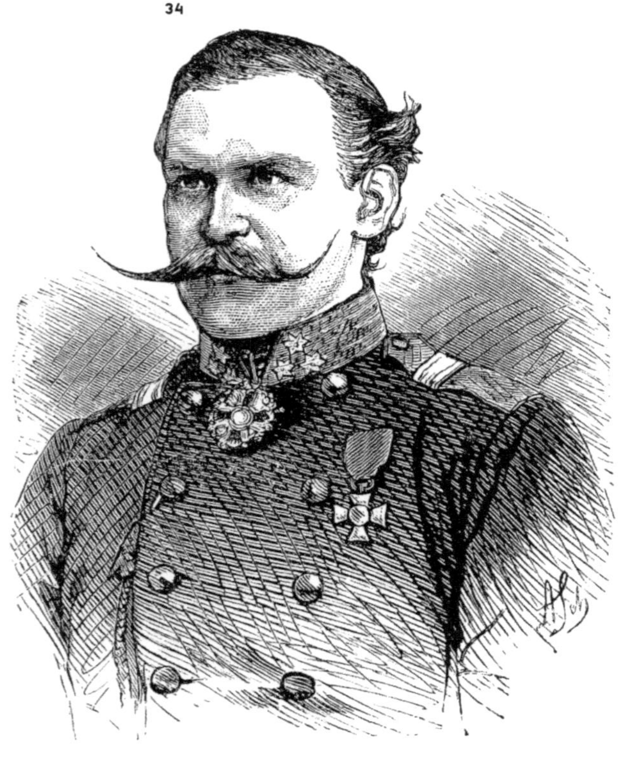

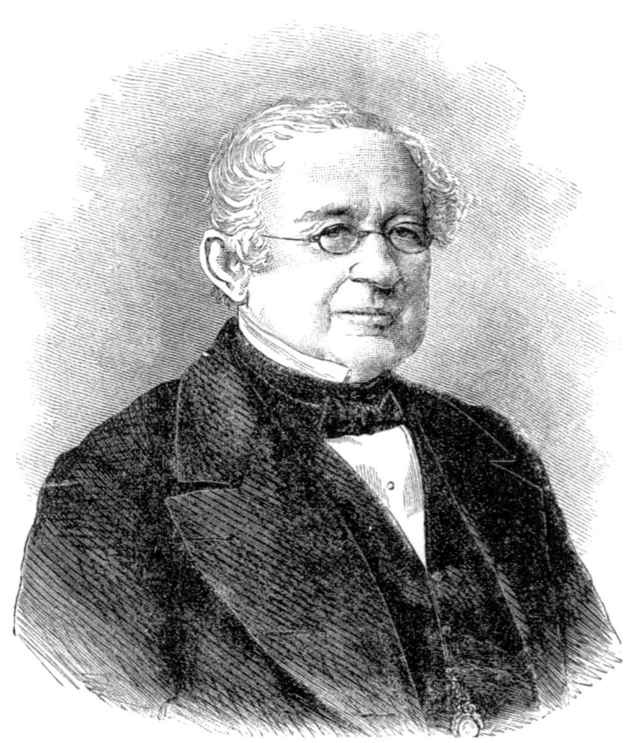

36

37

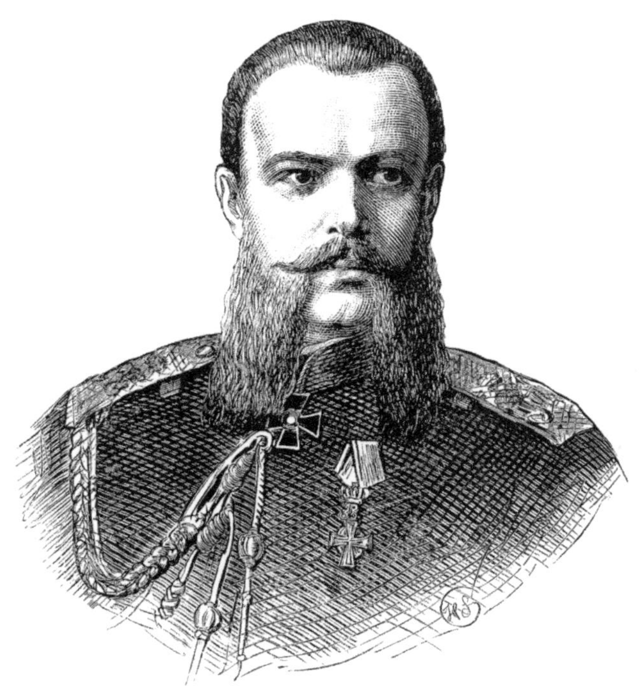

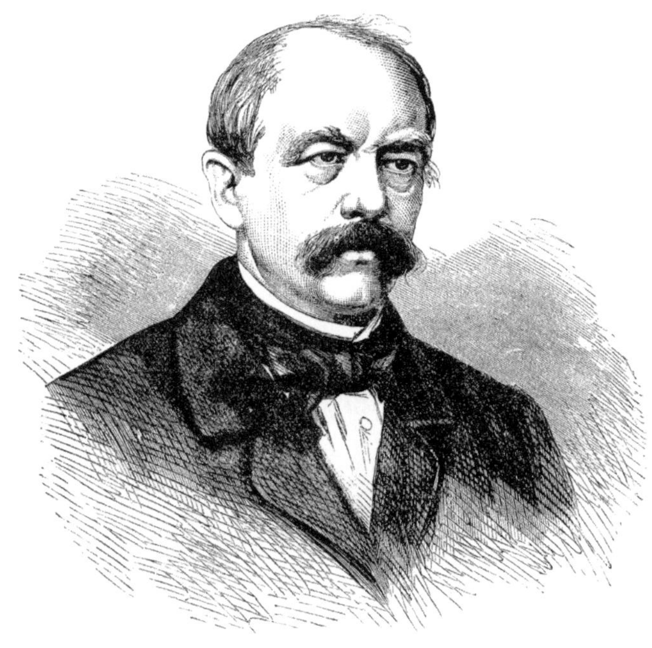

38

39

MEN

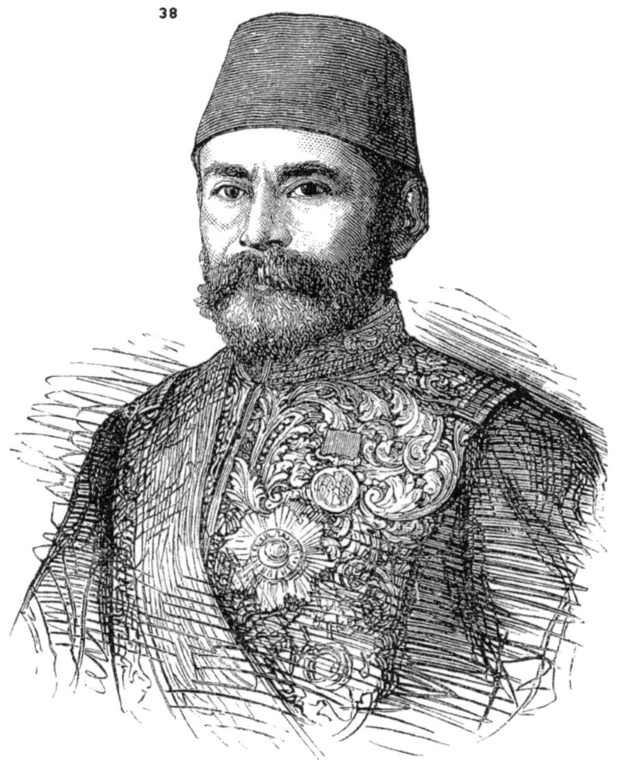

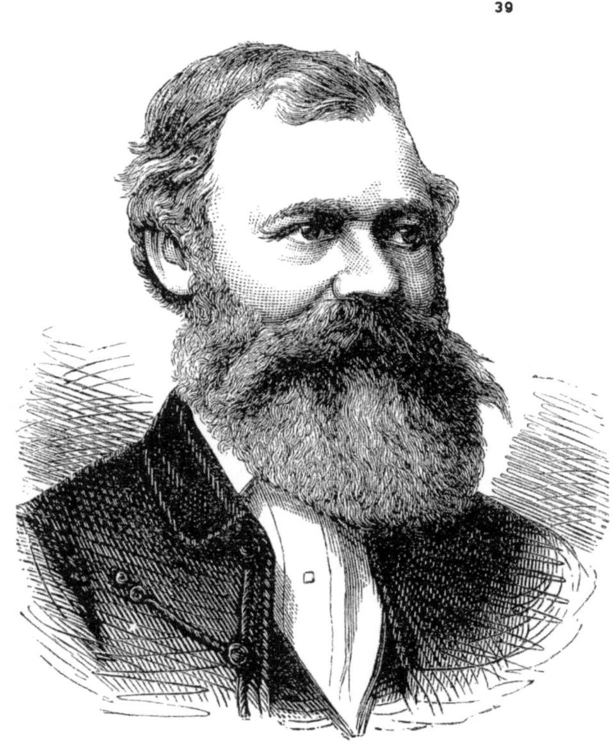

MEN

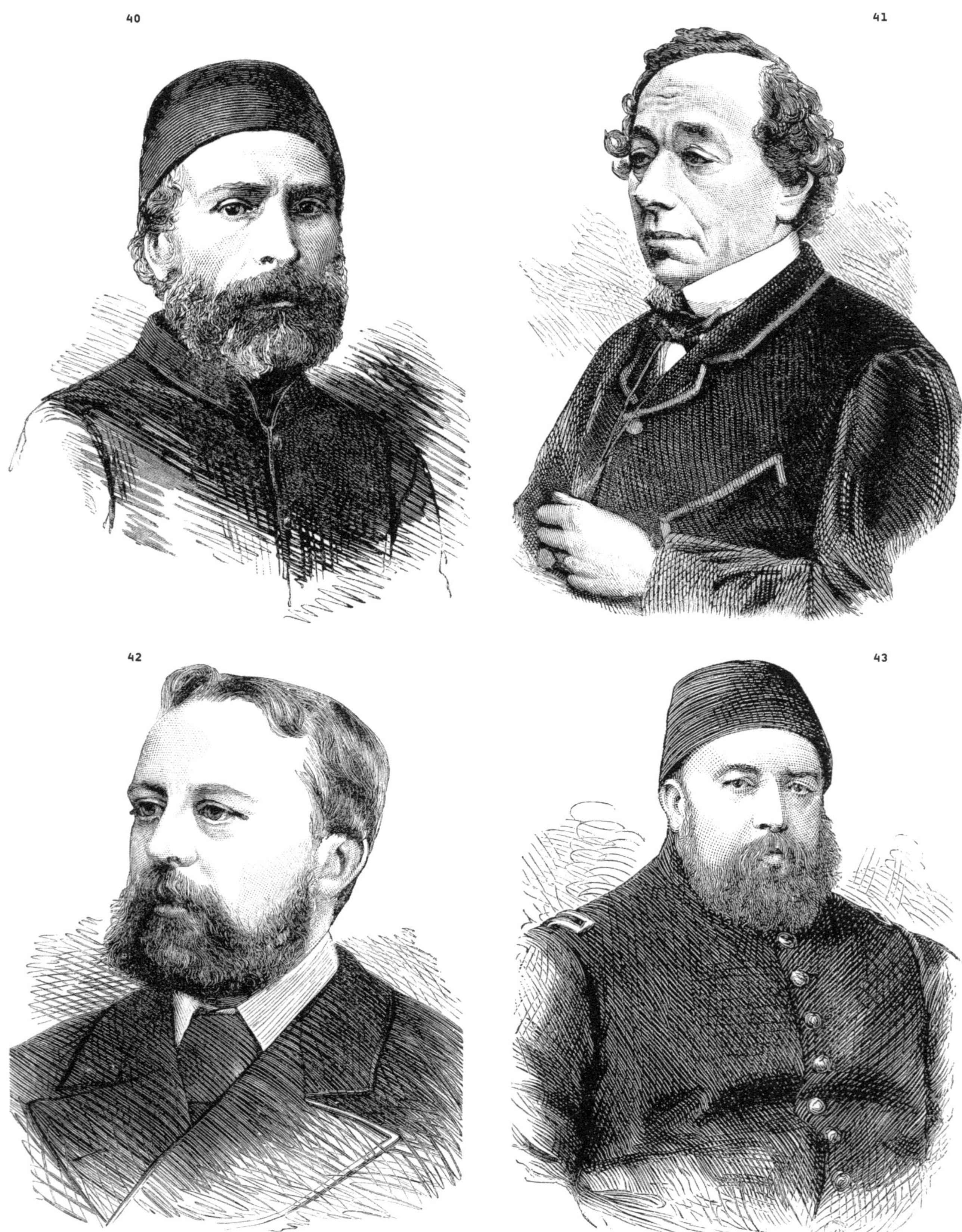

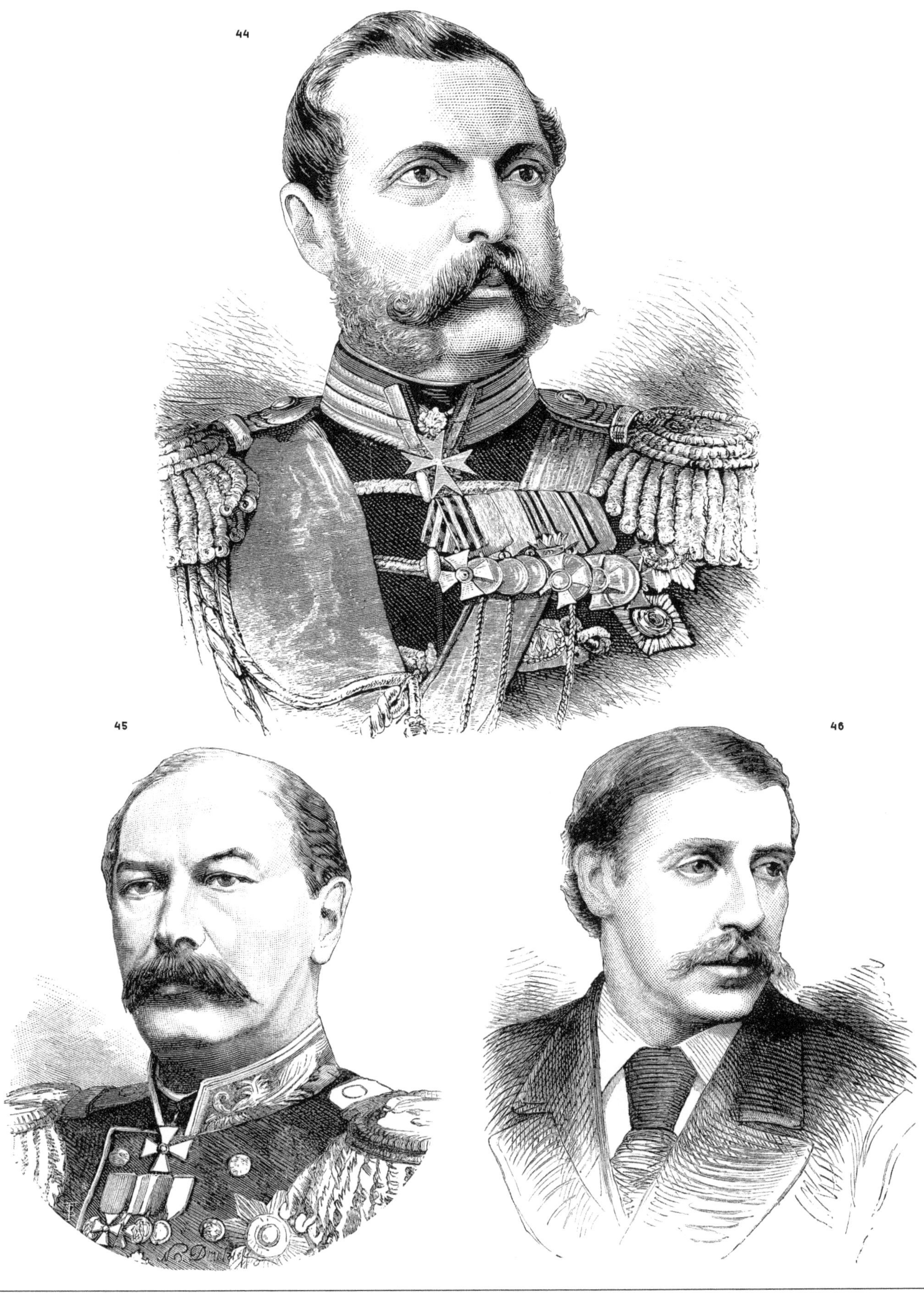

44
45
46
MEN

47

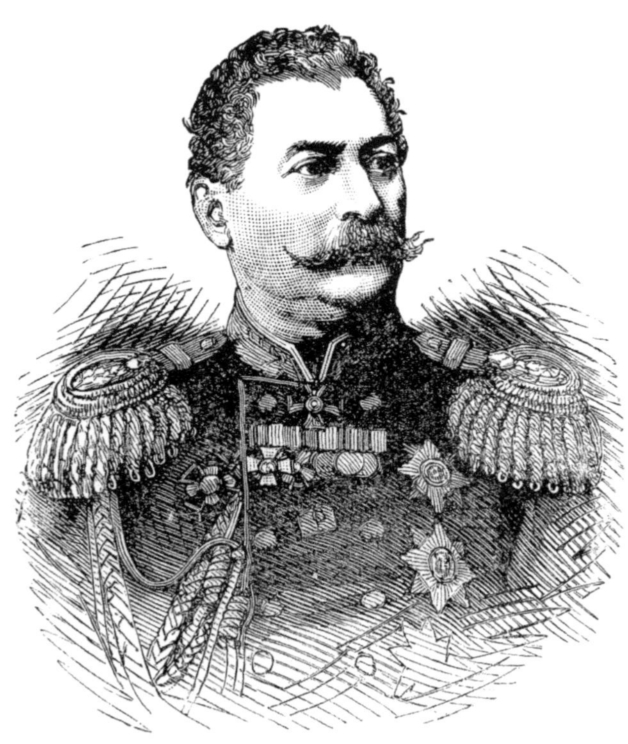

48

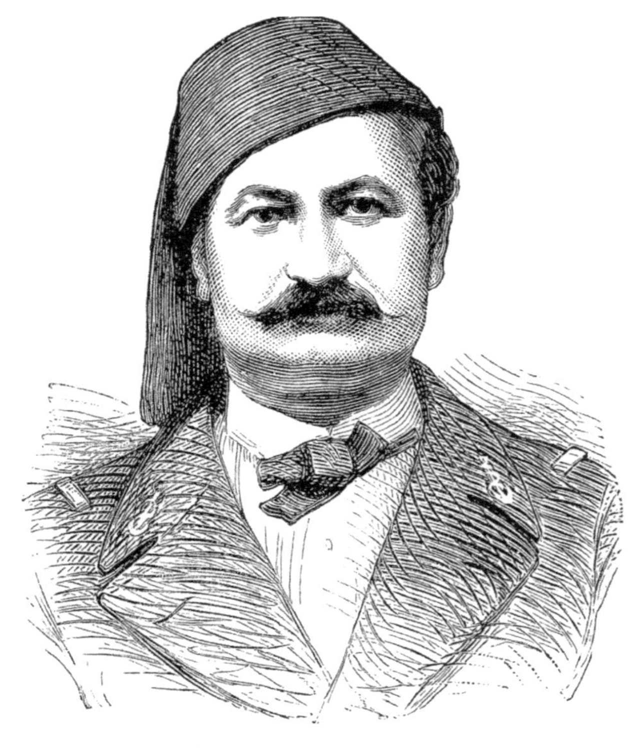

MEN

49

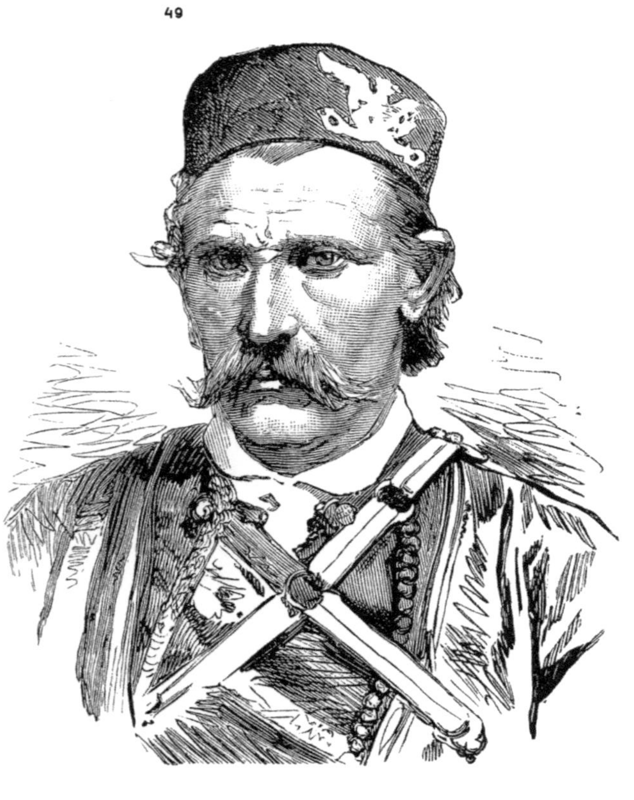

50

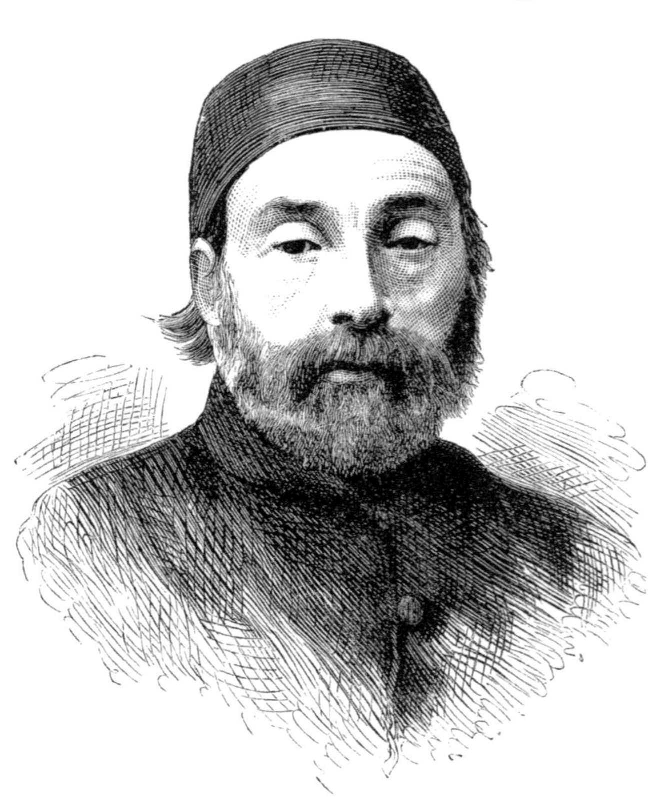

51

52

53

MEN

54

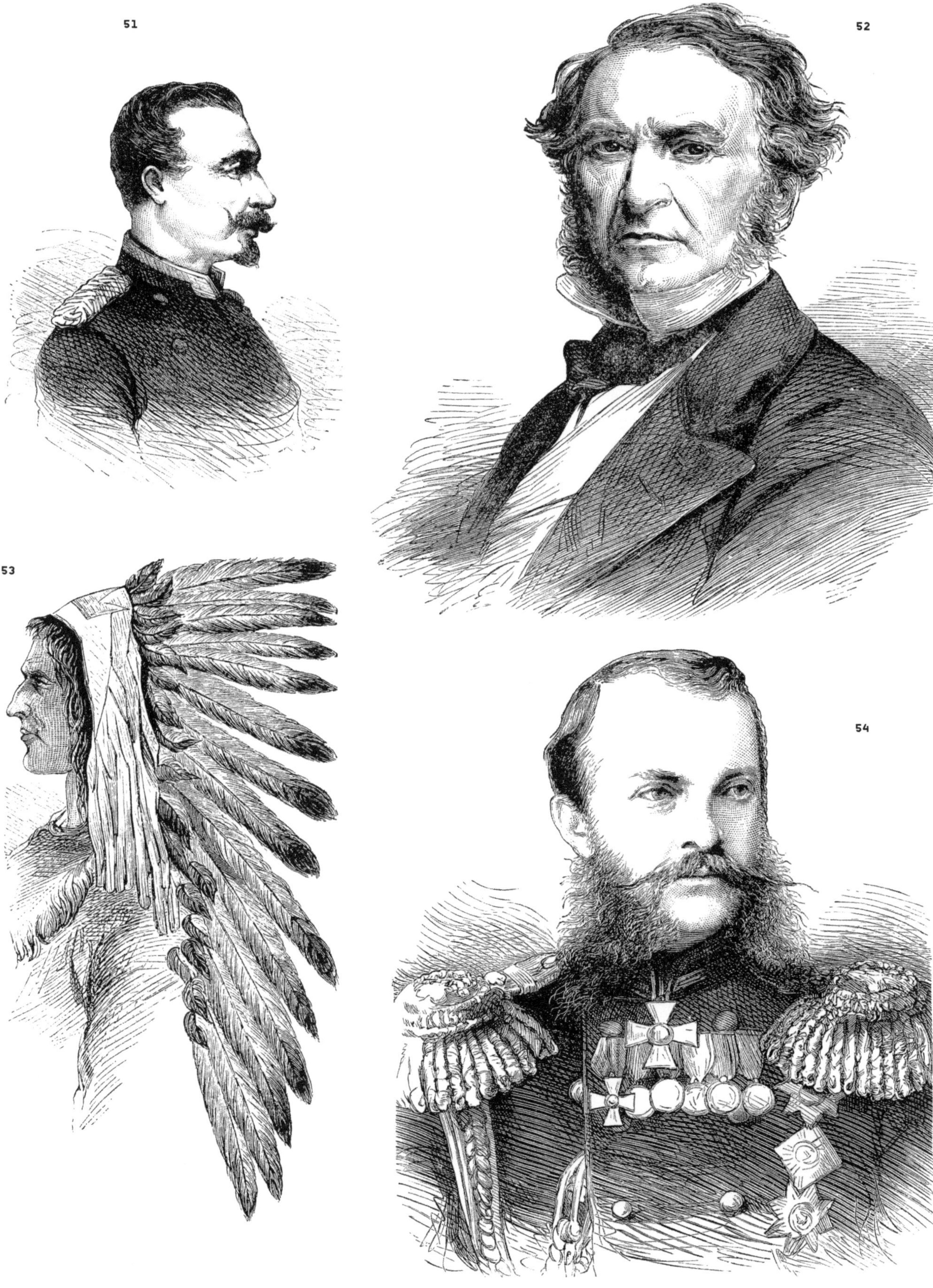

55

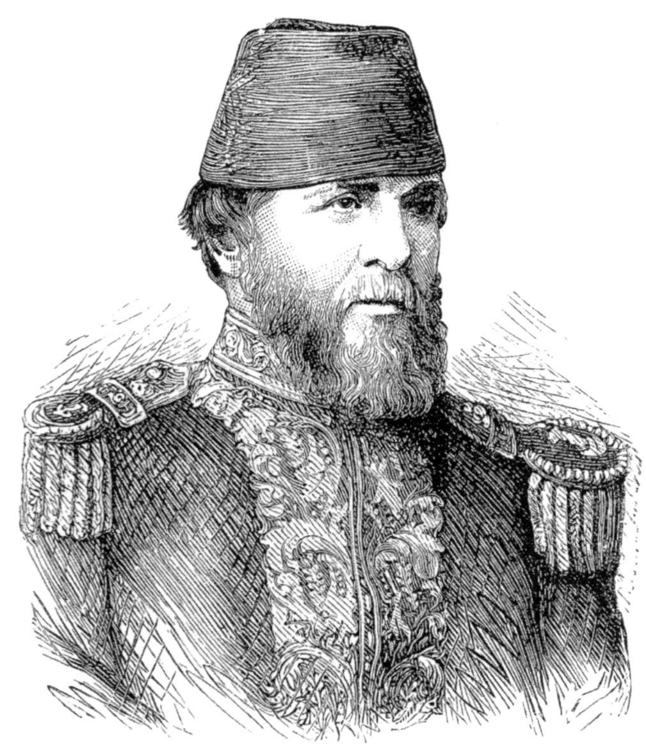

56

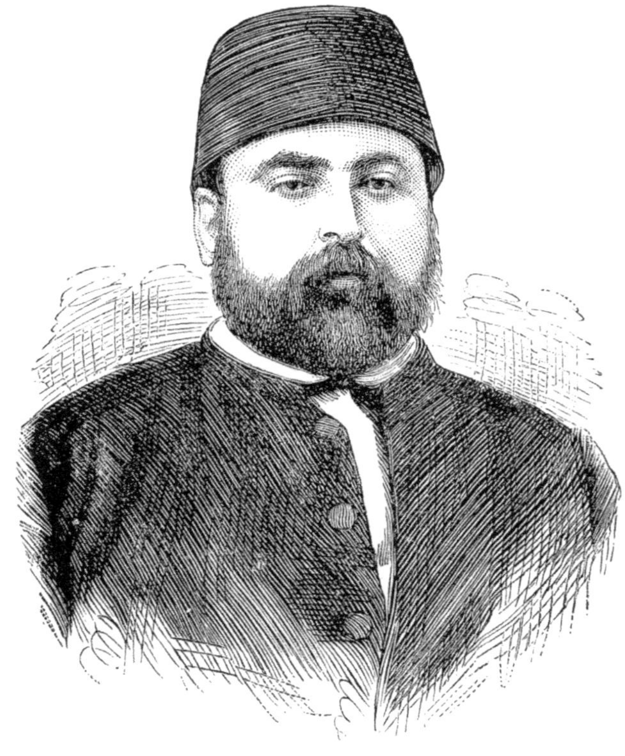

57

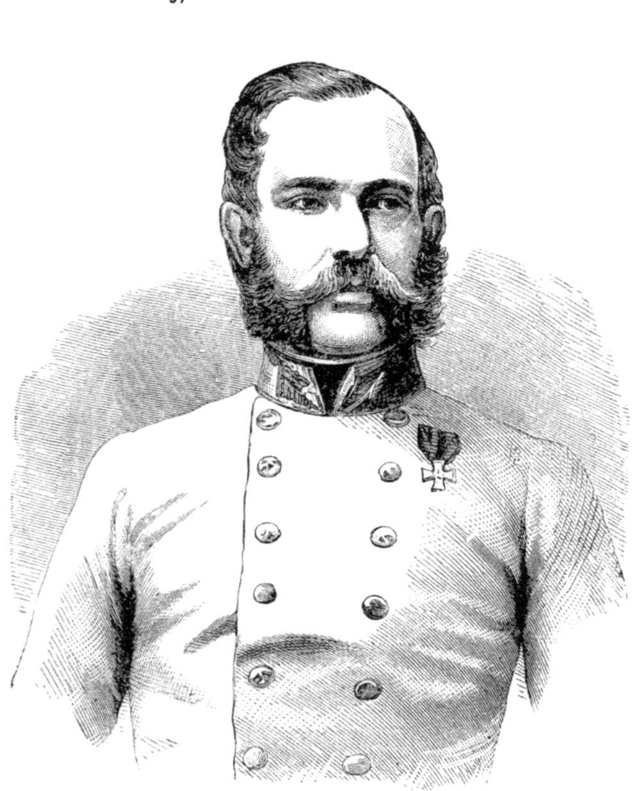

58

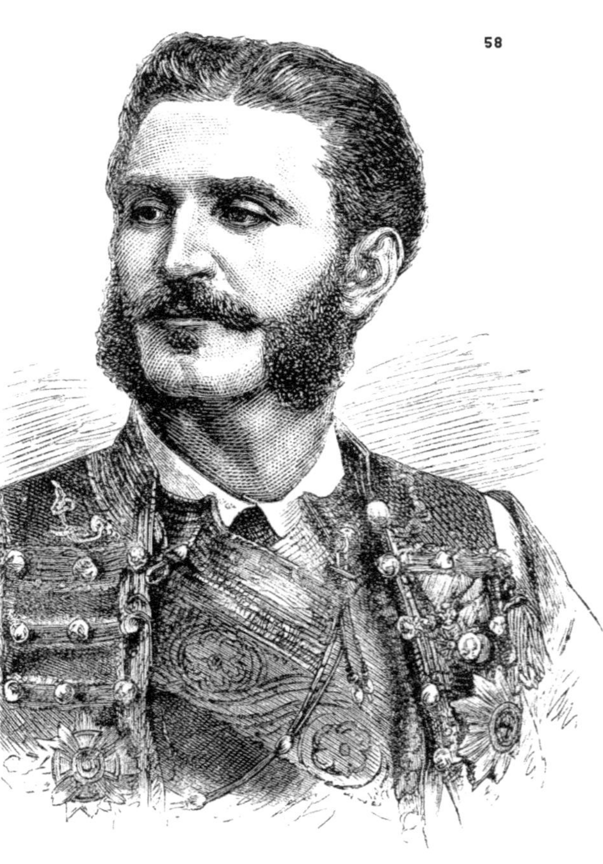

59

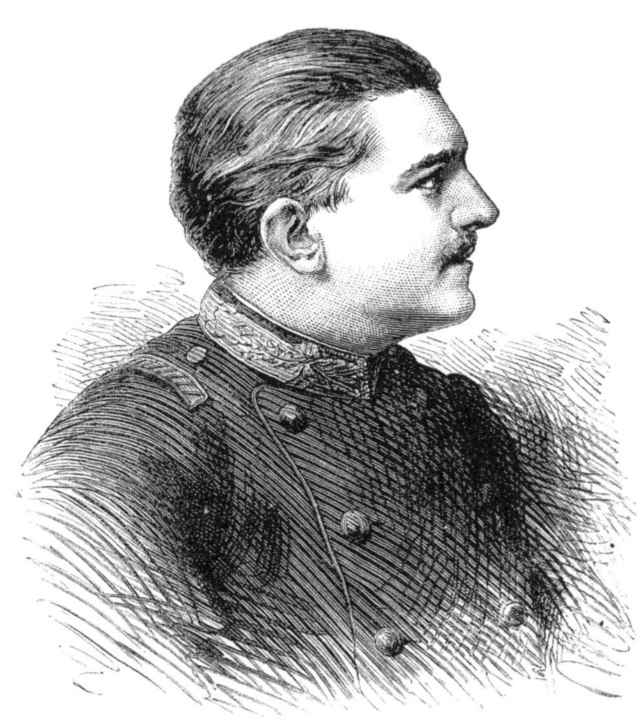

60

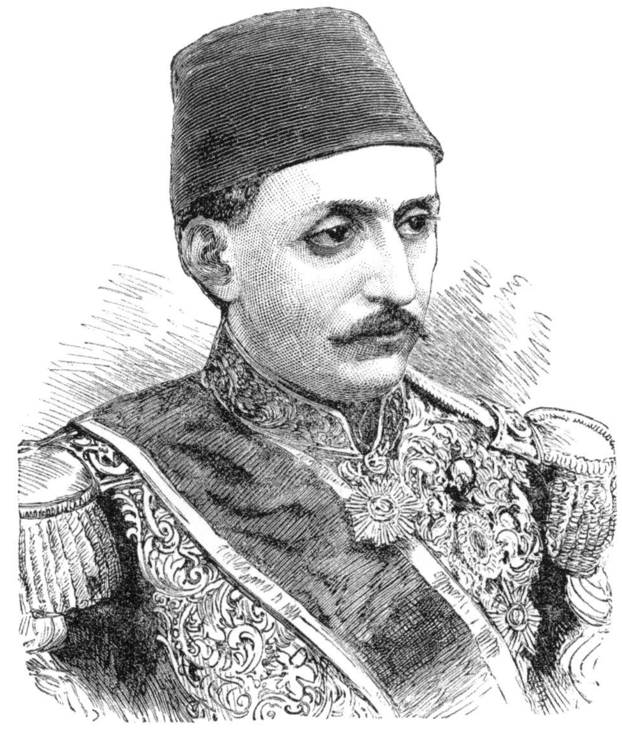

61

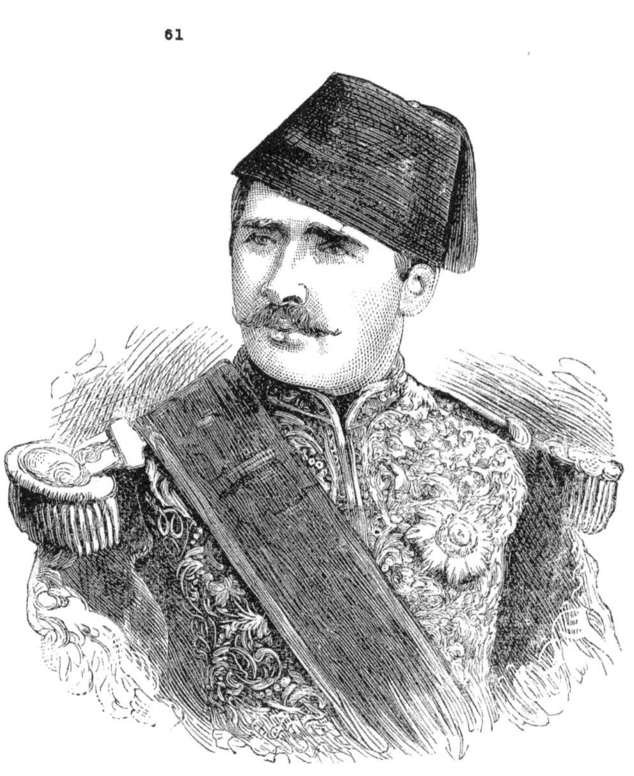

62

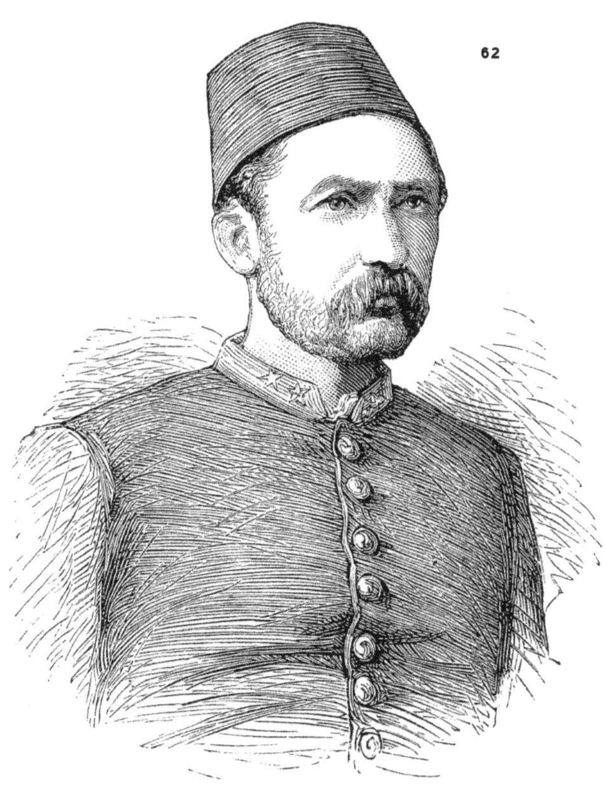

63

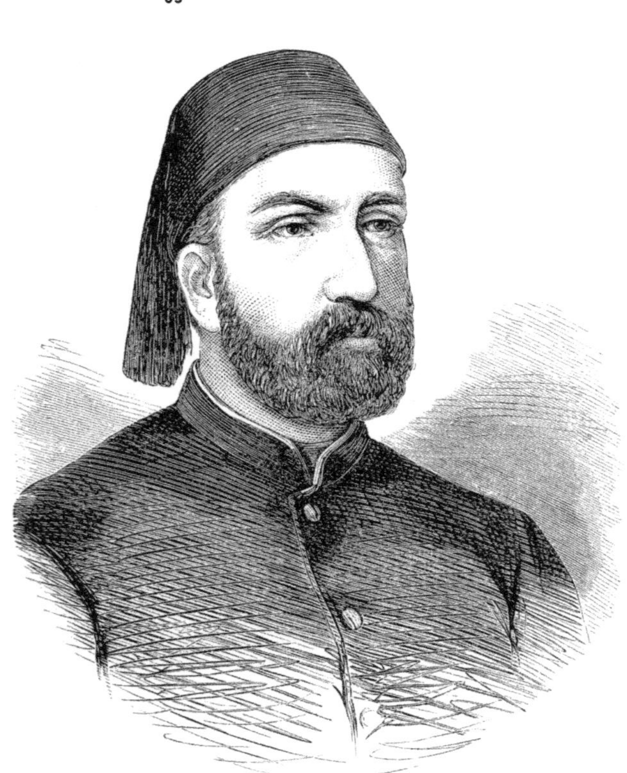

64

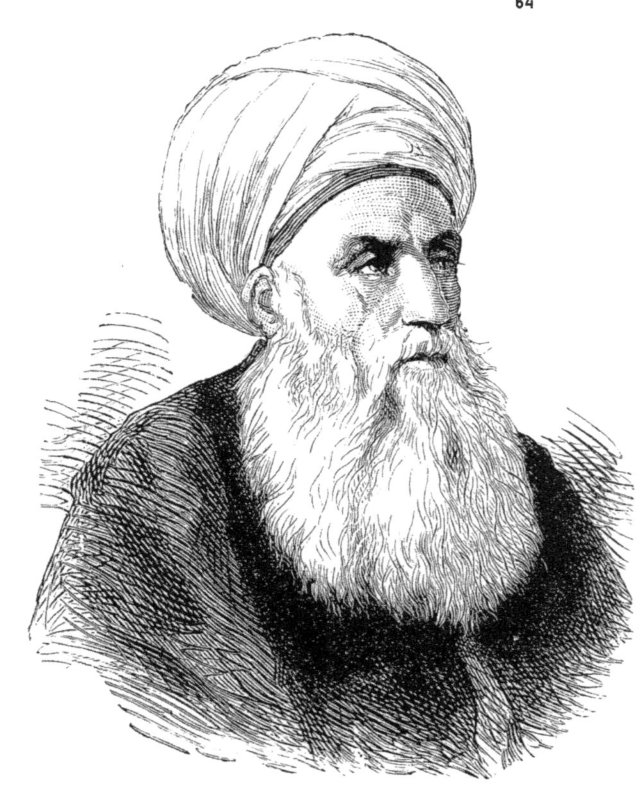

MEN

65

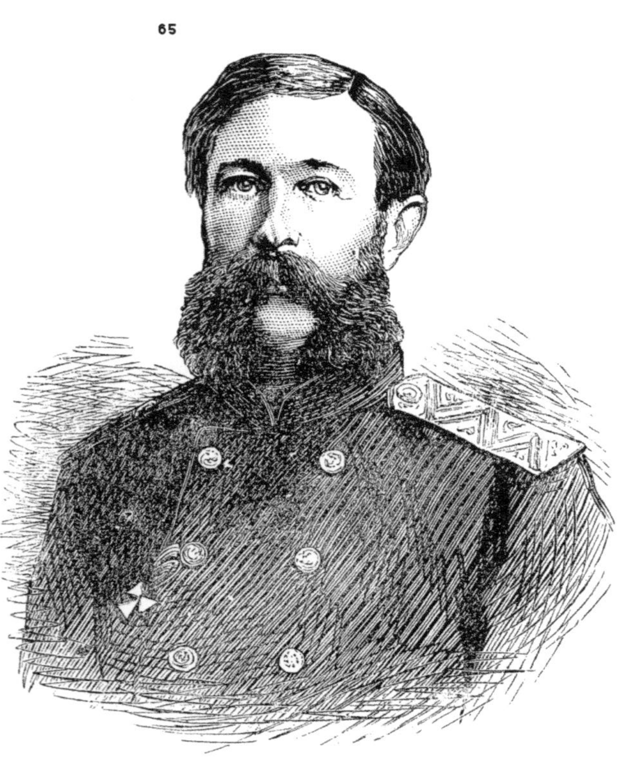

66

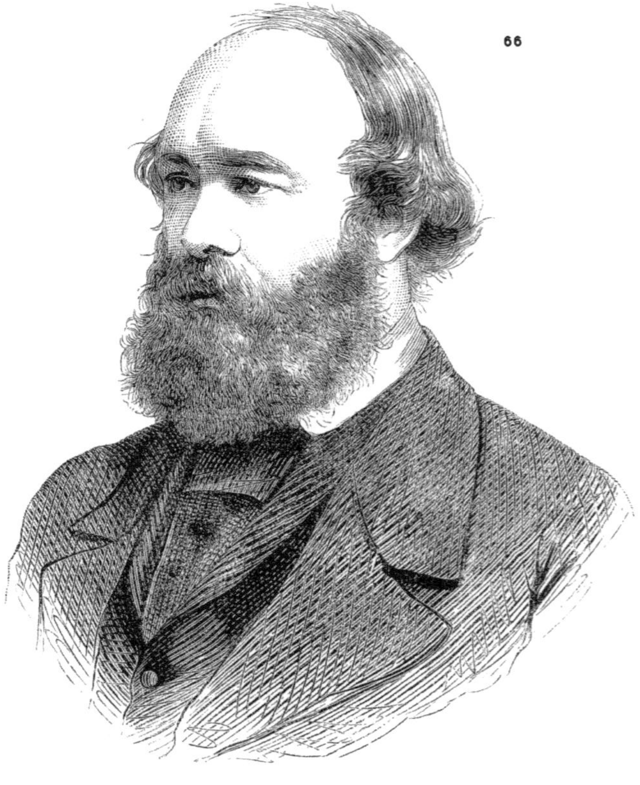

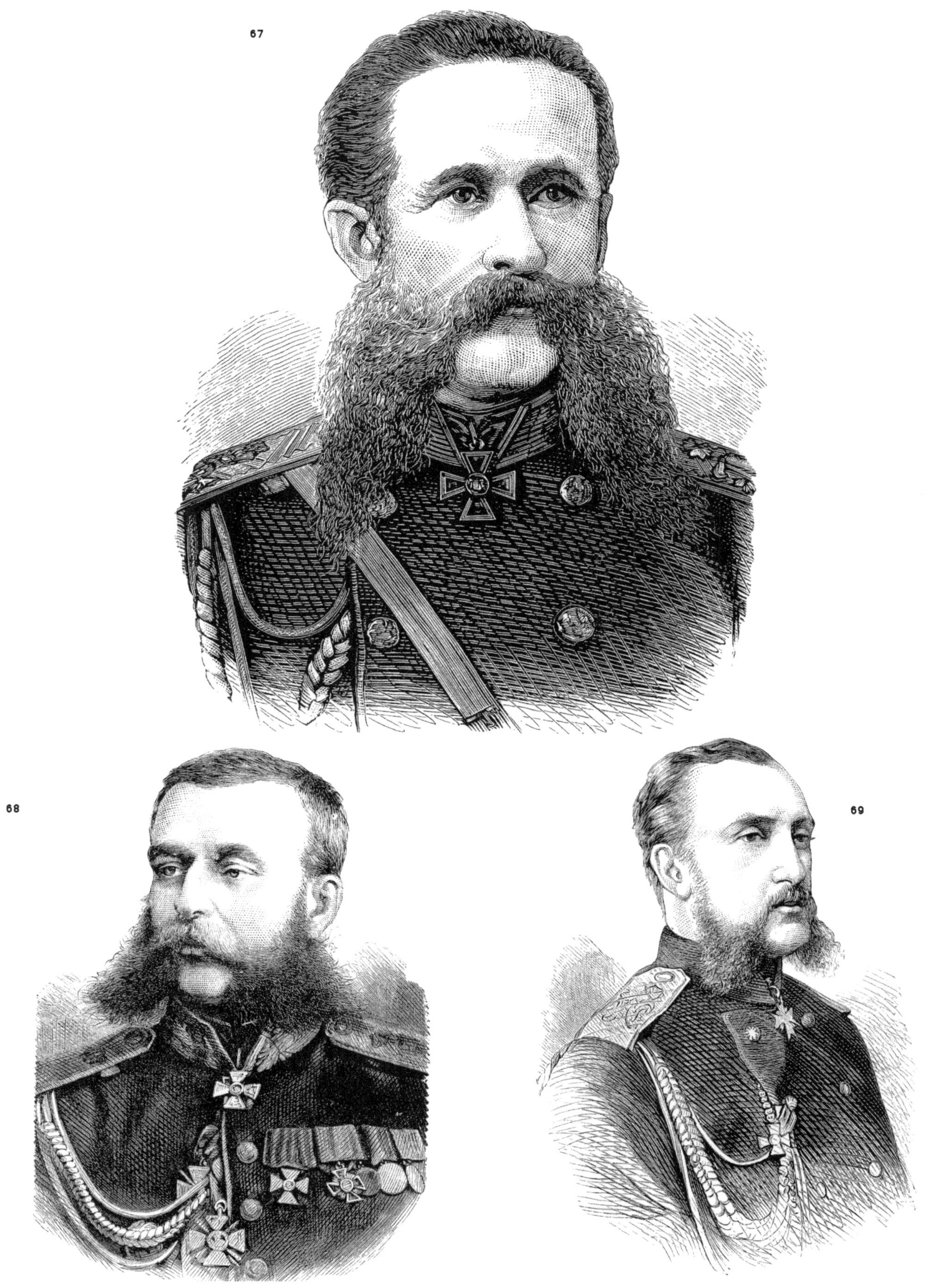

67
68
69
MEN

MEN

70

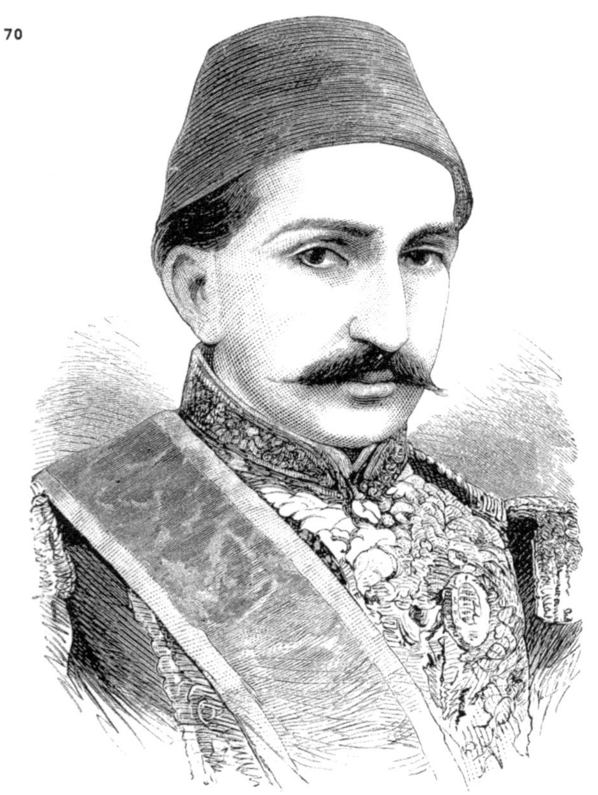

71

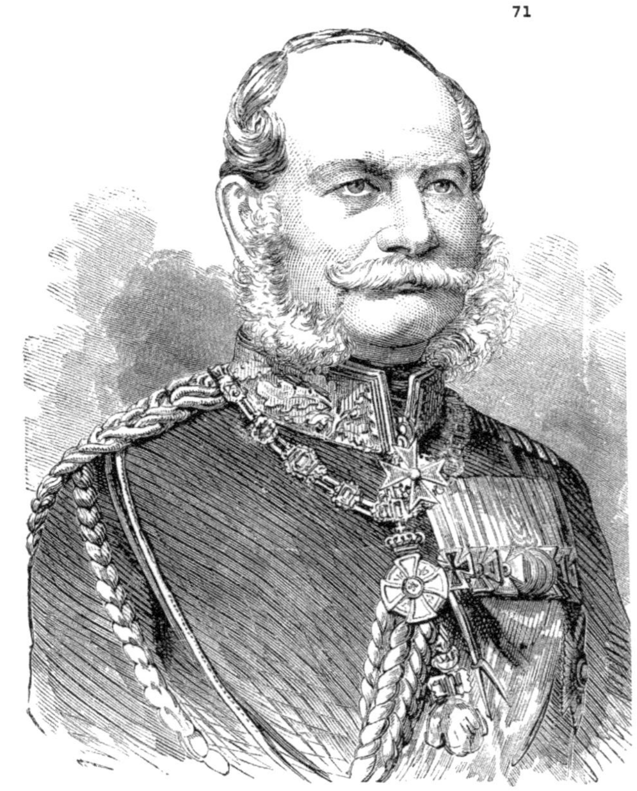

72

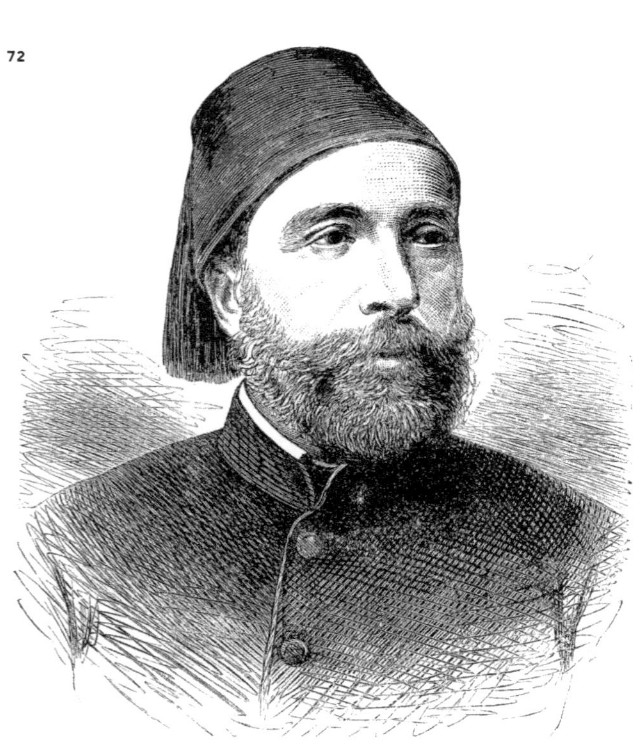

73

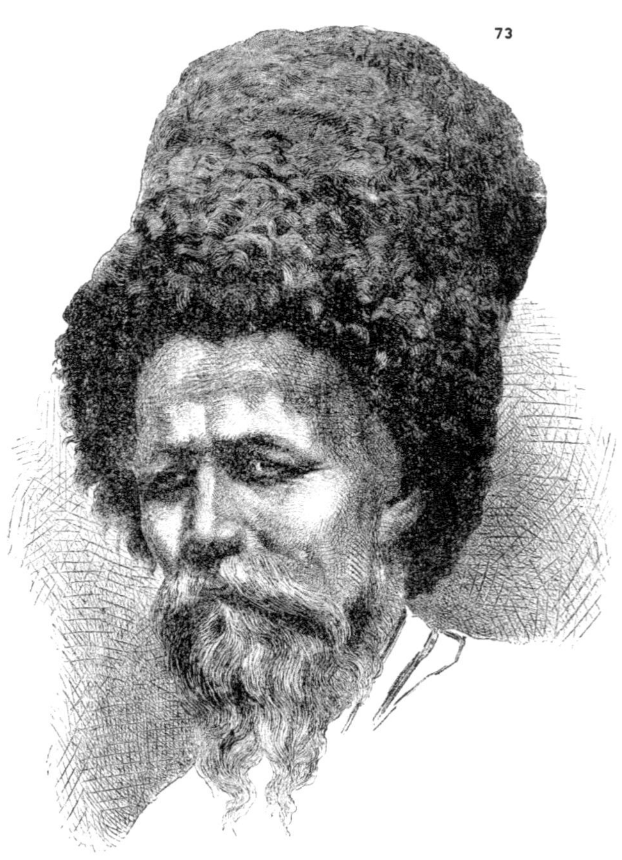

74

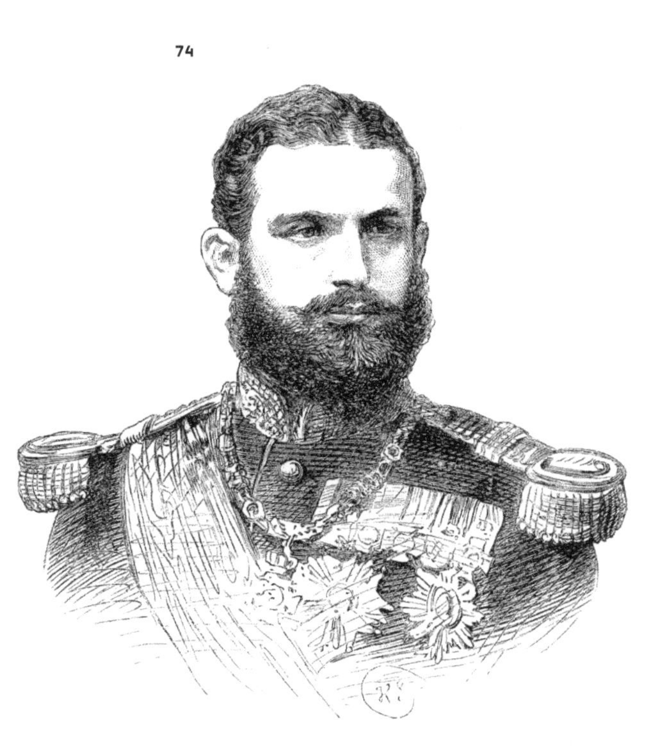

75

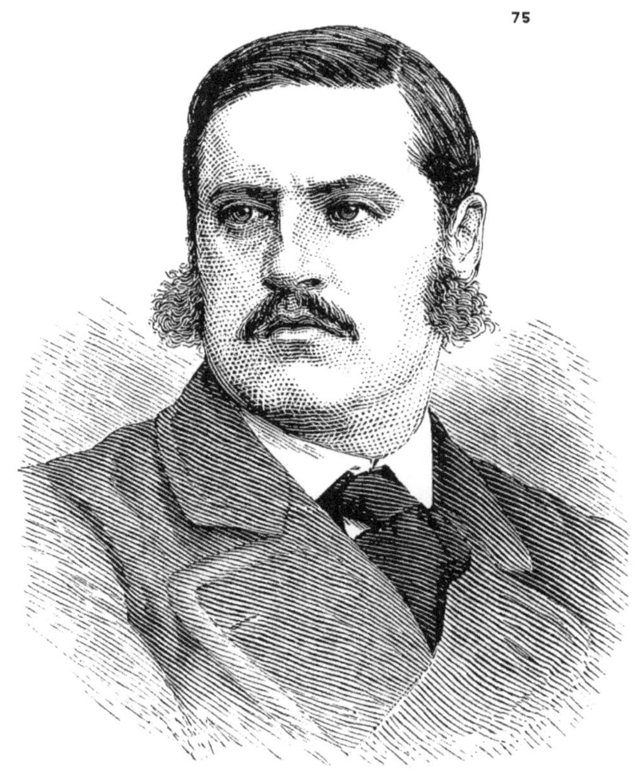

76

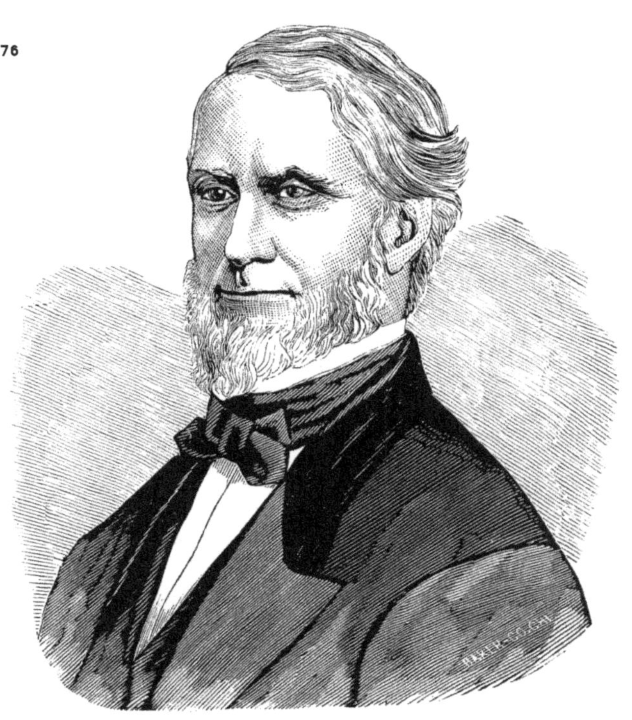

77

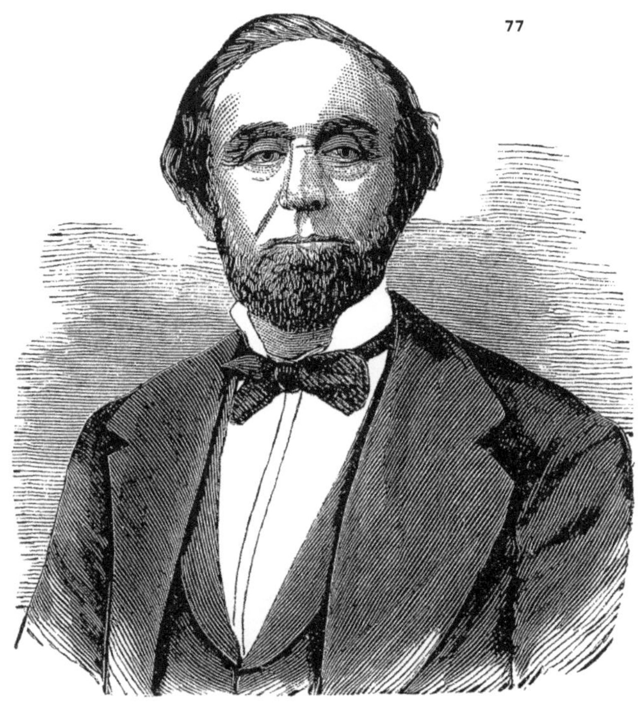

MEN

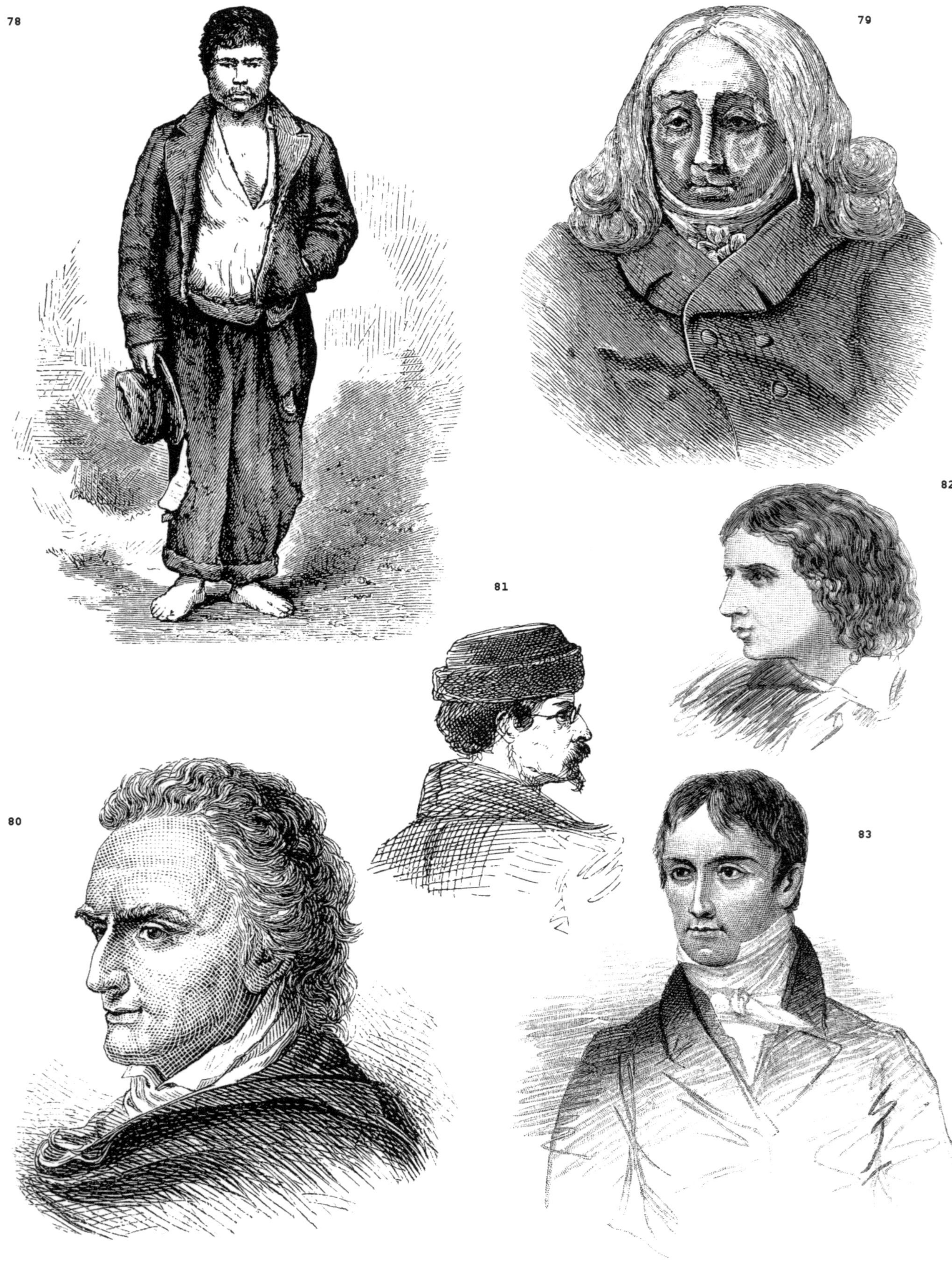

84

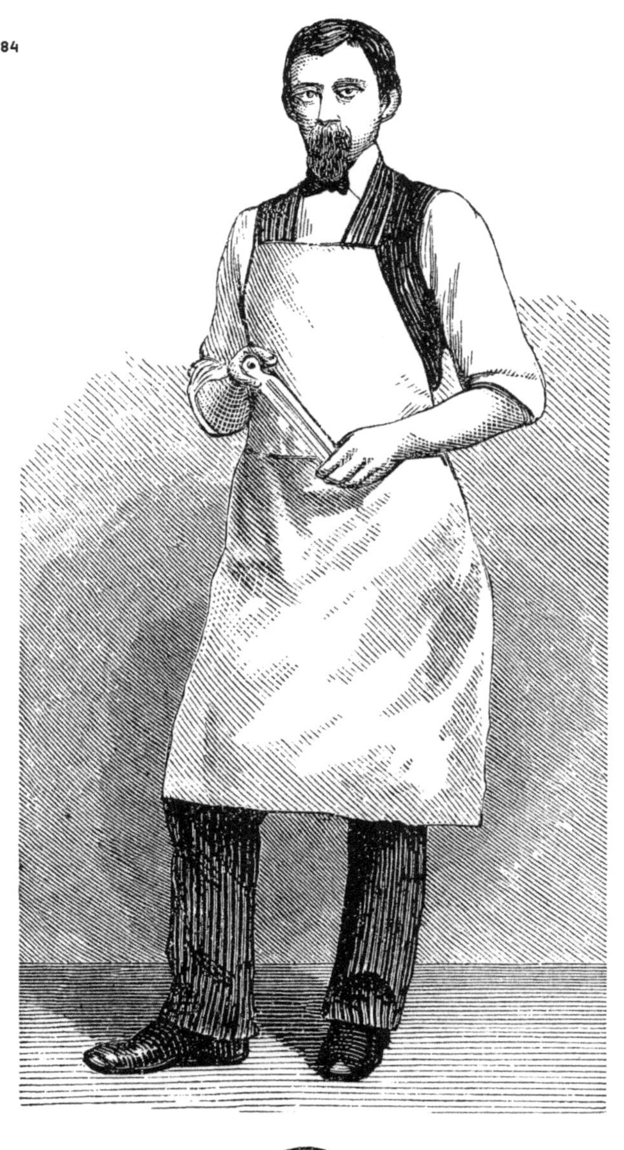

85

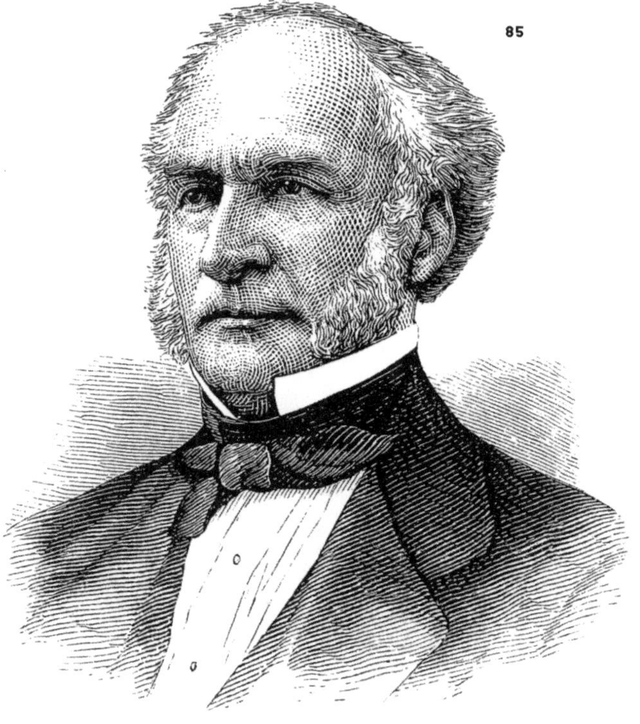

87

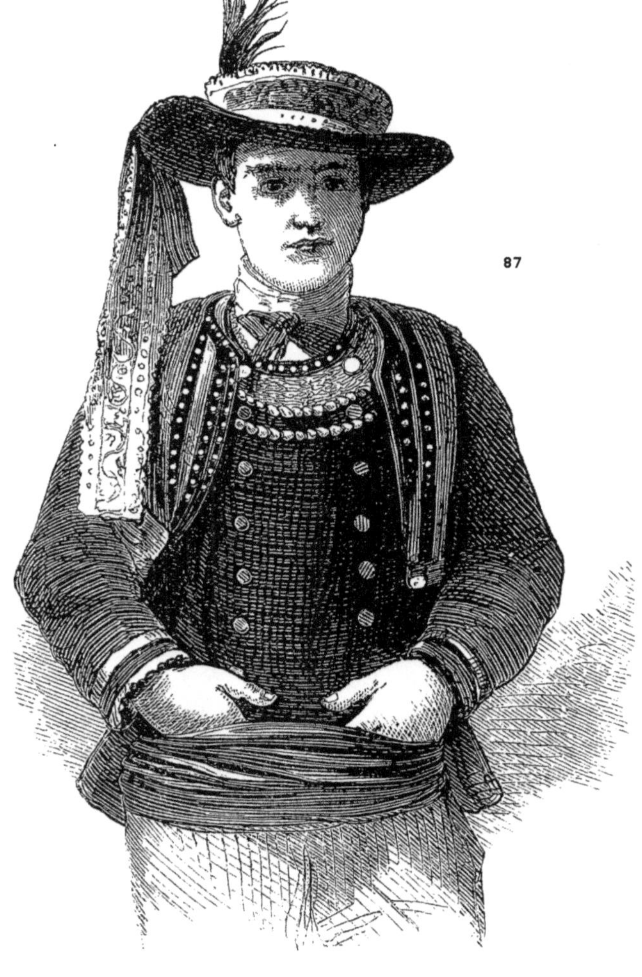

86

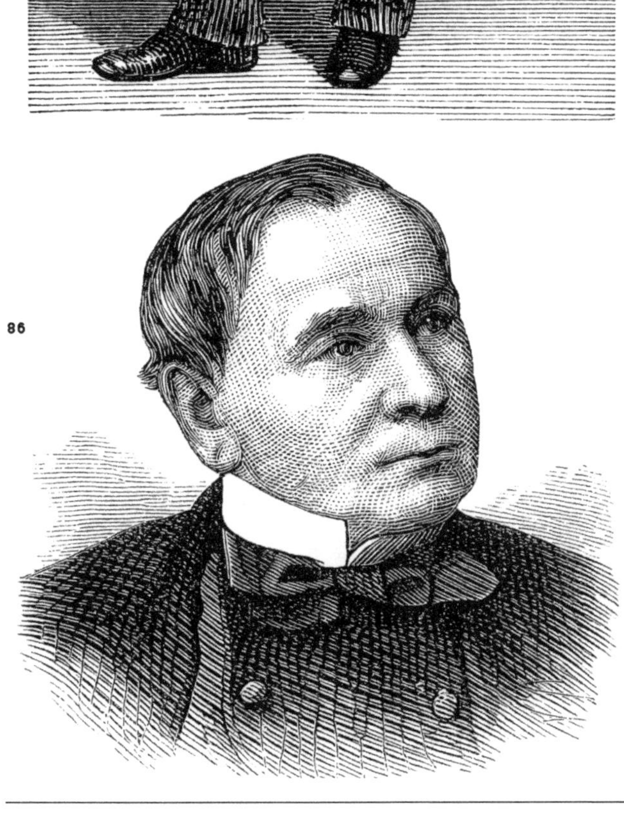

88

89

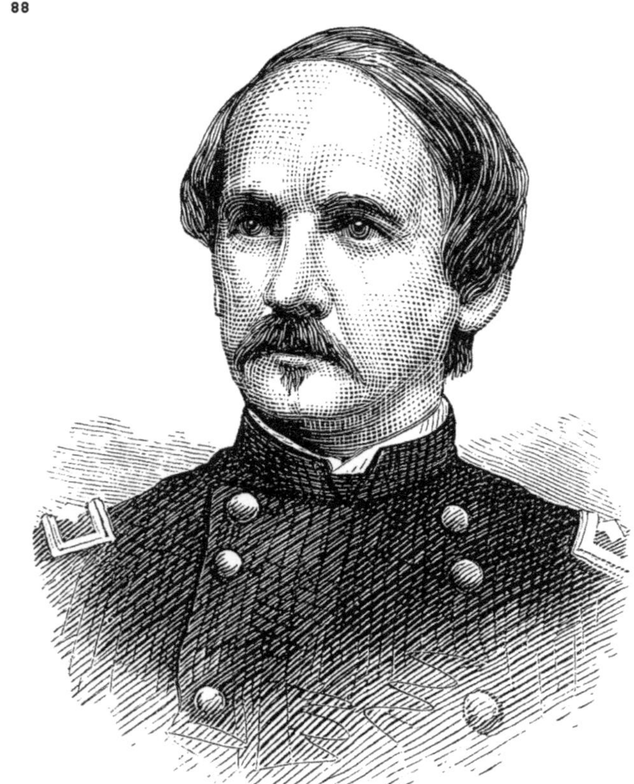

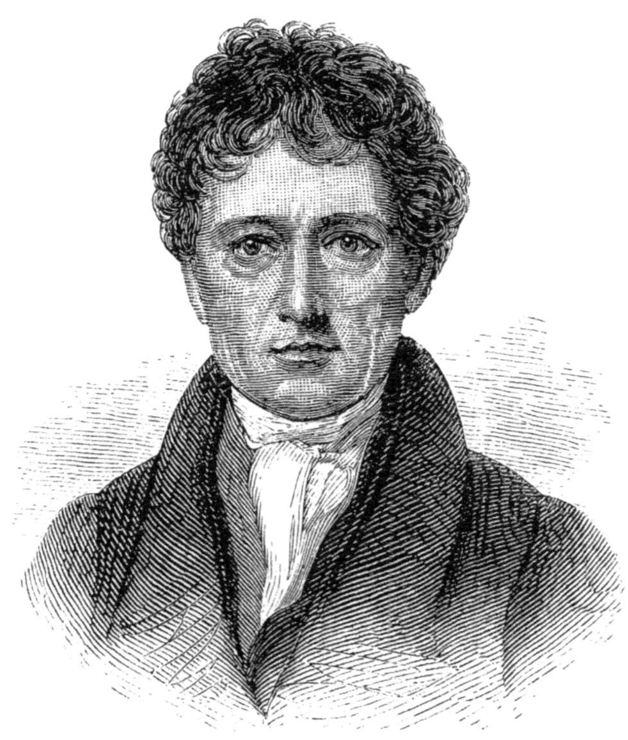

MEN

90

91

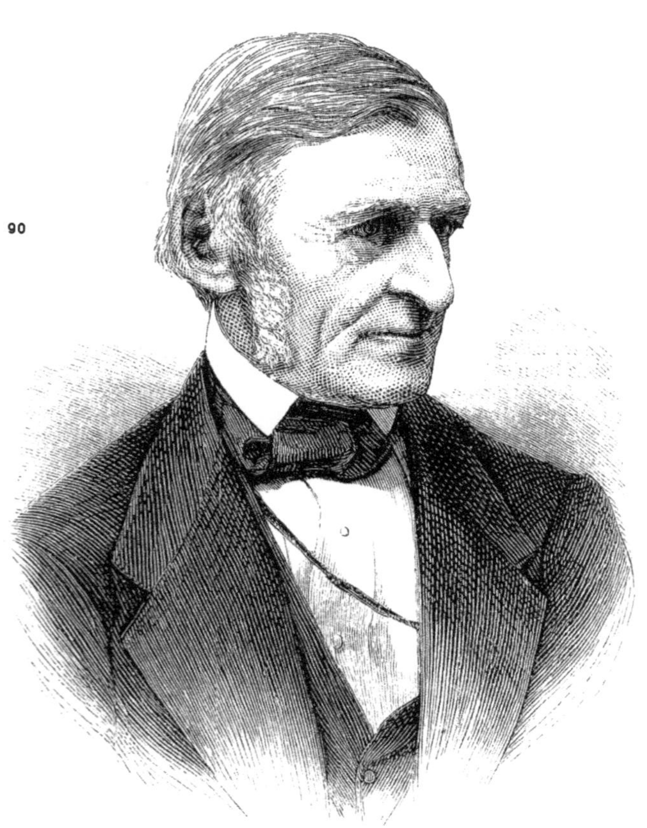

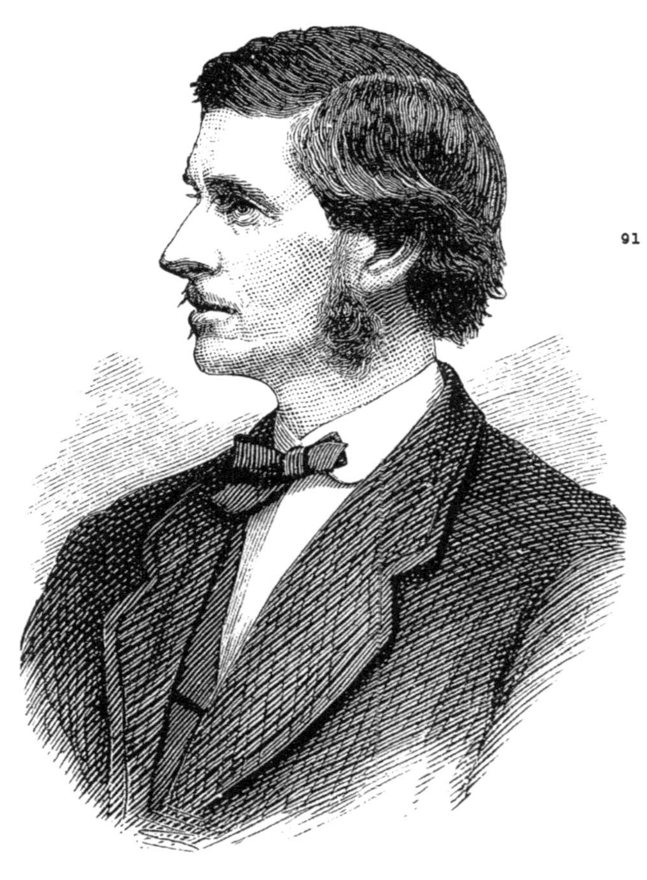

92

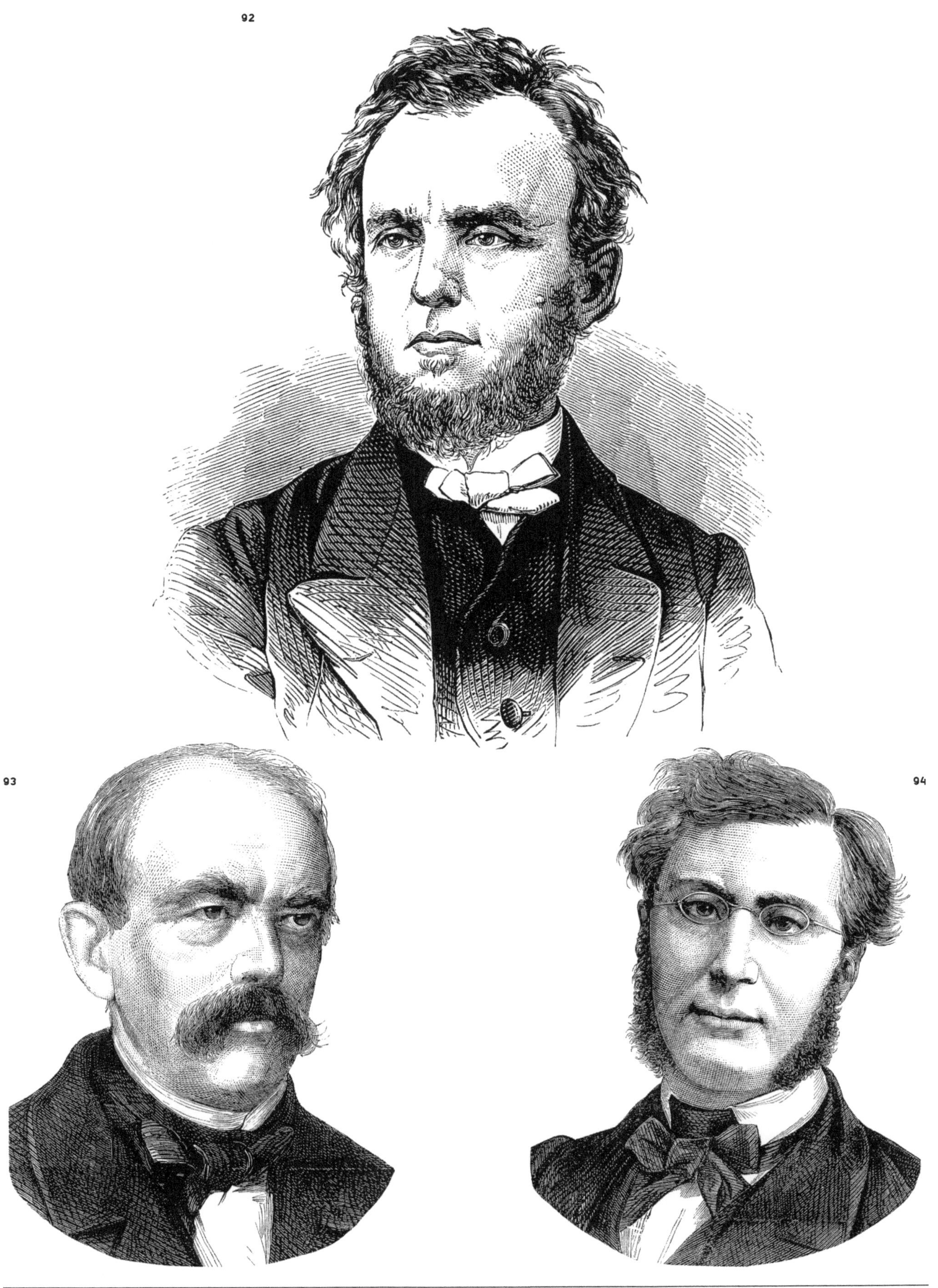

93

94

MEN

95

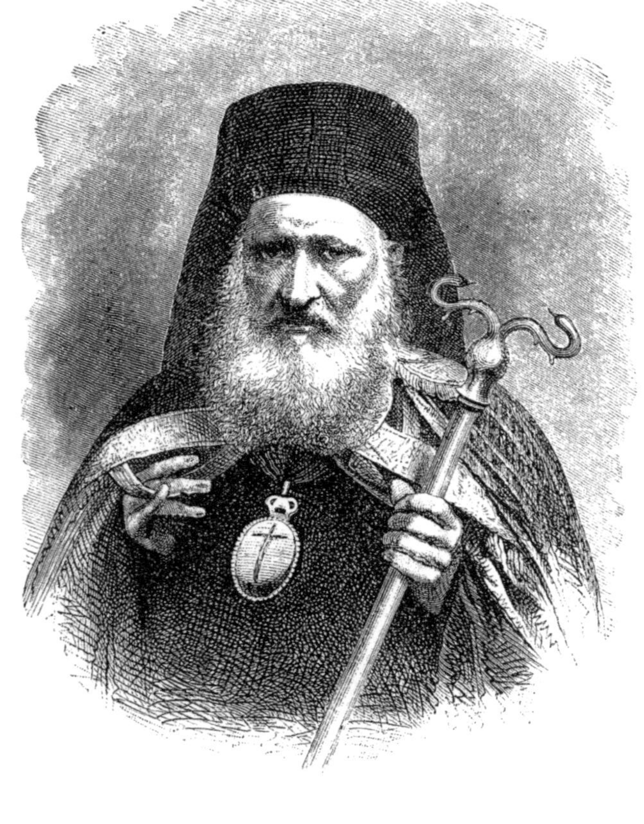

96

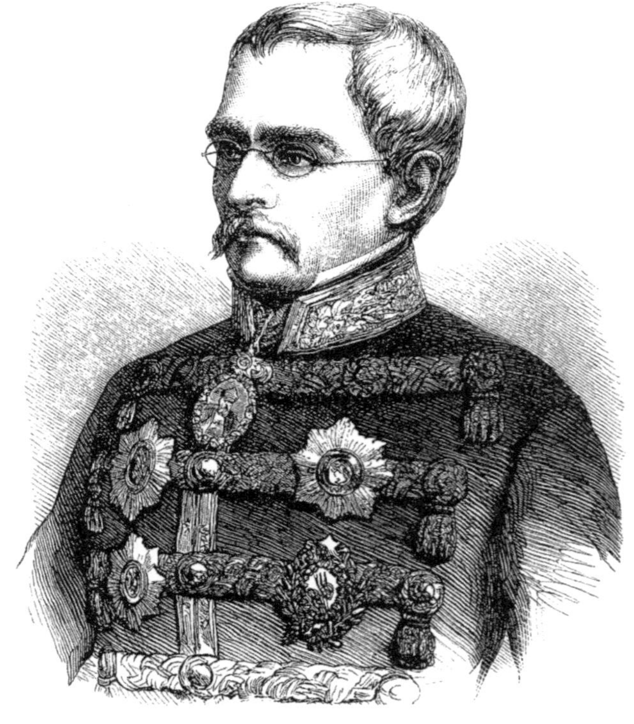

MEN

97

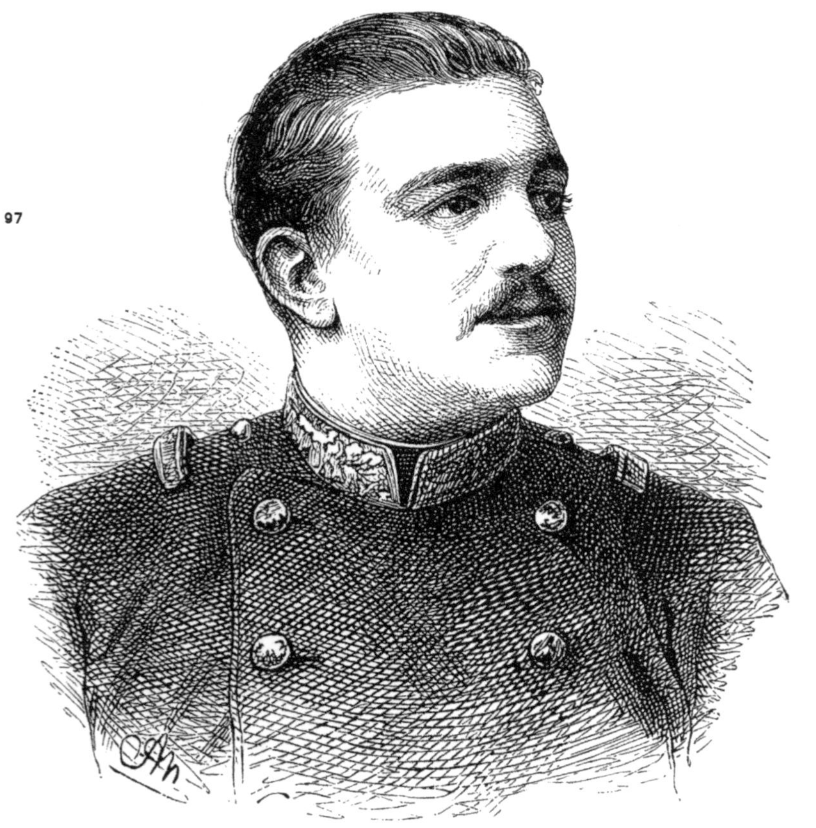

98

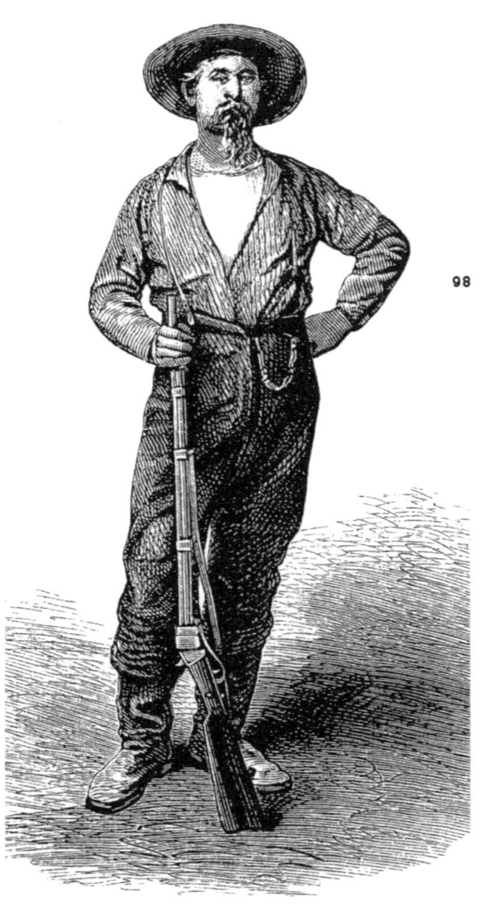

99

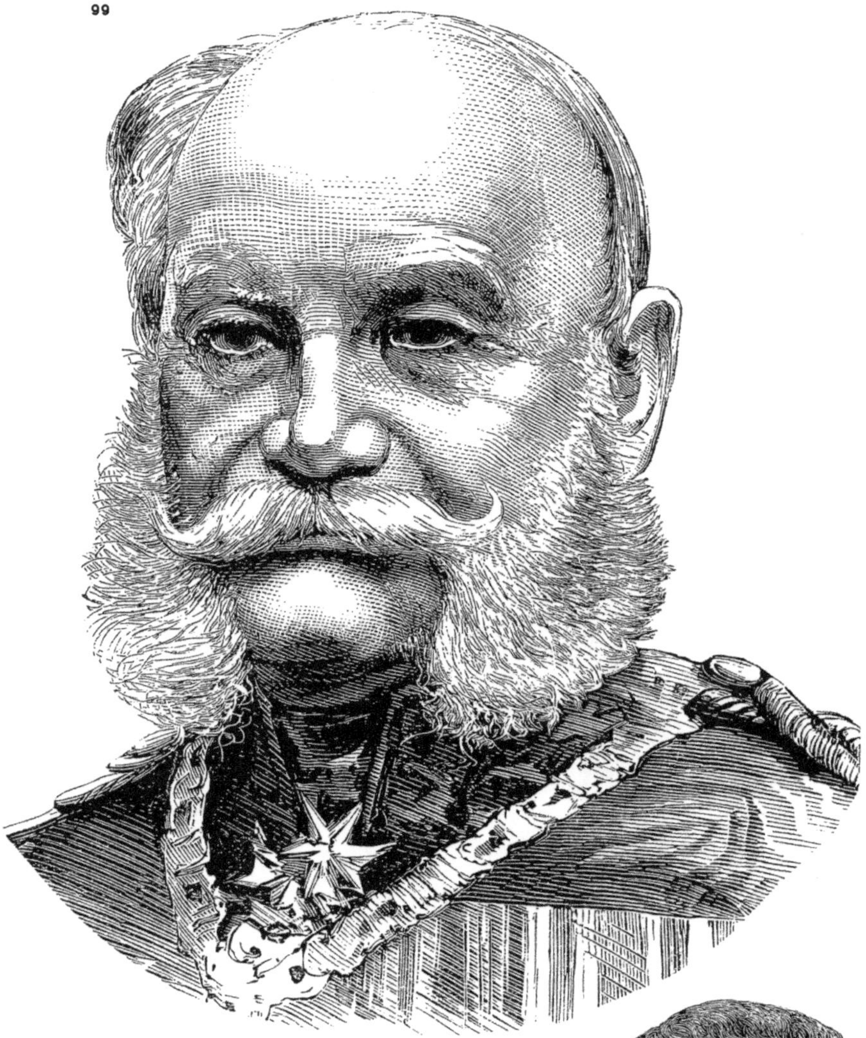

100

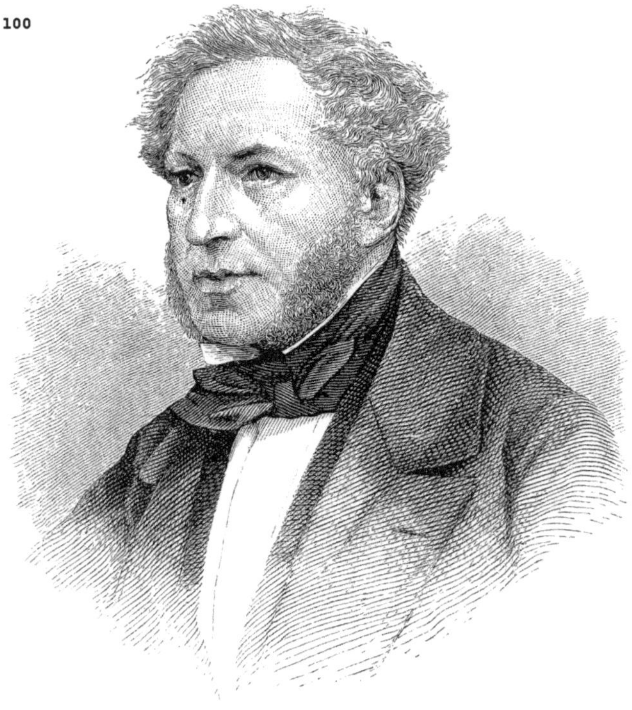

101

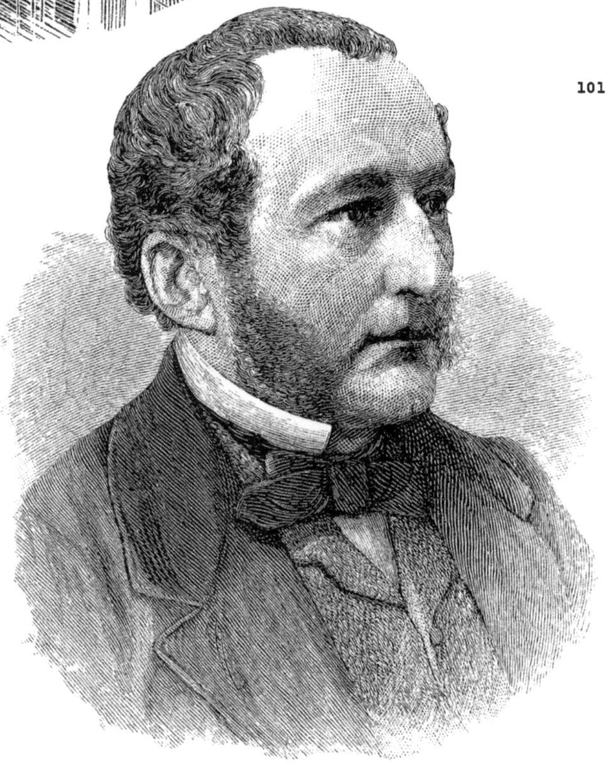

102

103

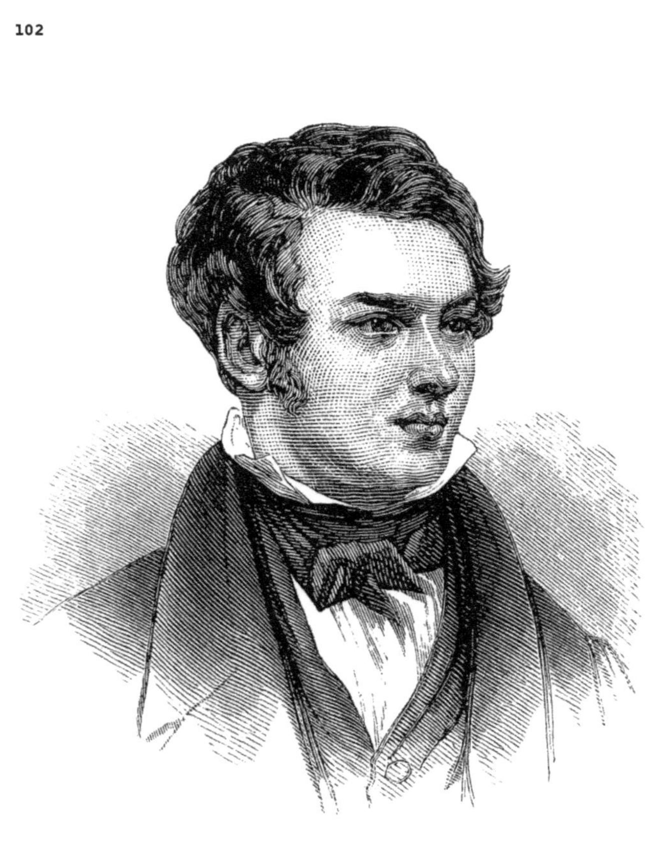

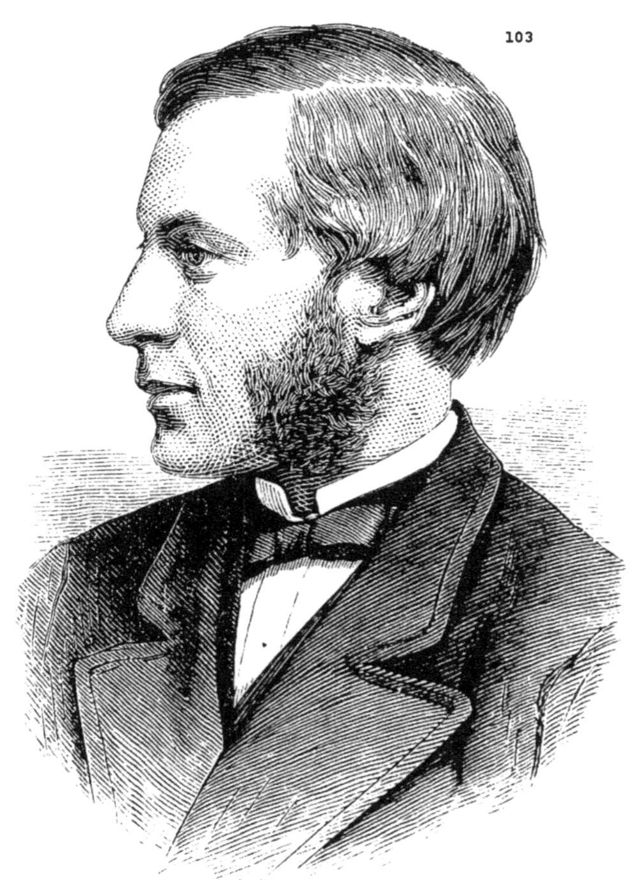

MEN

104

105

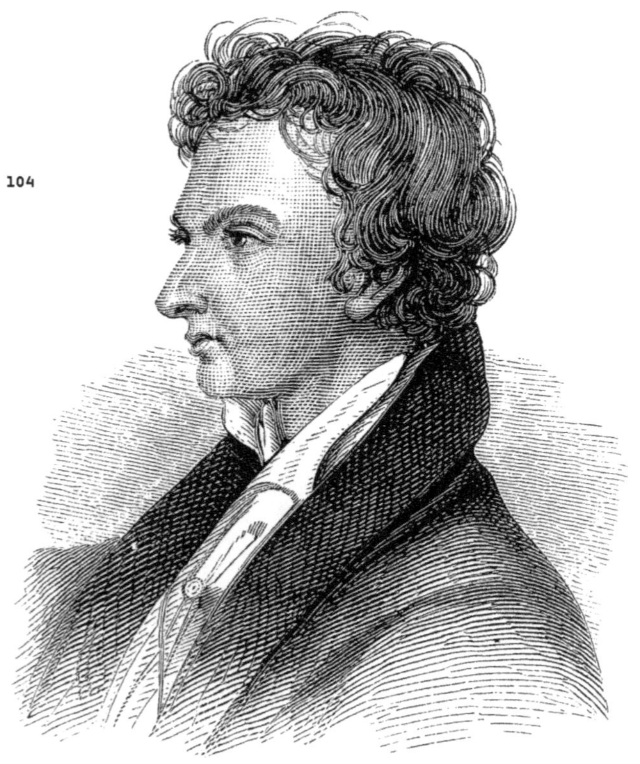

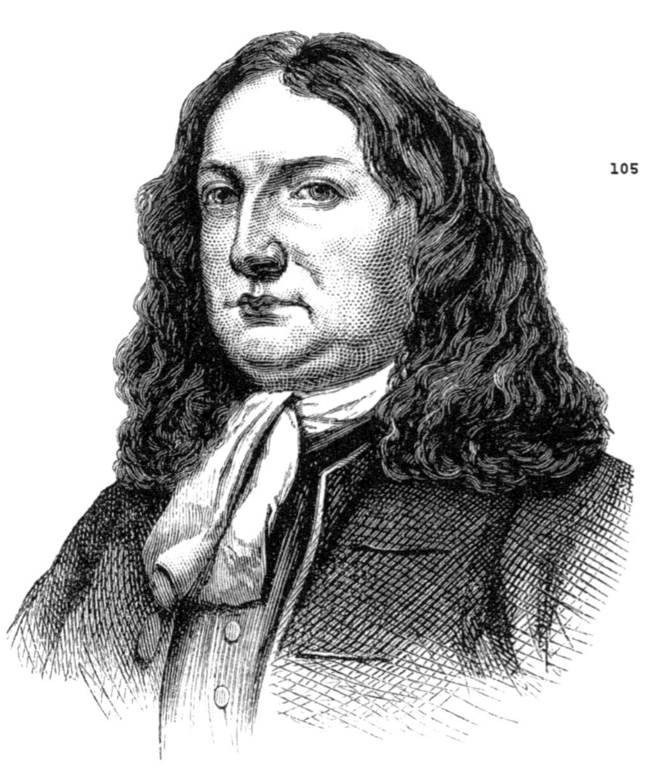

106

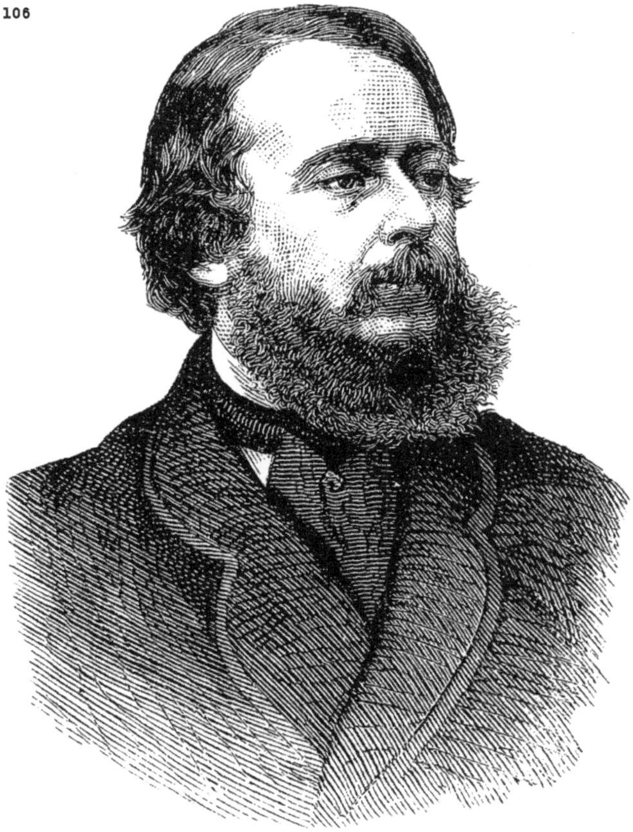

107

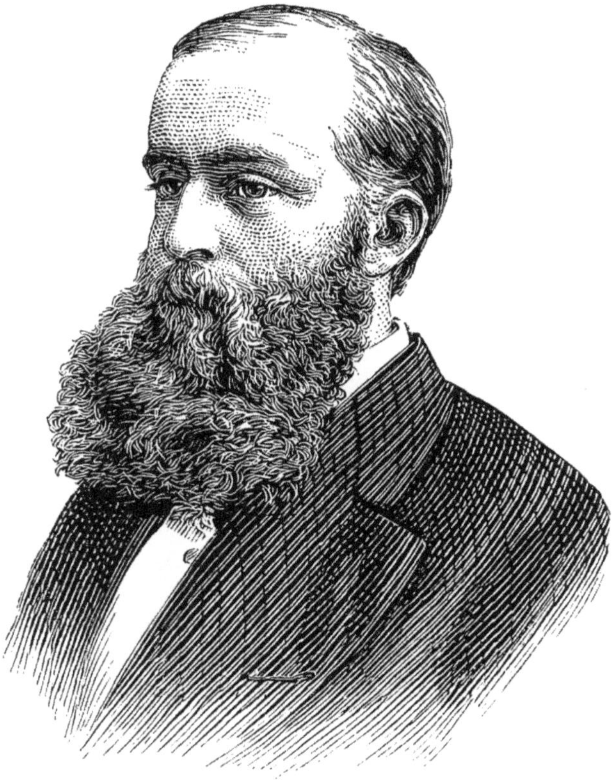

108

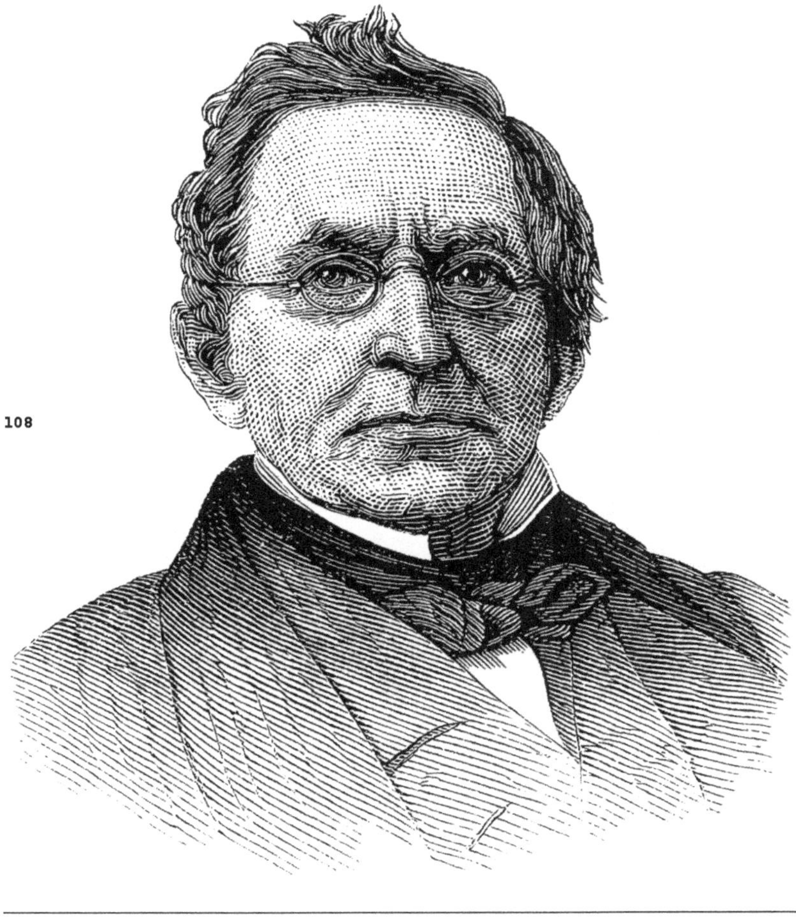

109

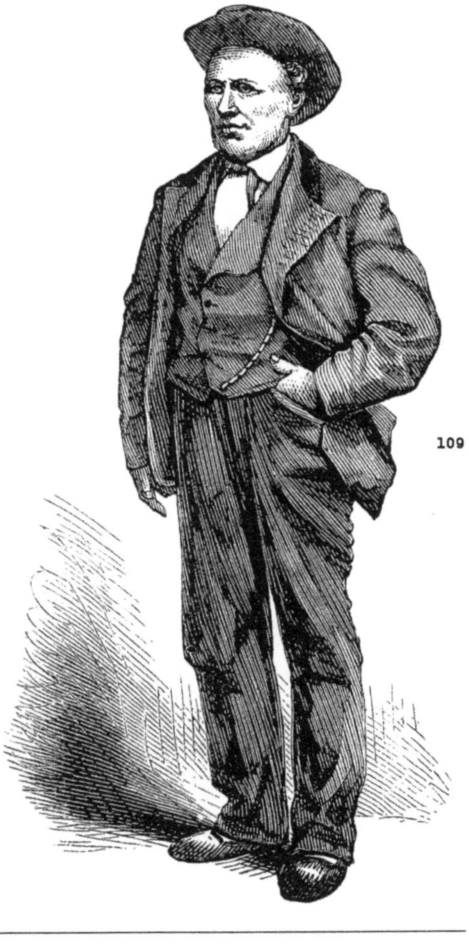

110

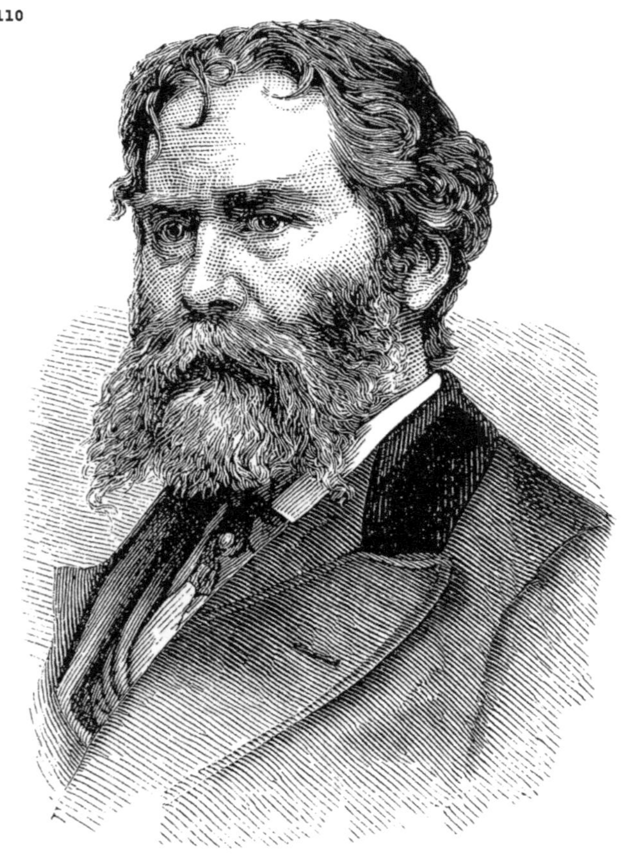

111

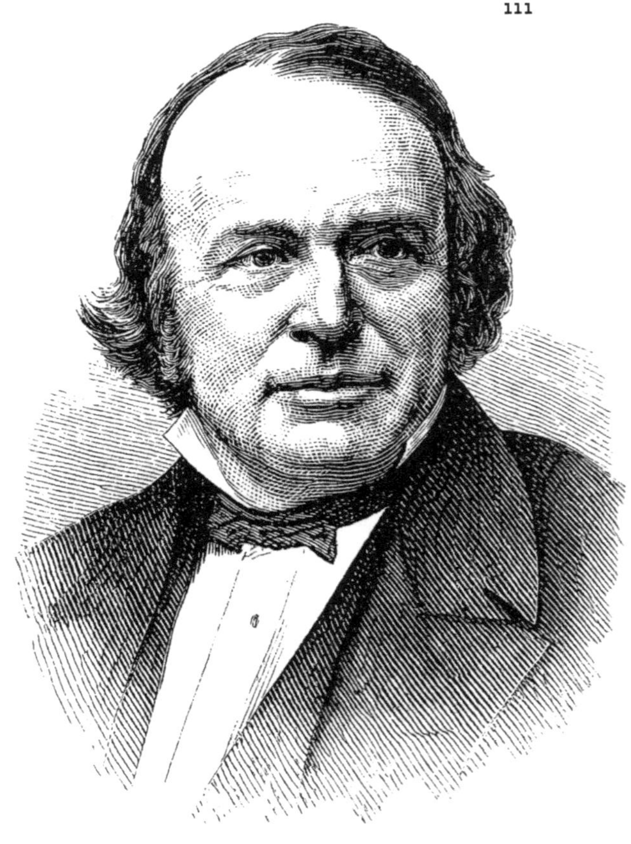

MEN

112

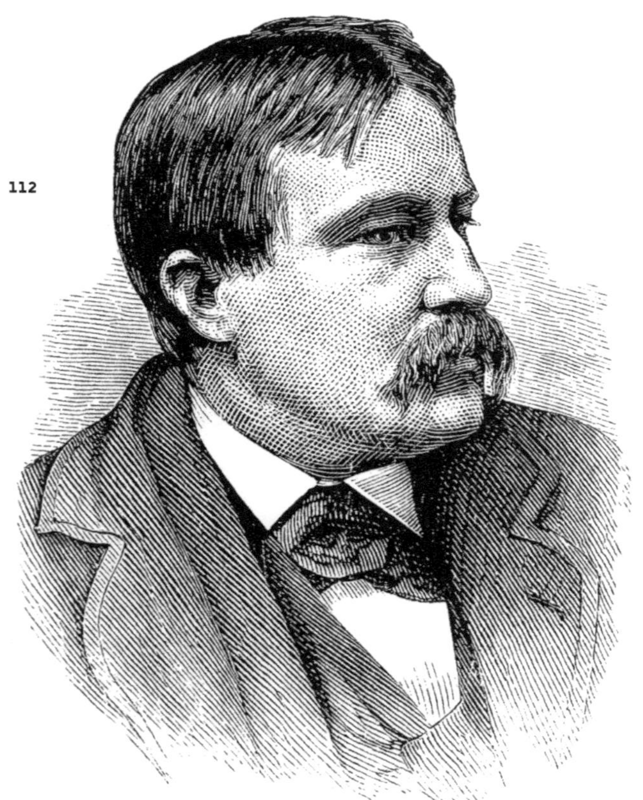

113

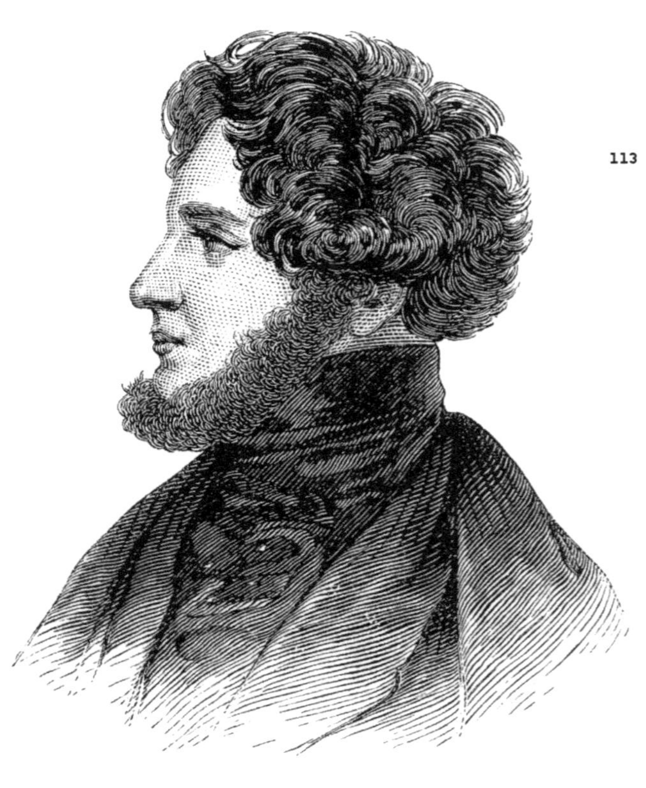

114

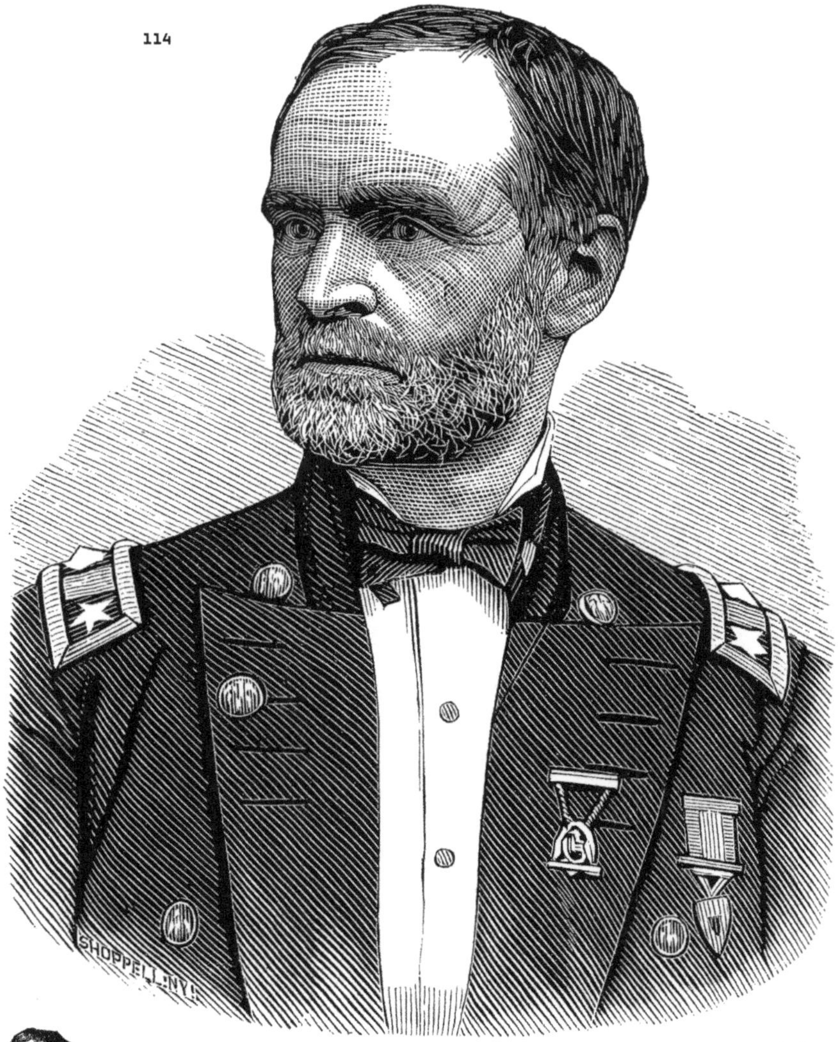

115

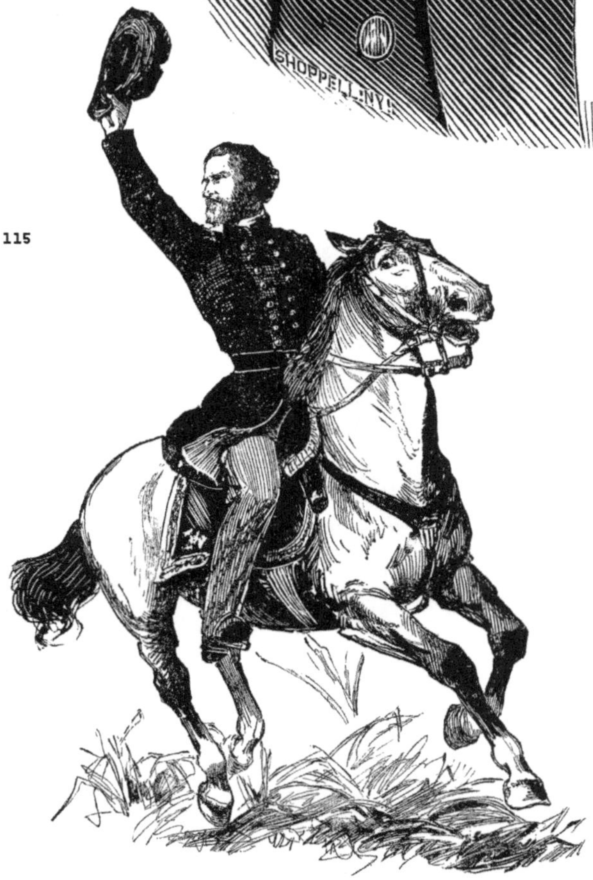

116

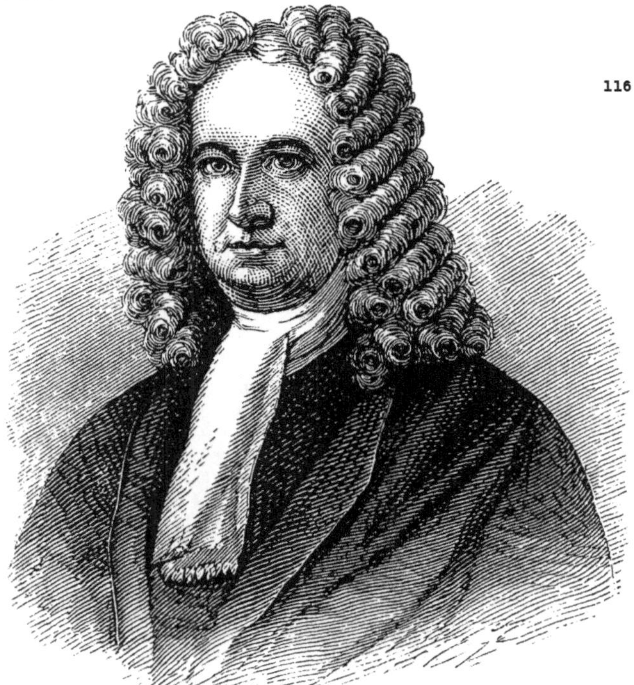

117

118

MEN

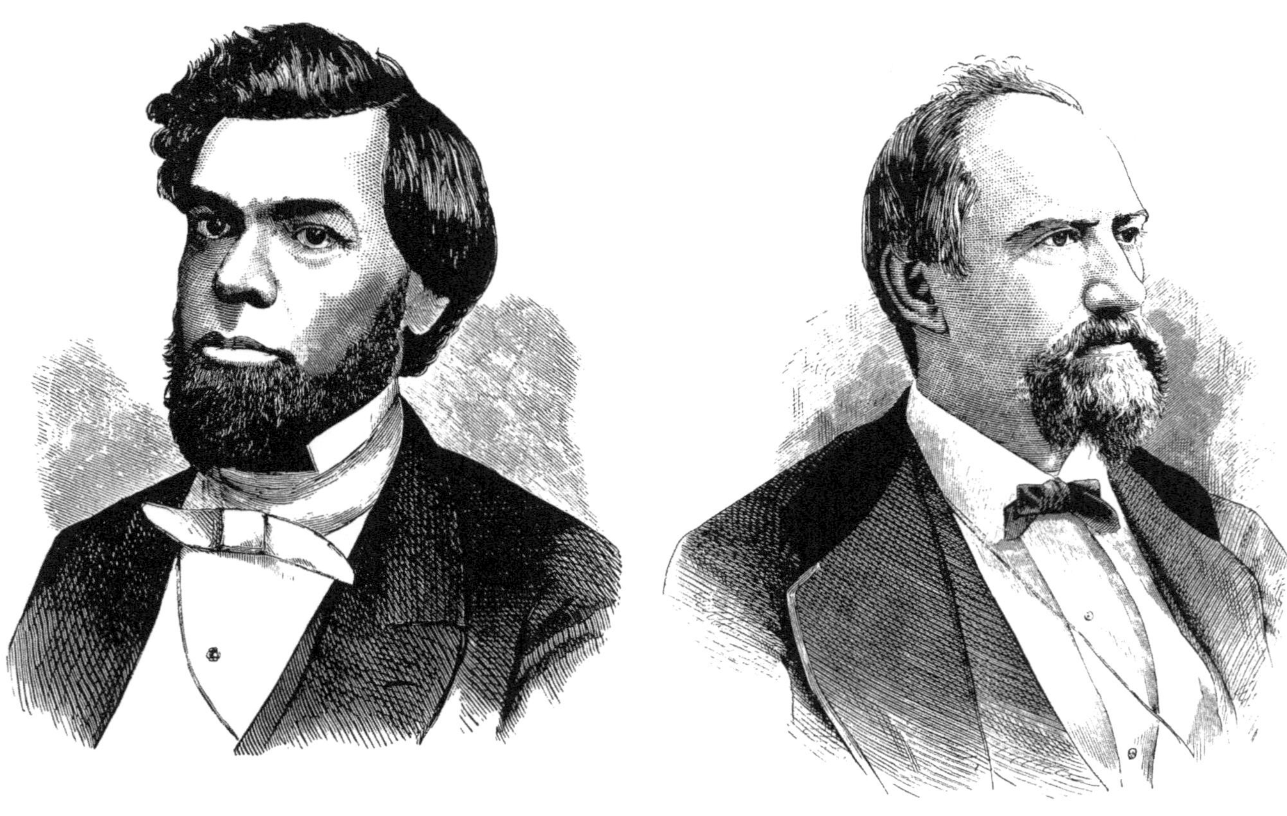

119

120

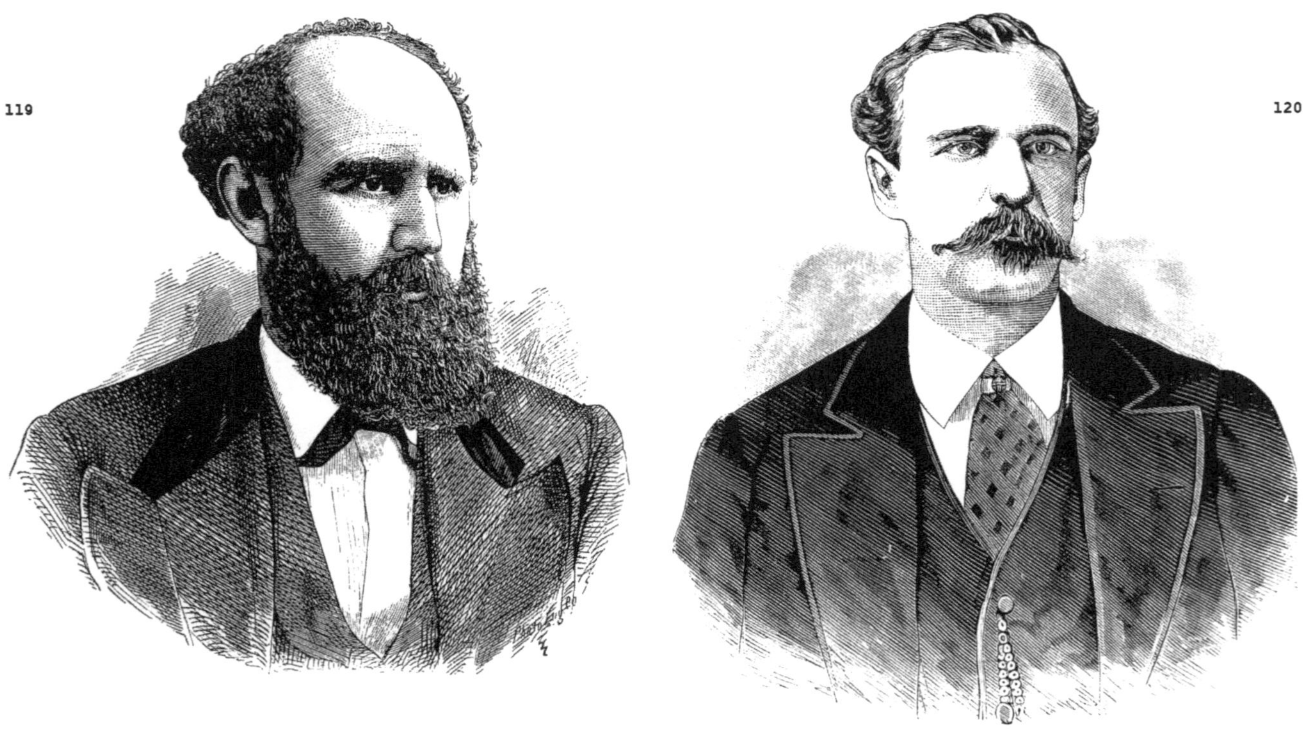

121

122

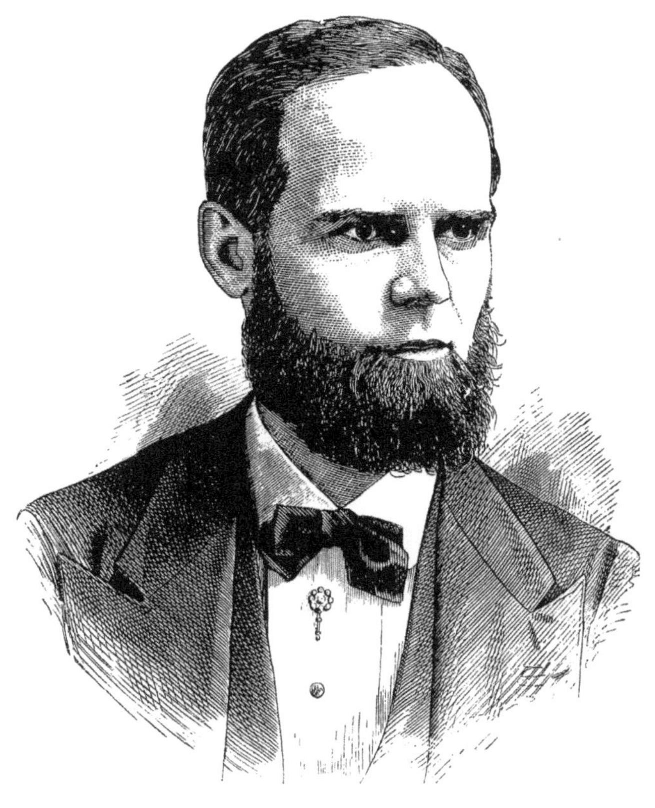

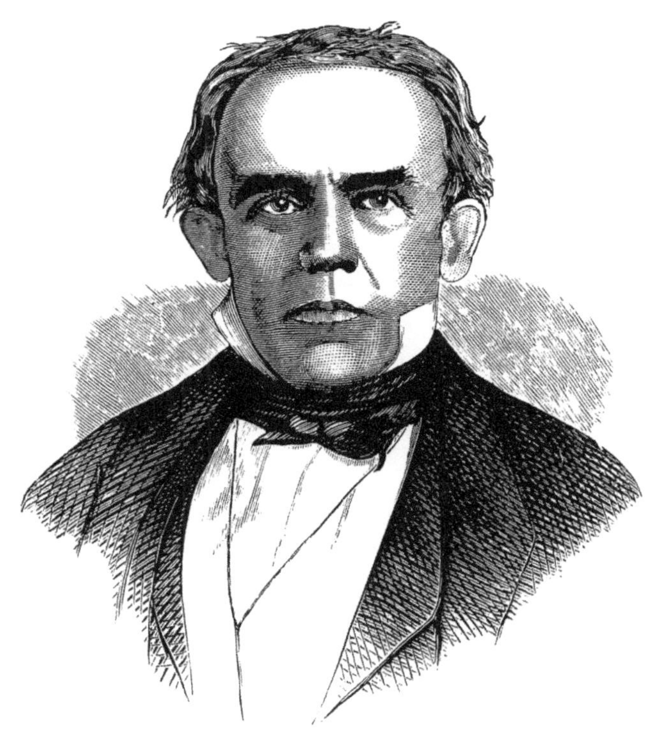

MEN

123

124

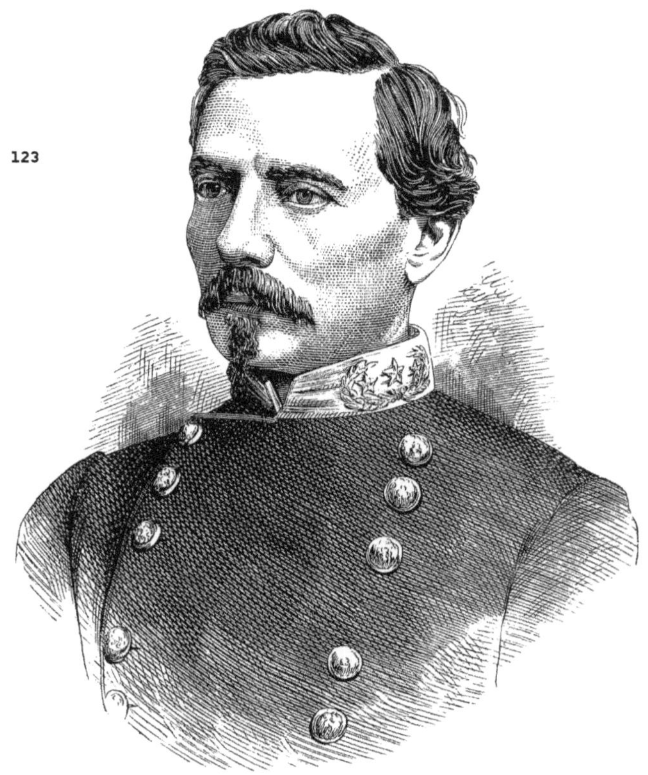

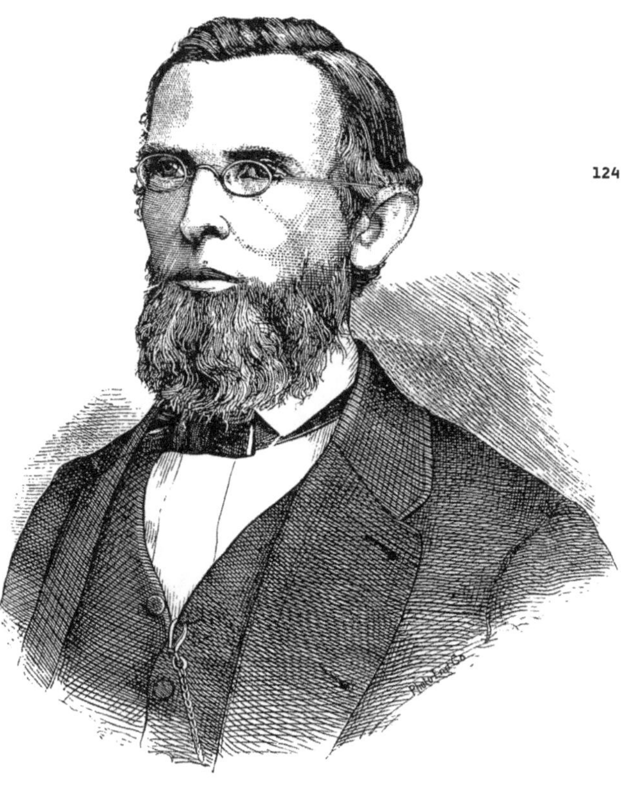

125

126

MEN

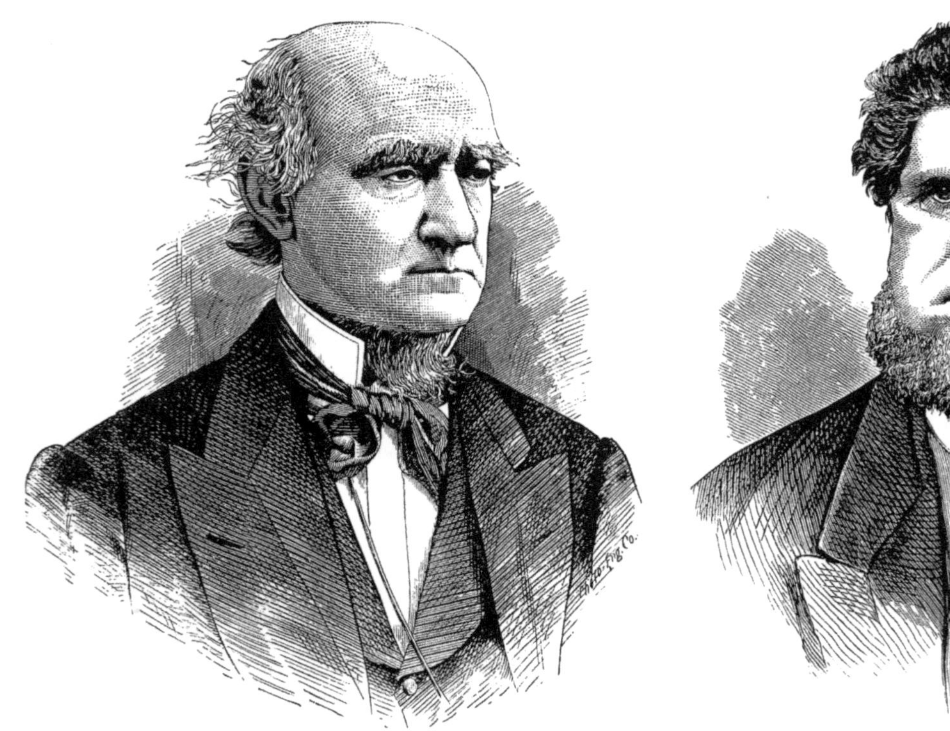

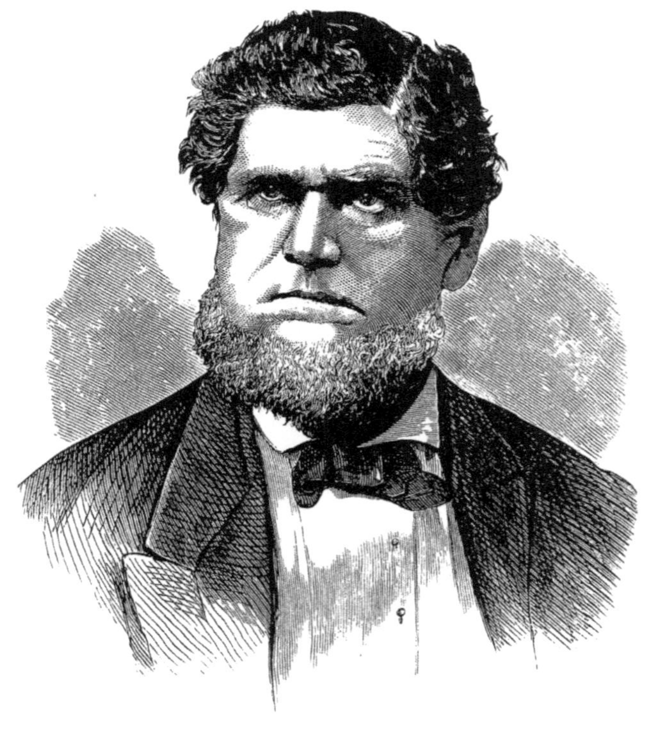

127

128

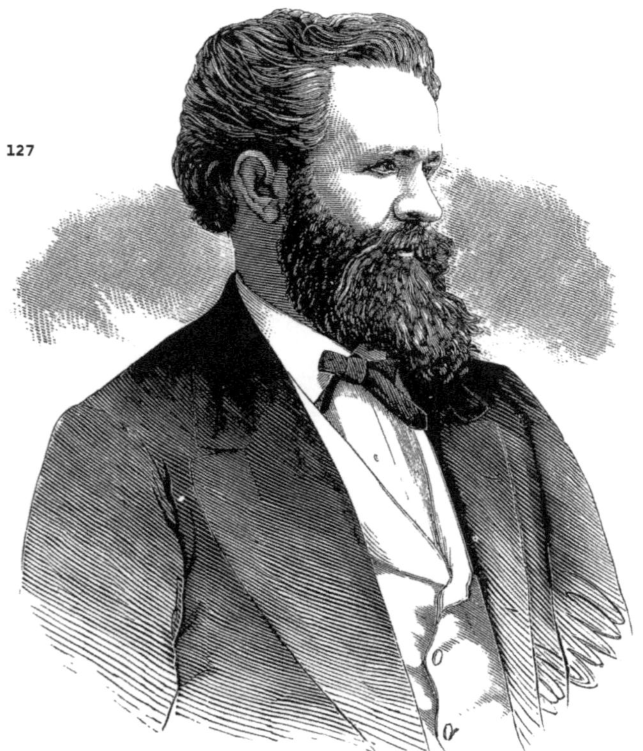

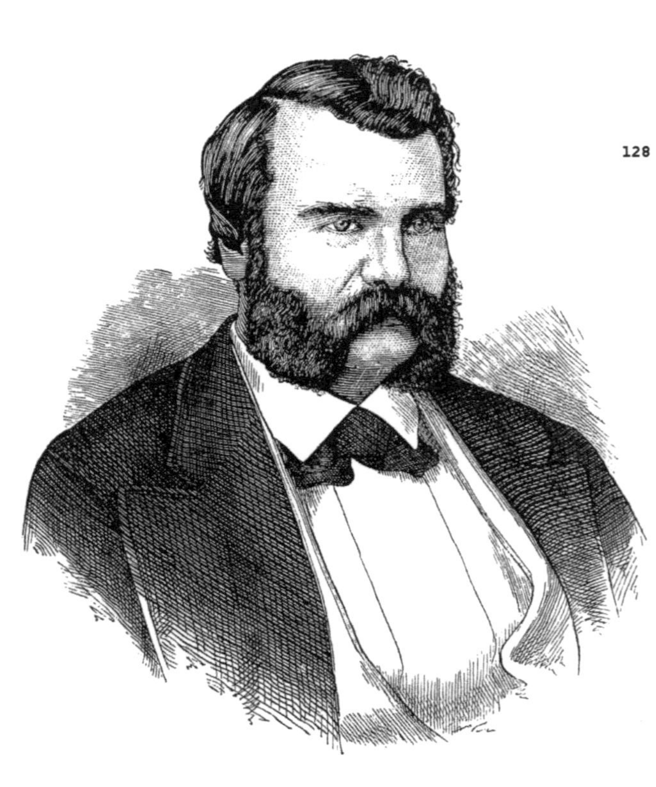

129

130

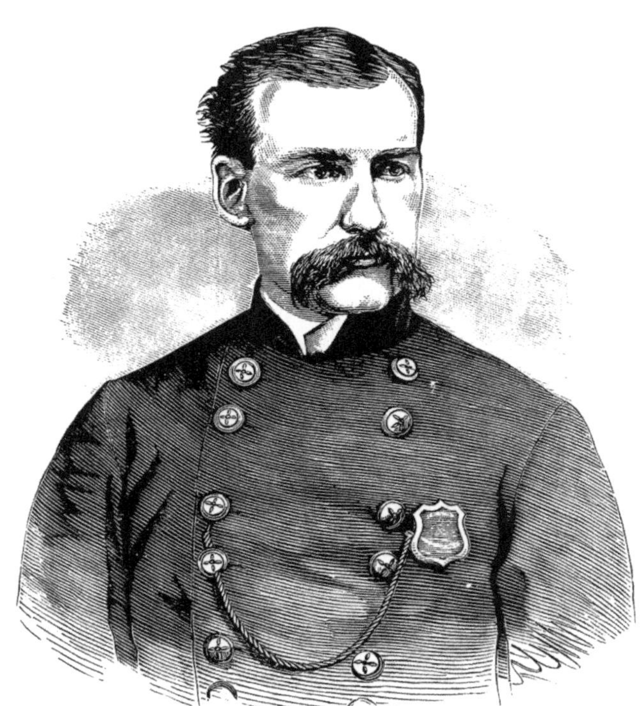

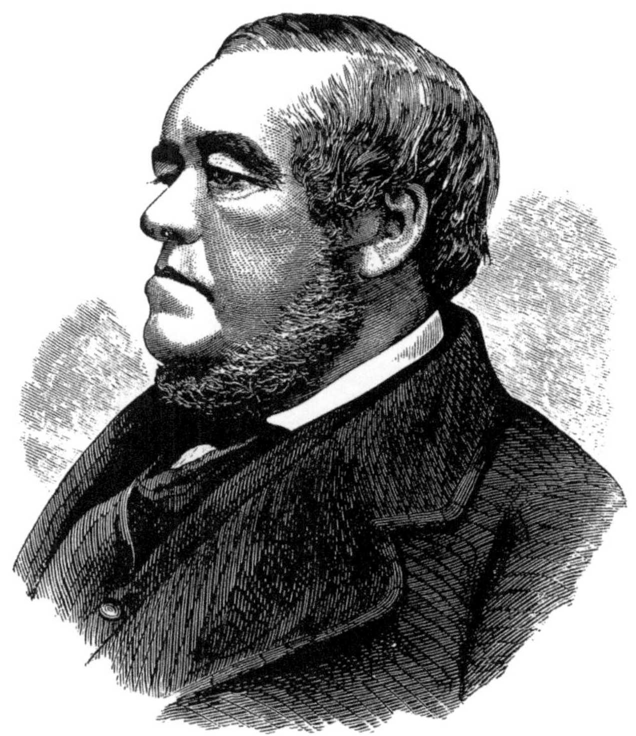

MEN

131

132

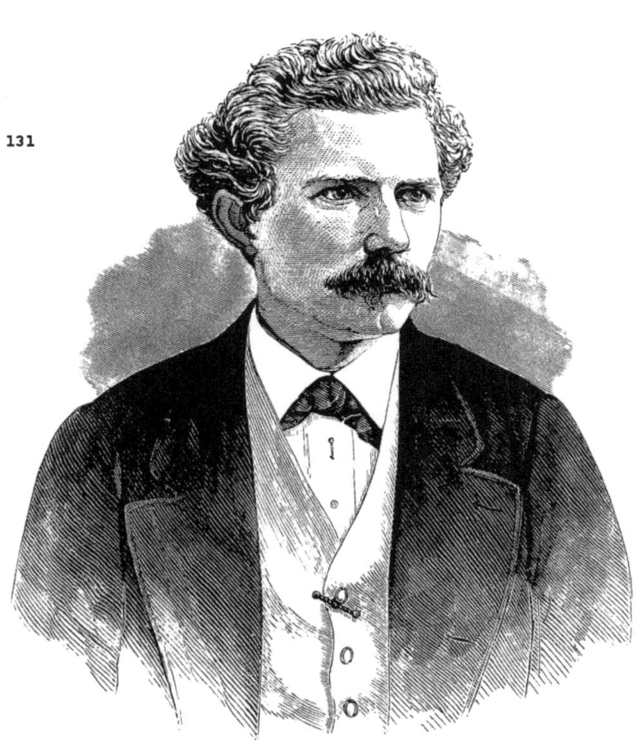

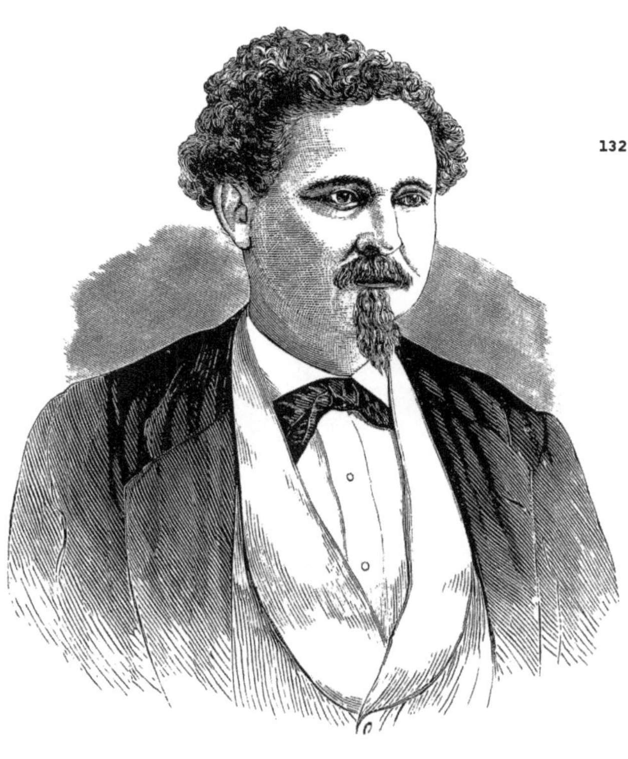

133

134

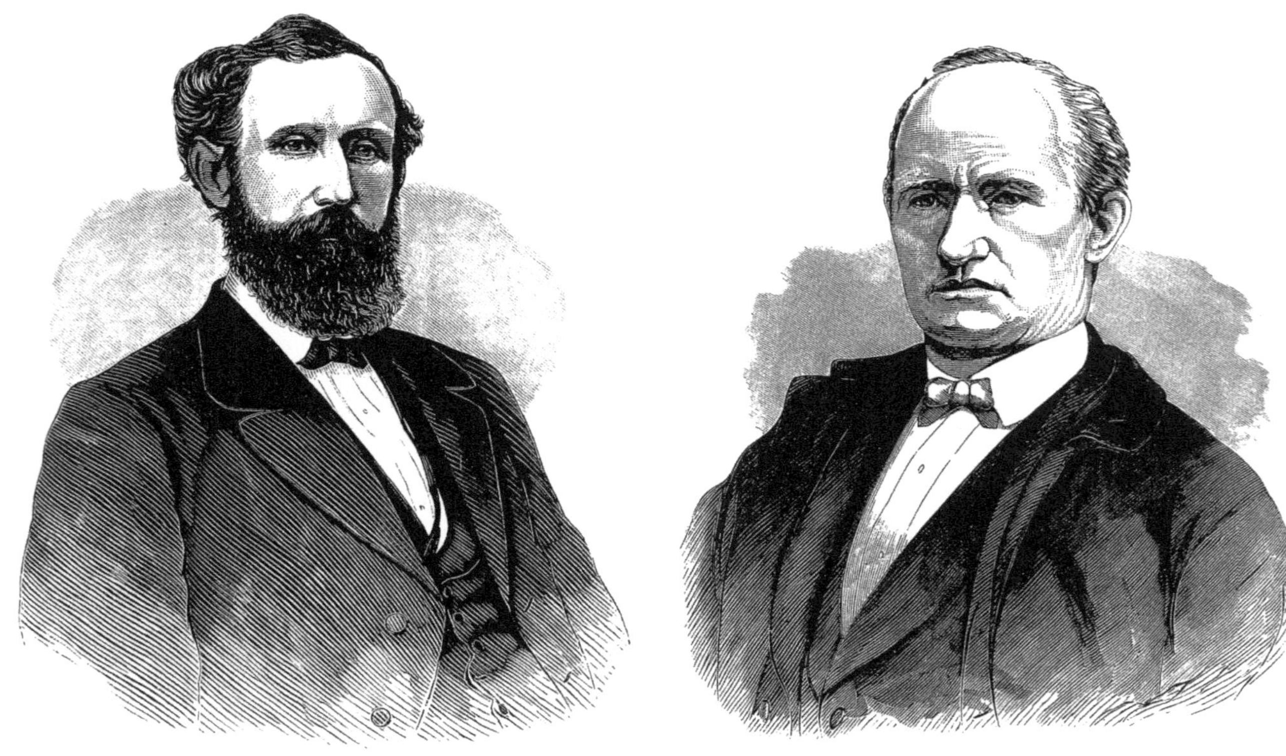

MEN

135

136

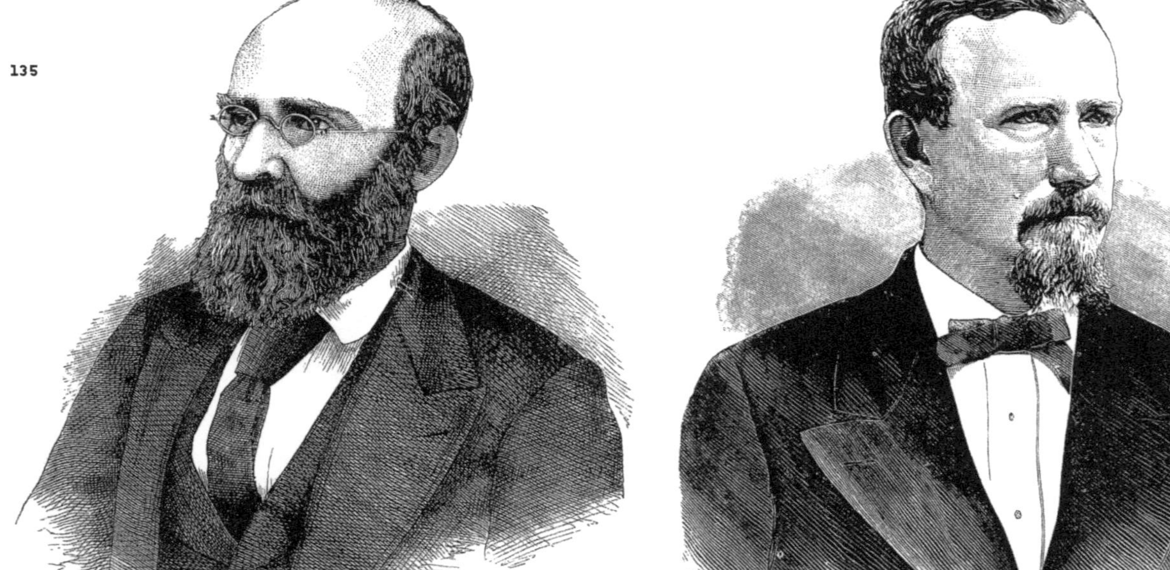

137

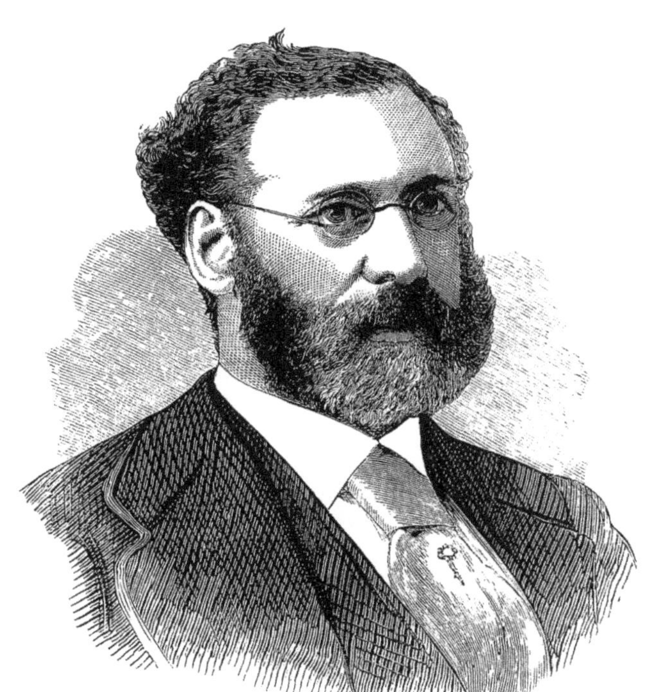

138

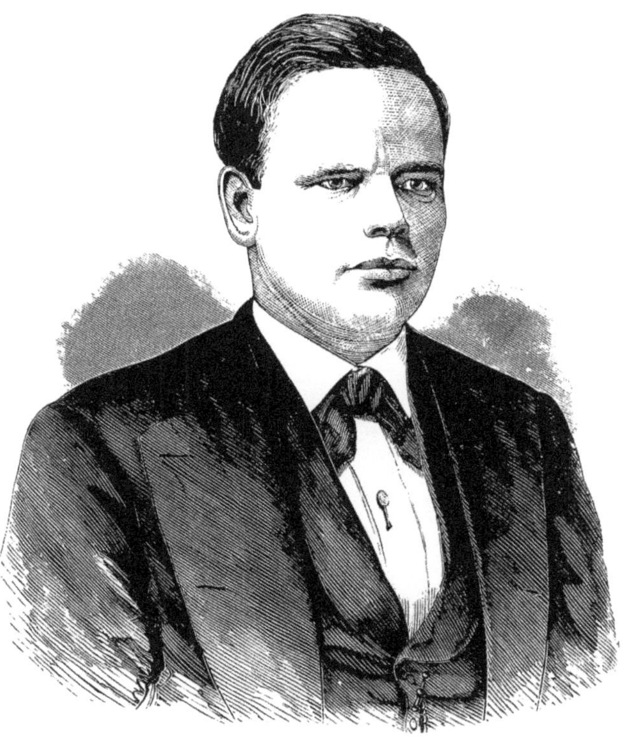

139

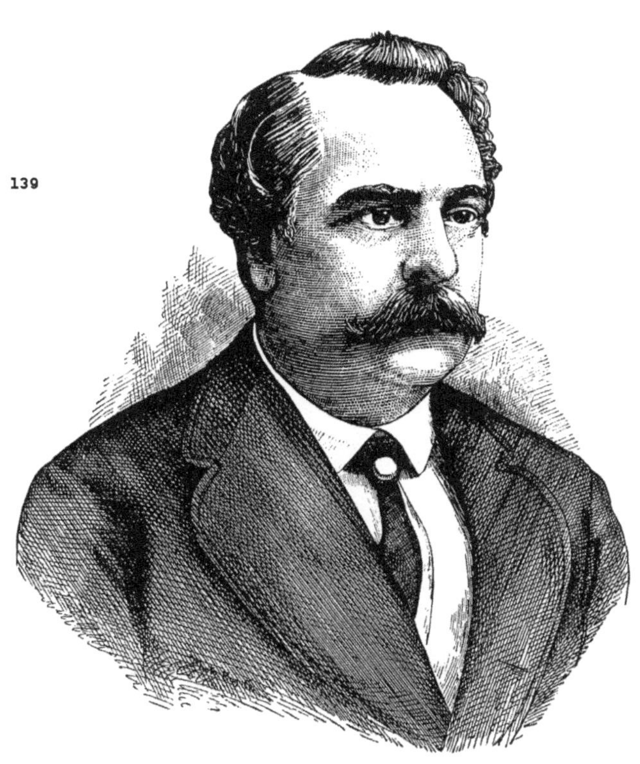

140

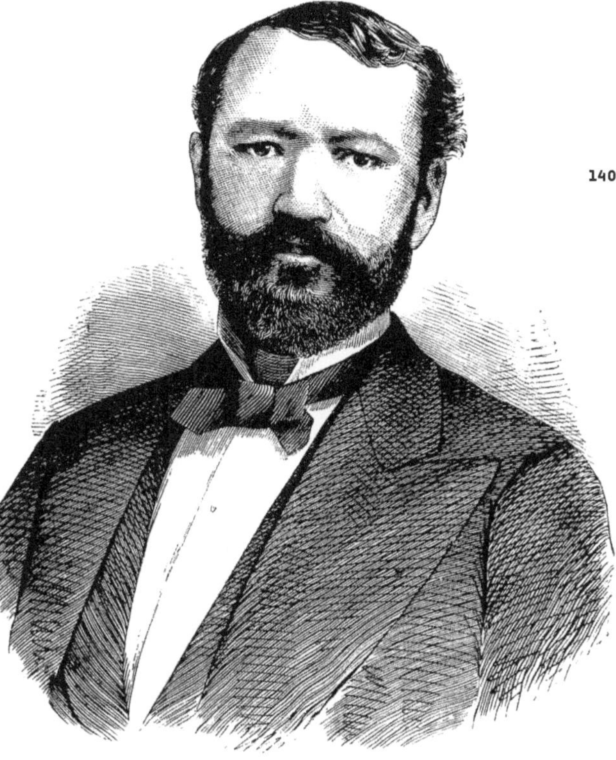

141

142

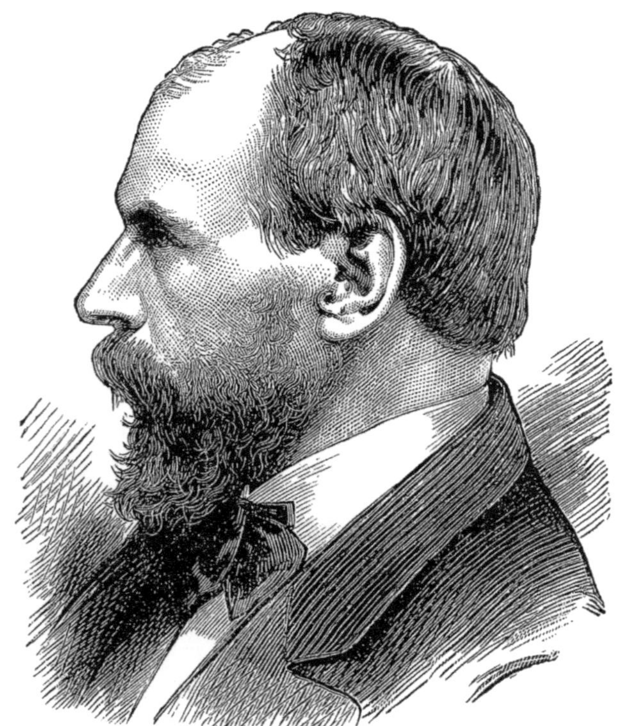

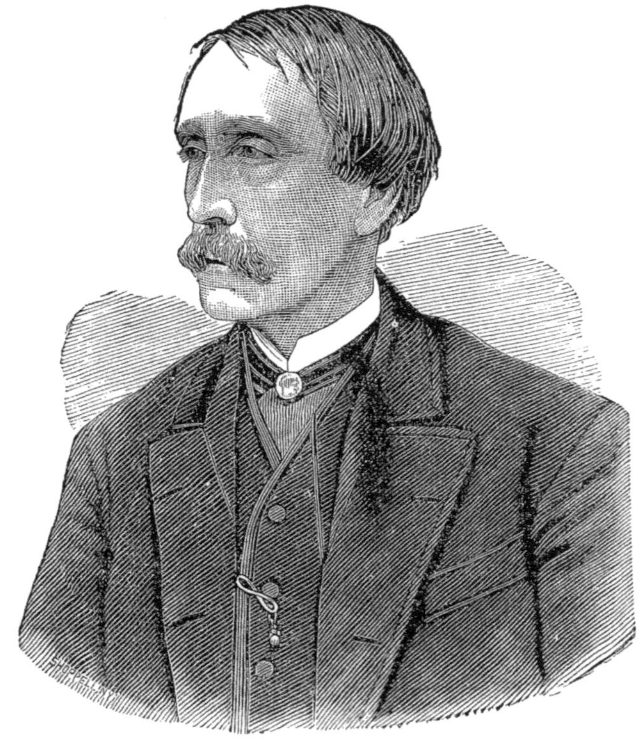

MEN

143

144

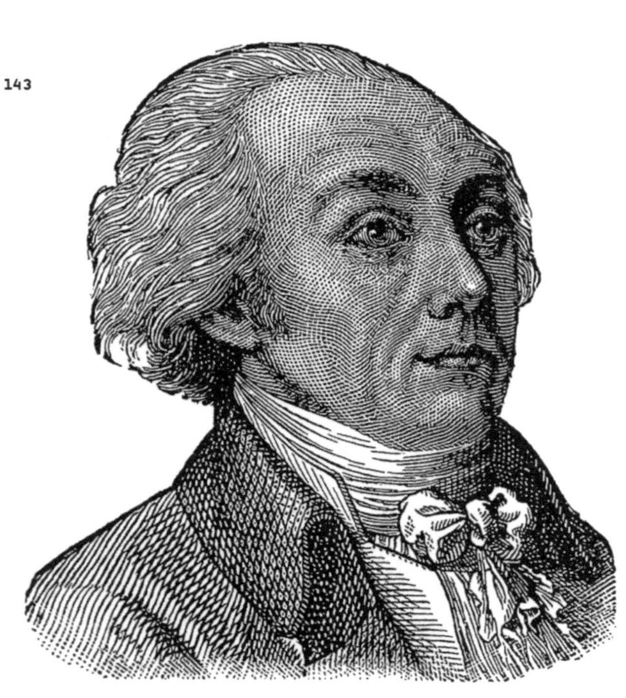

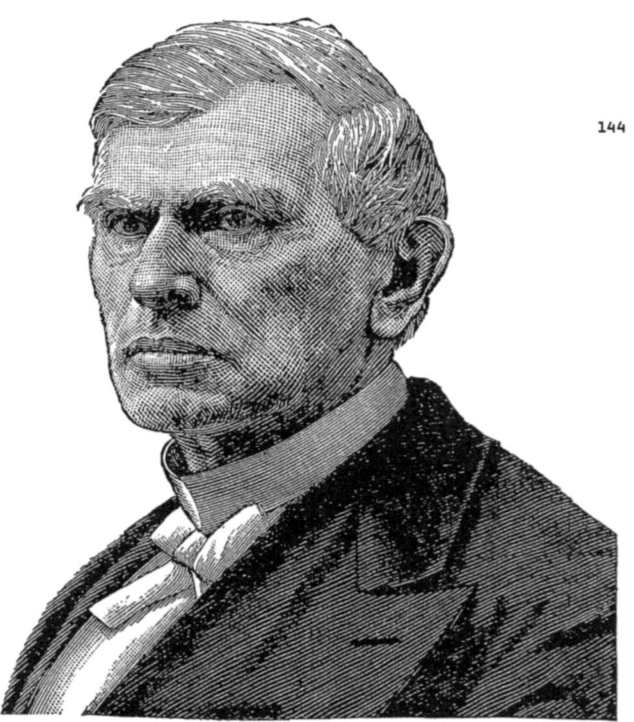

145

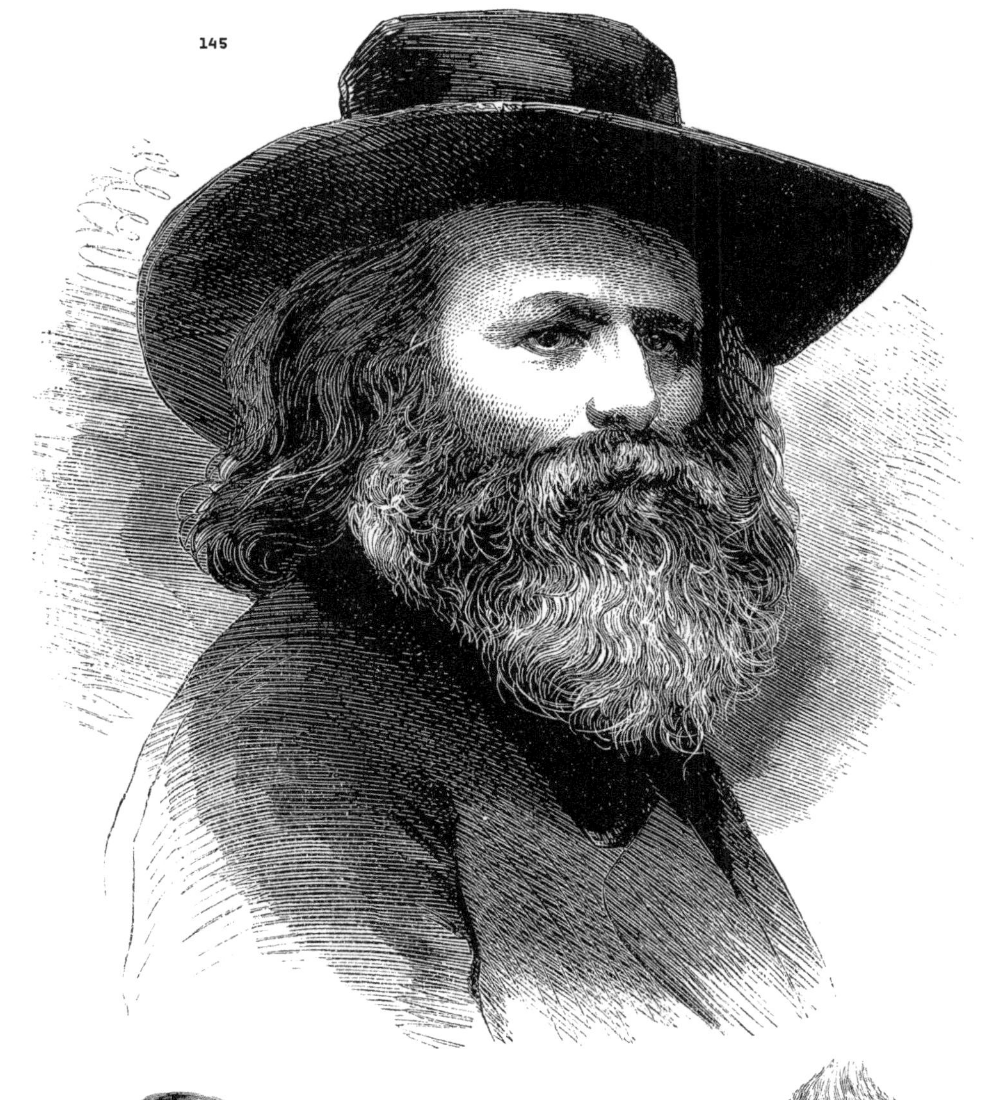

MEN

146

147

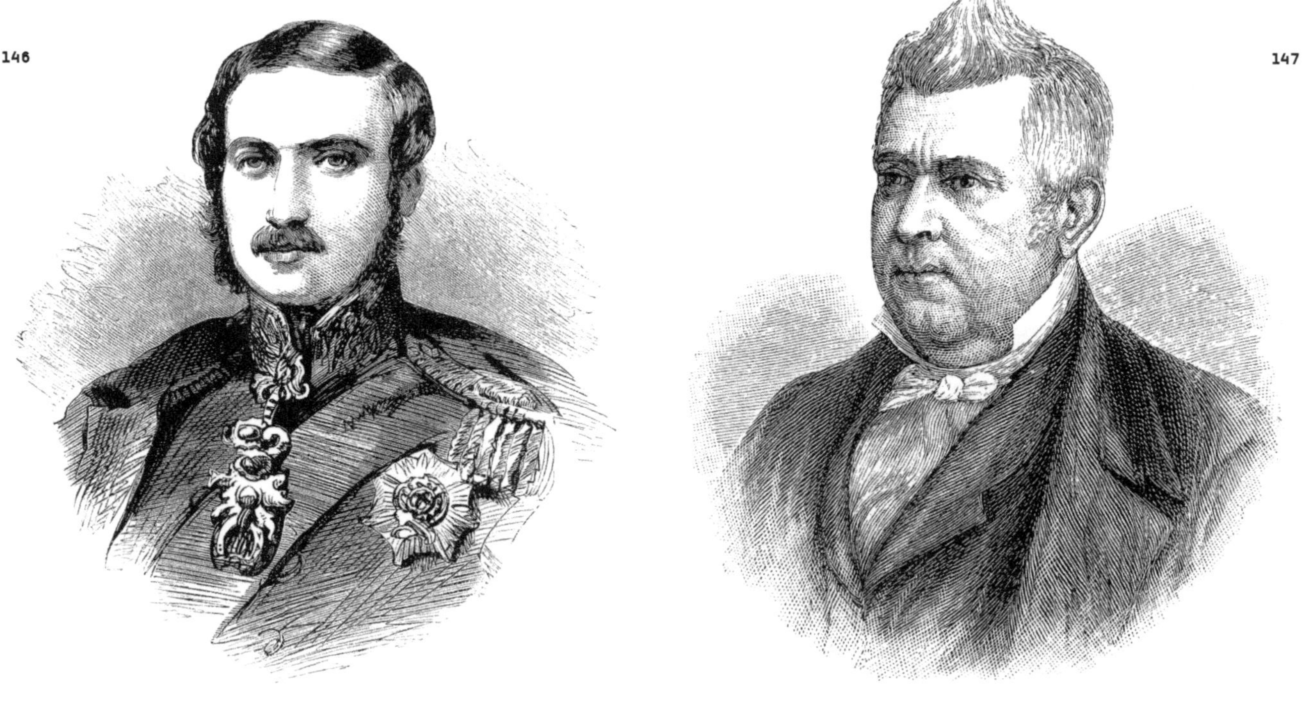

MEN

148

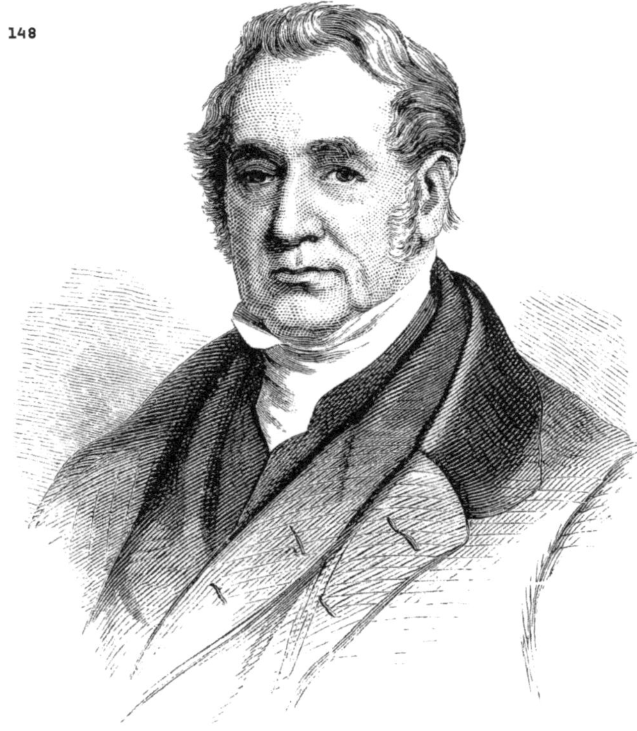

149

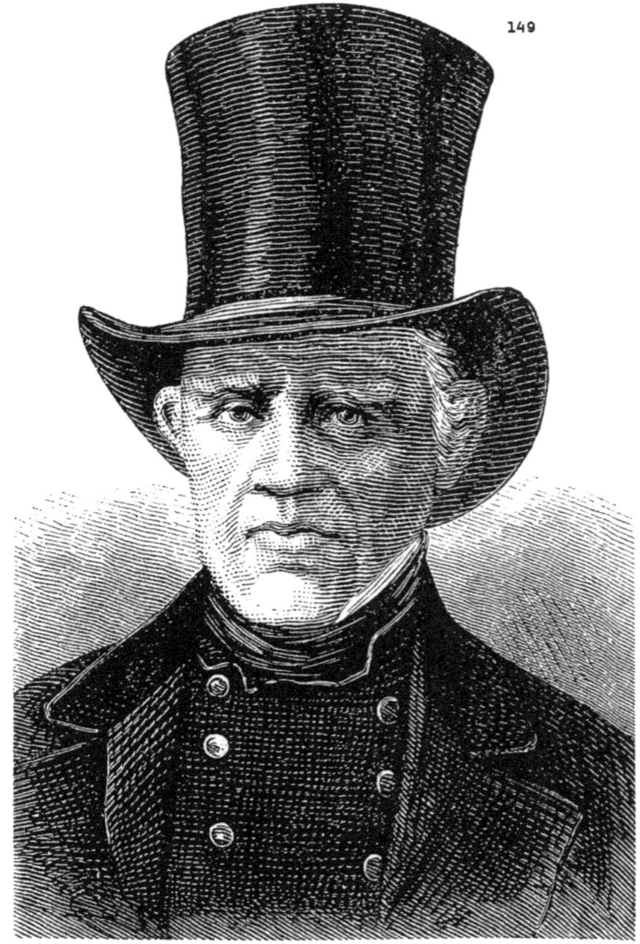

150

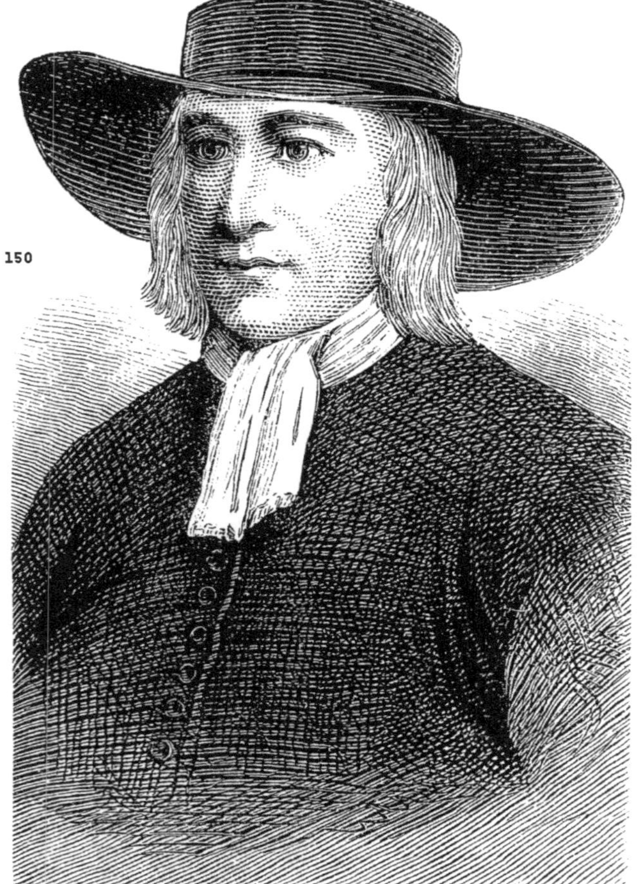

151

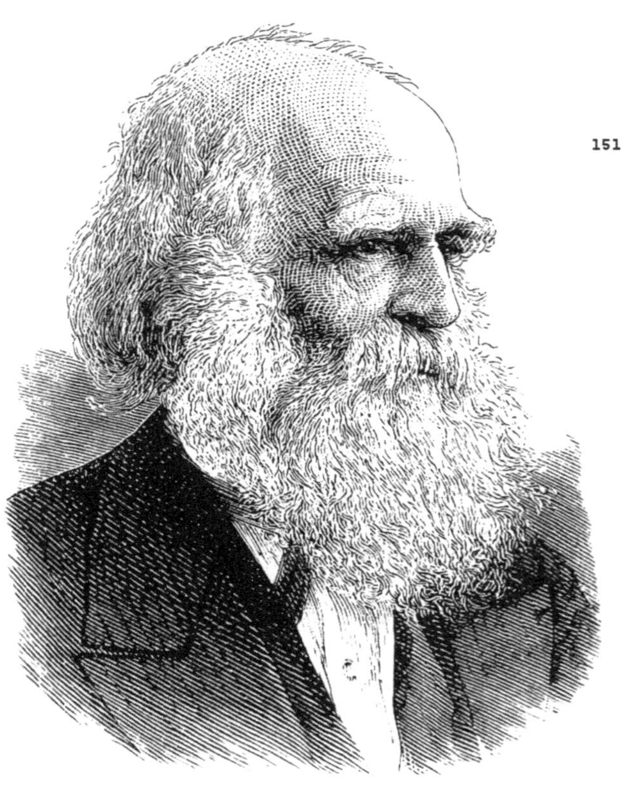

152

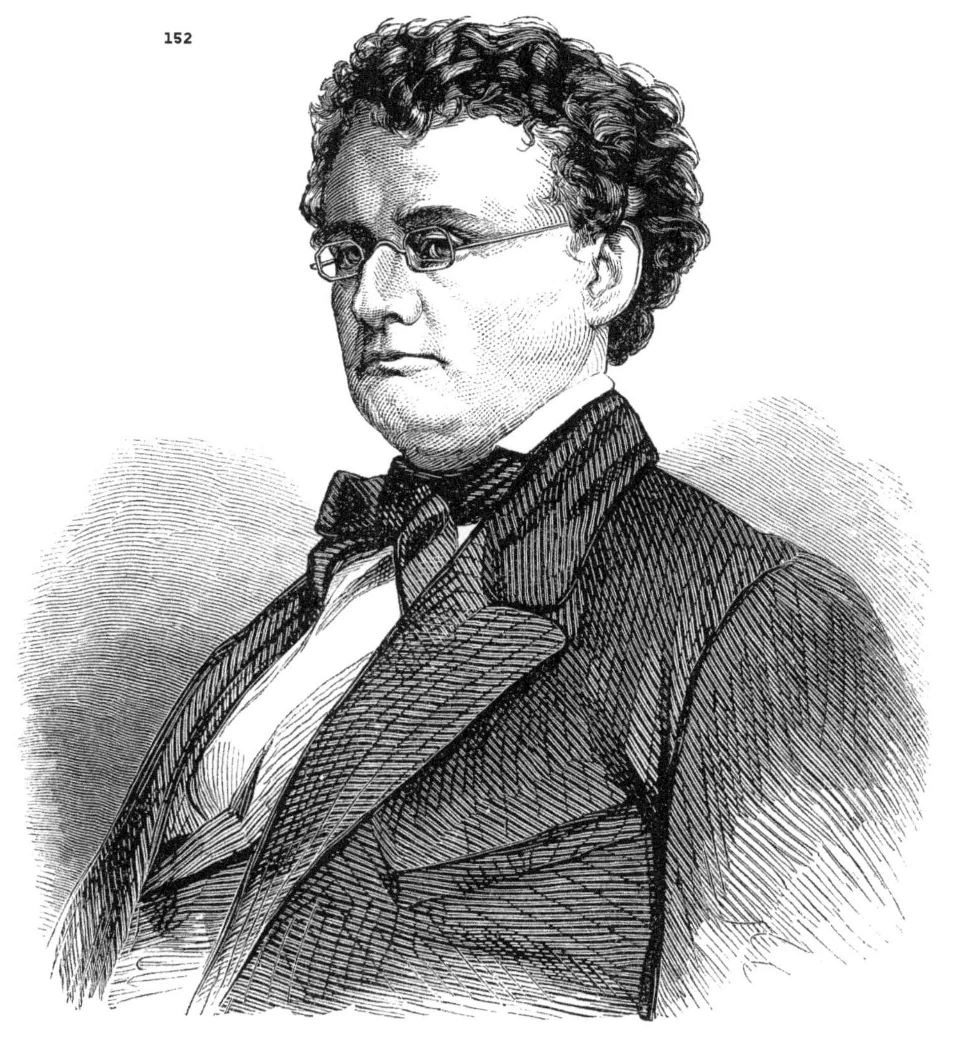

MEN

153

154

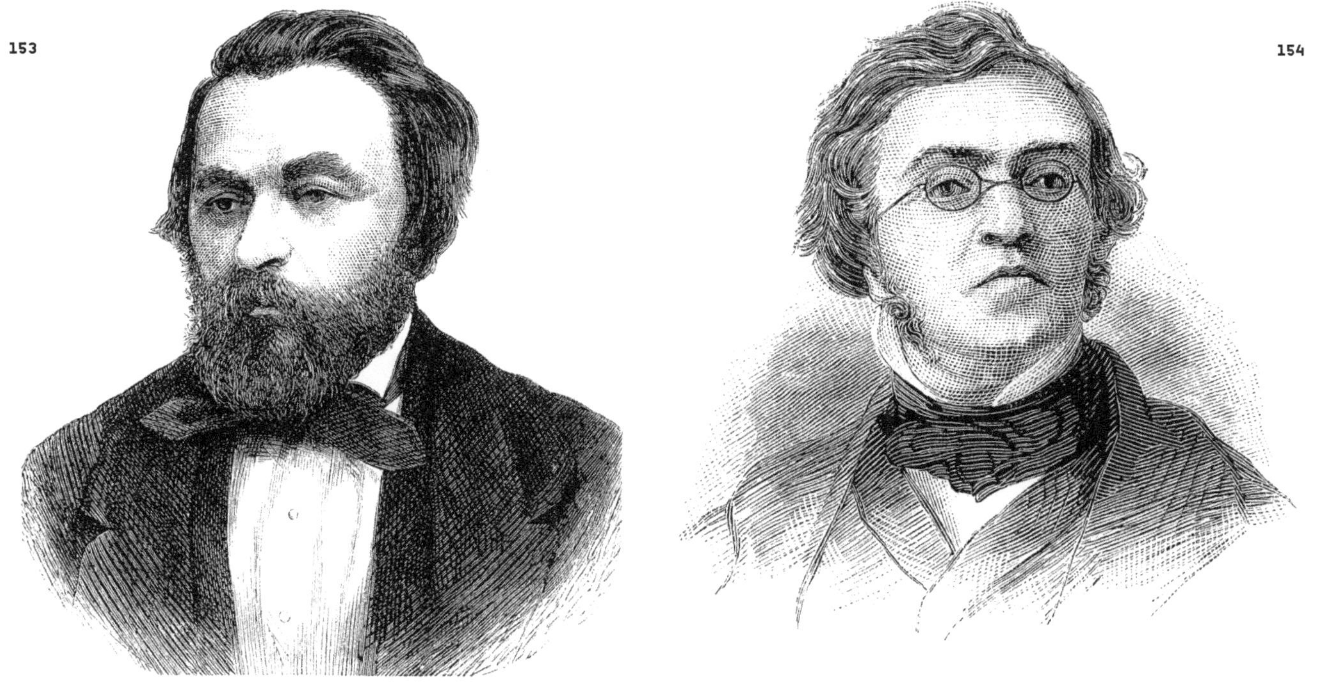

155

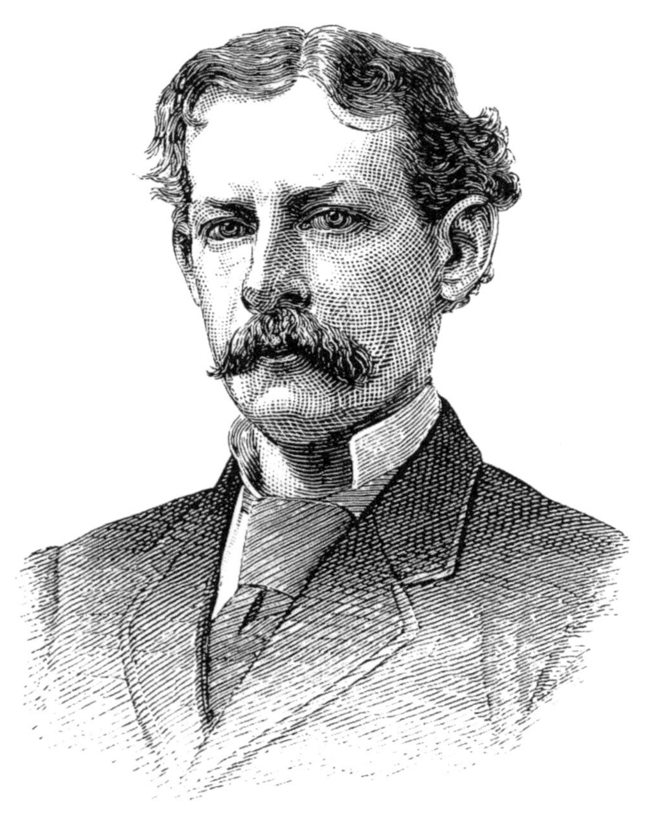

156

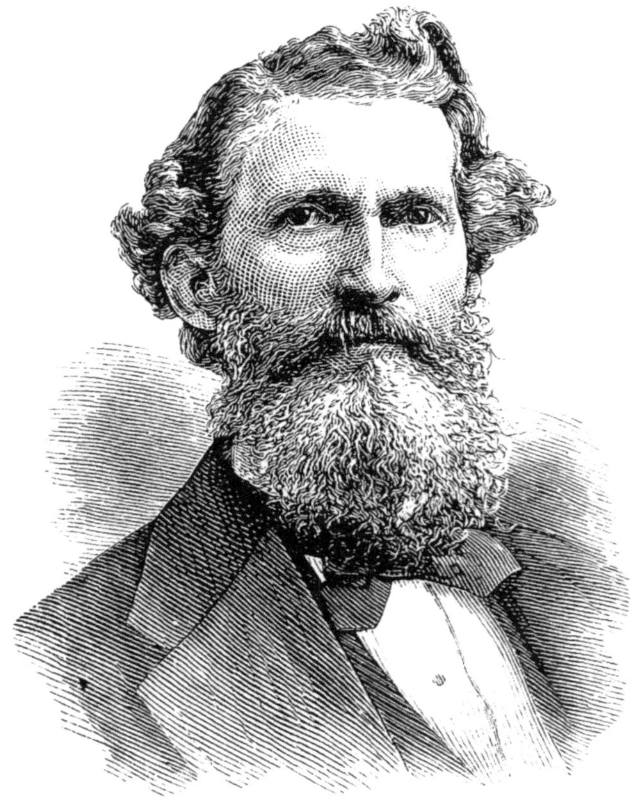

MEN

157

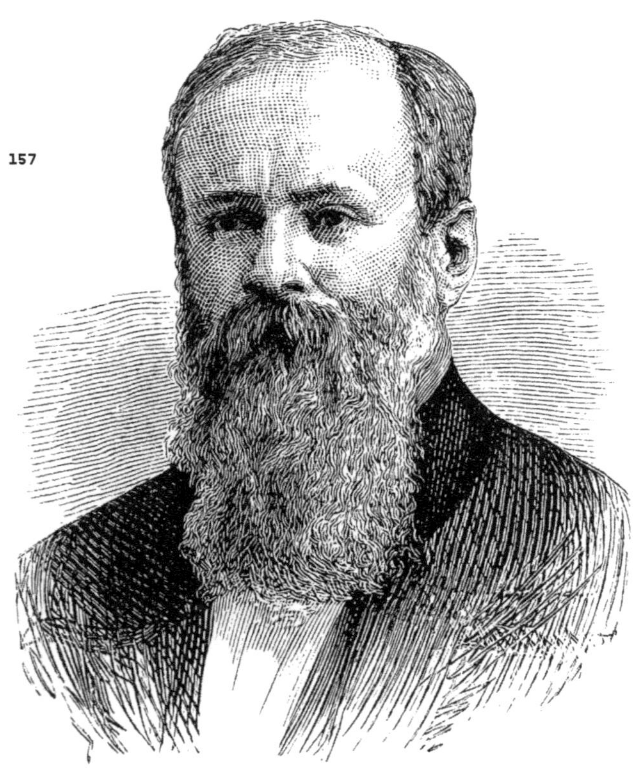

158

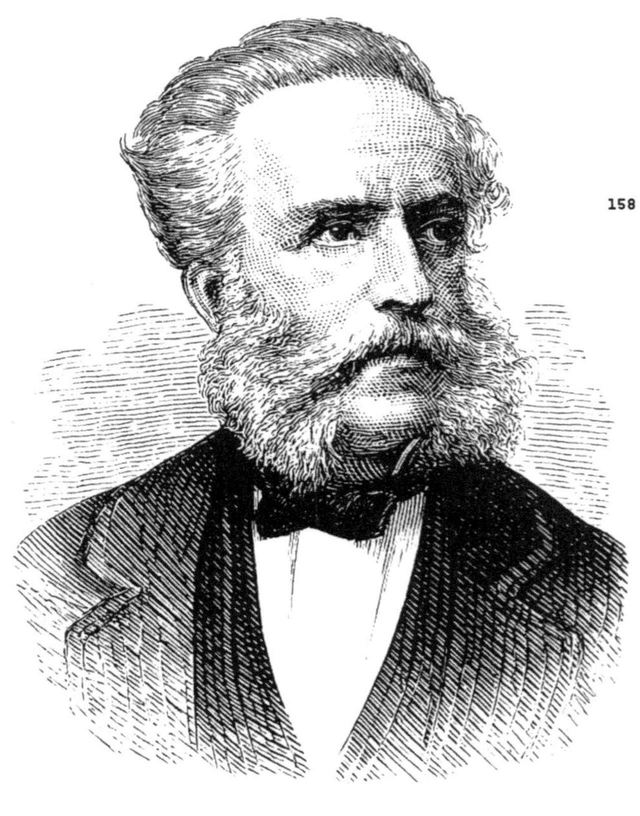

159

160

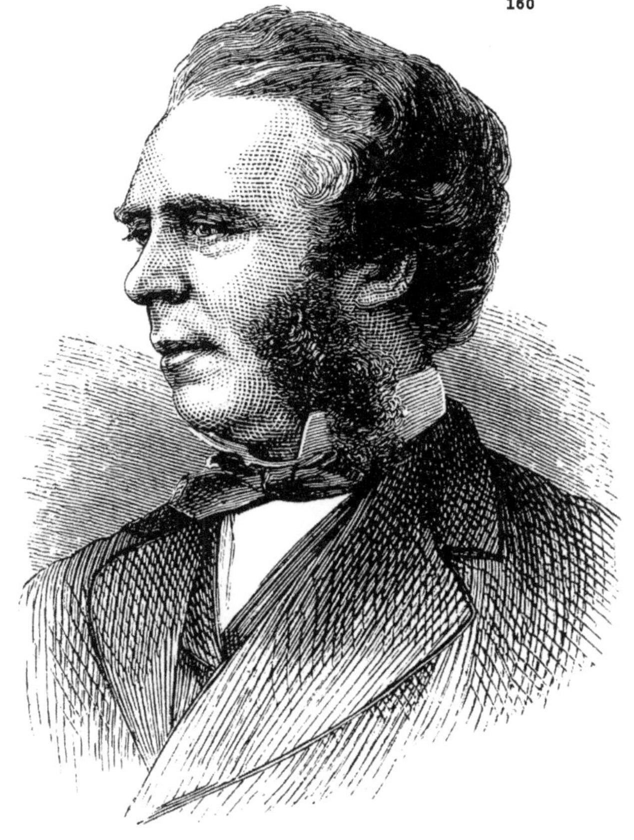

MEN

161

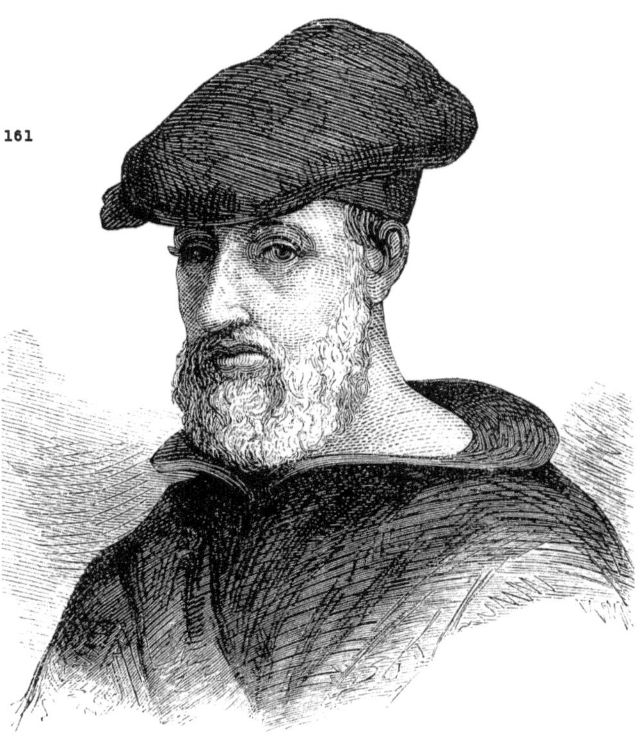

162

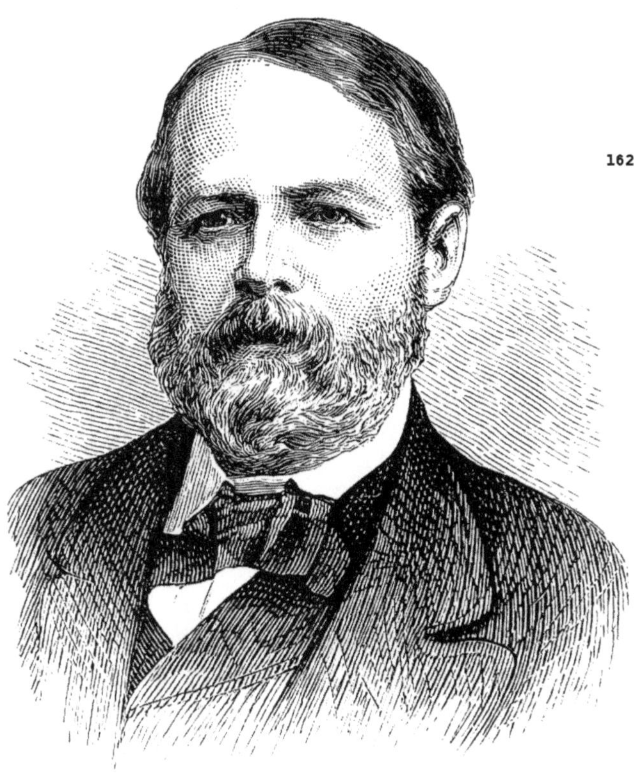

163

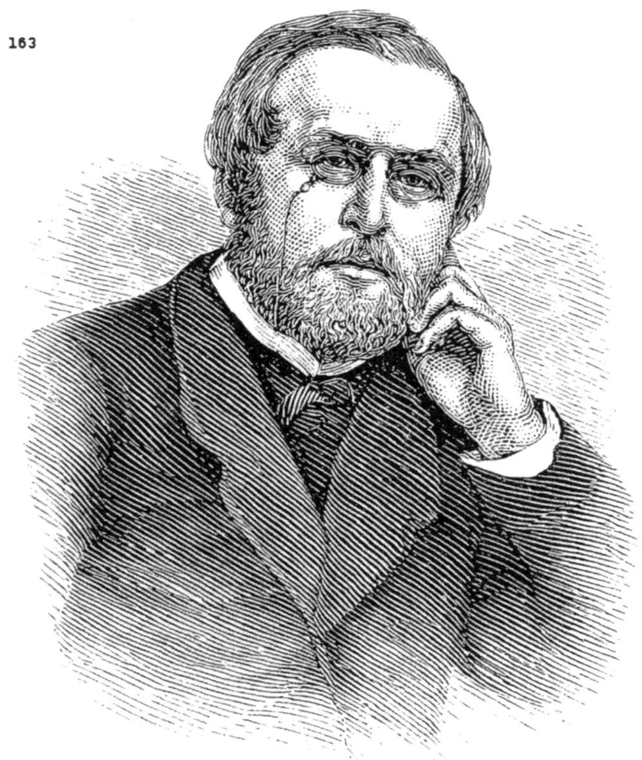

164

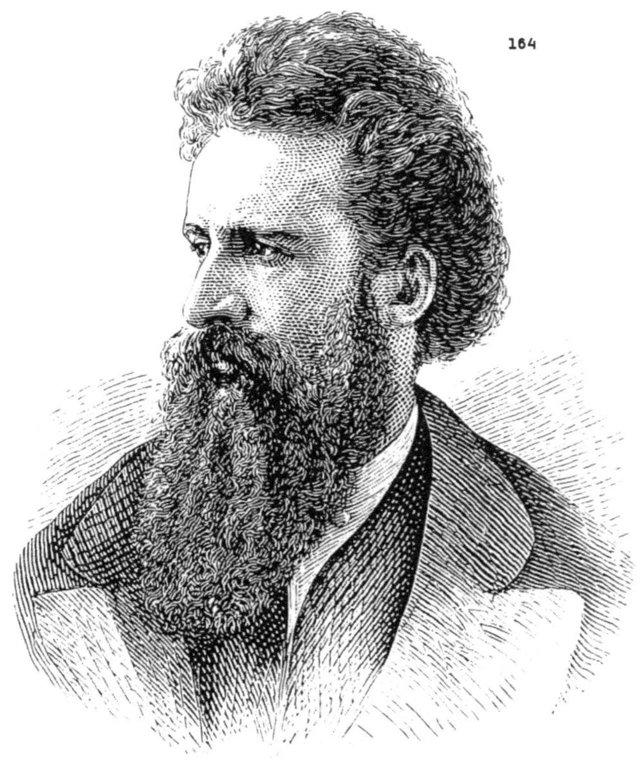

165

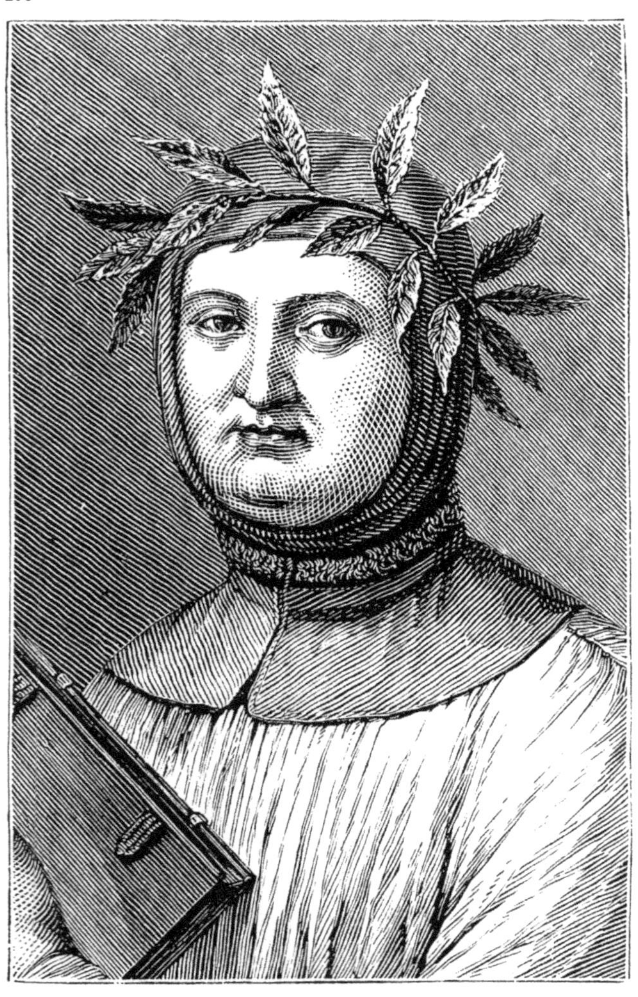

166

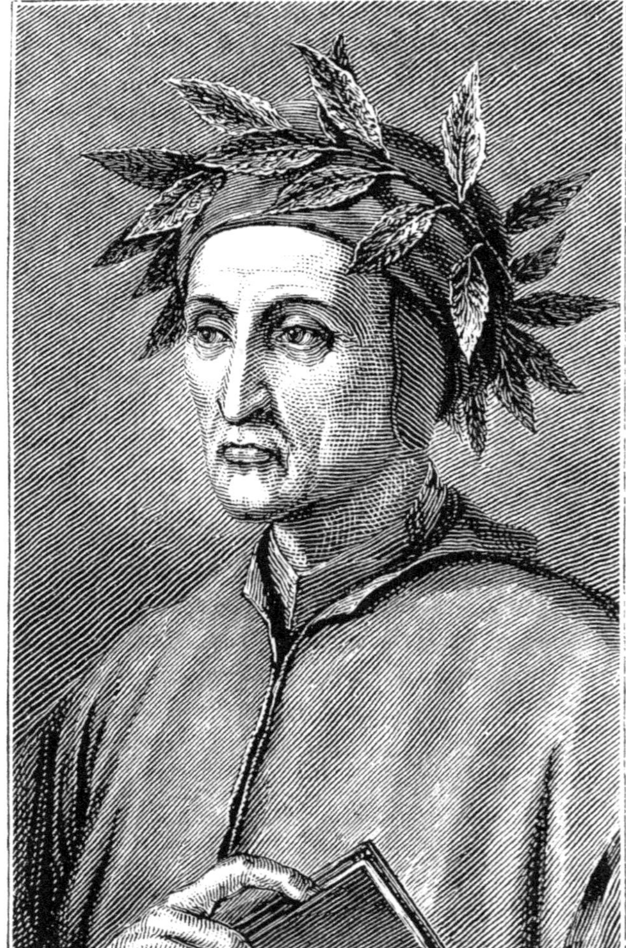

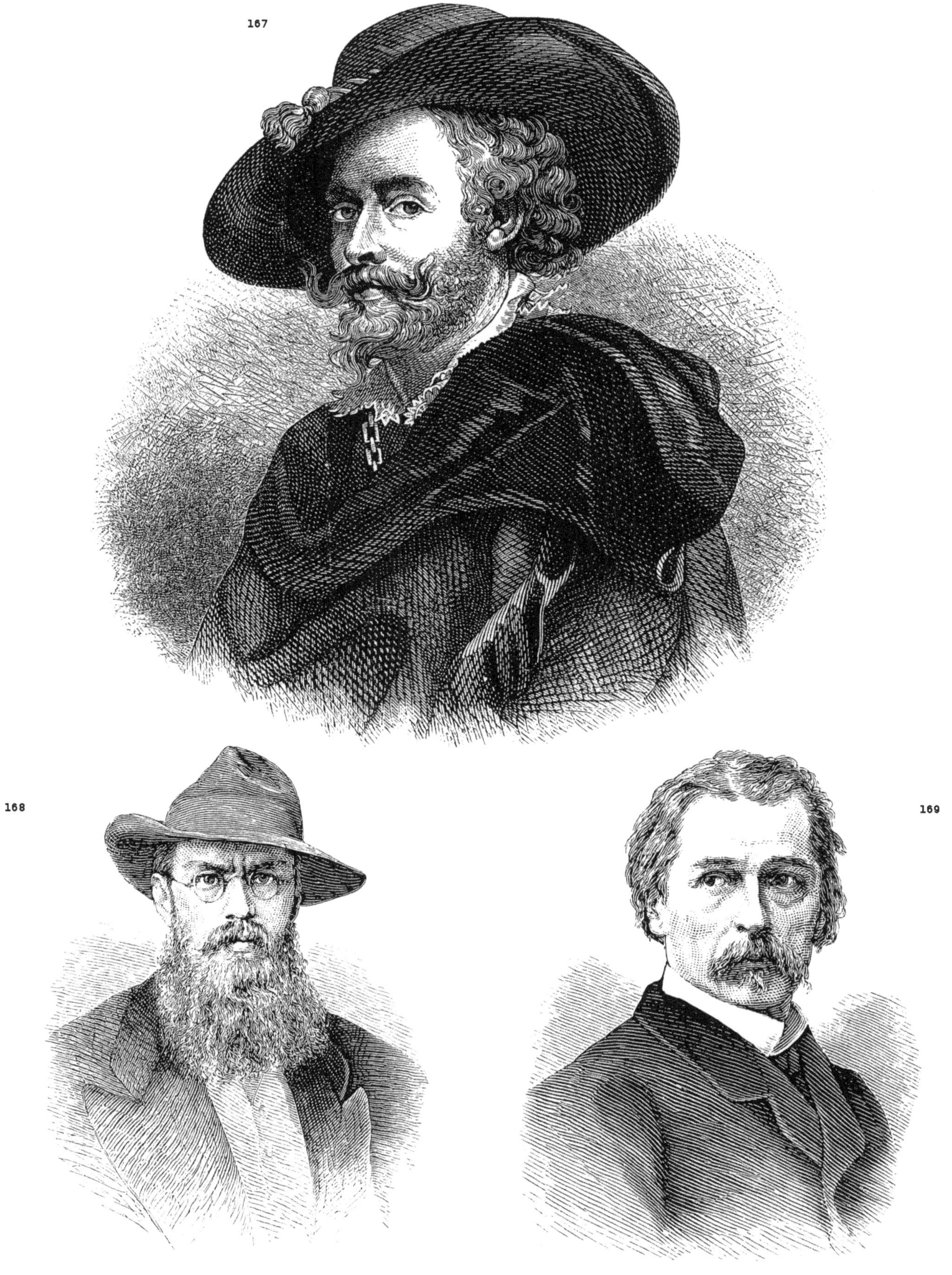

167

168

169

MEN

170

171

MEN

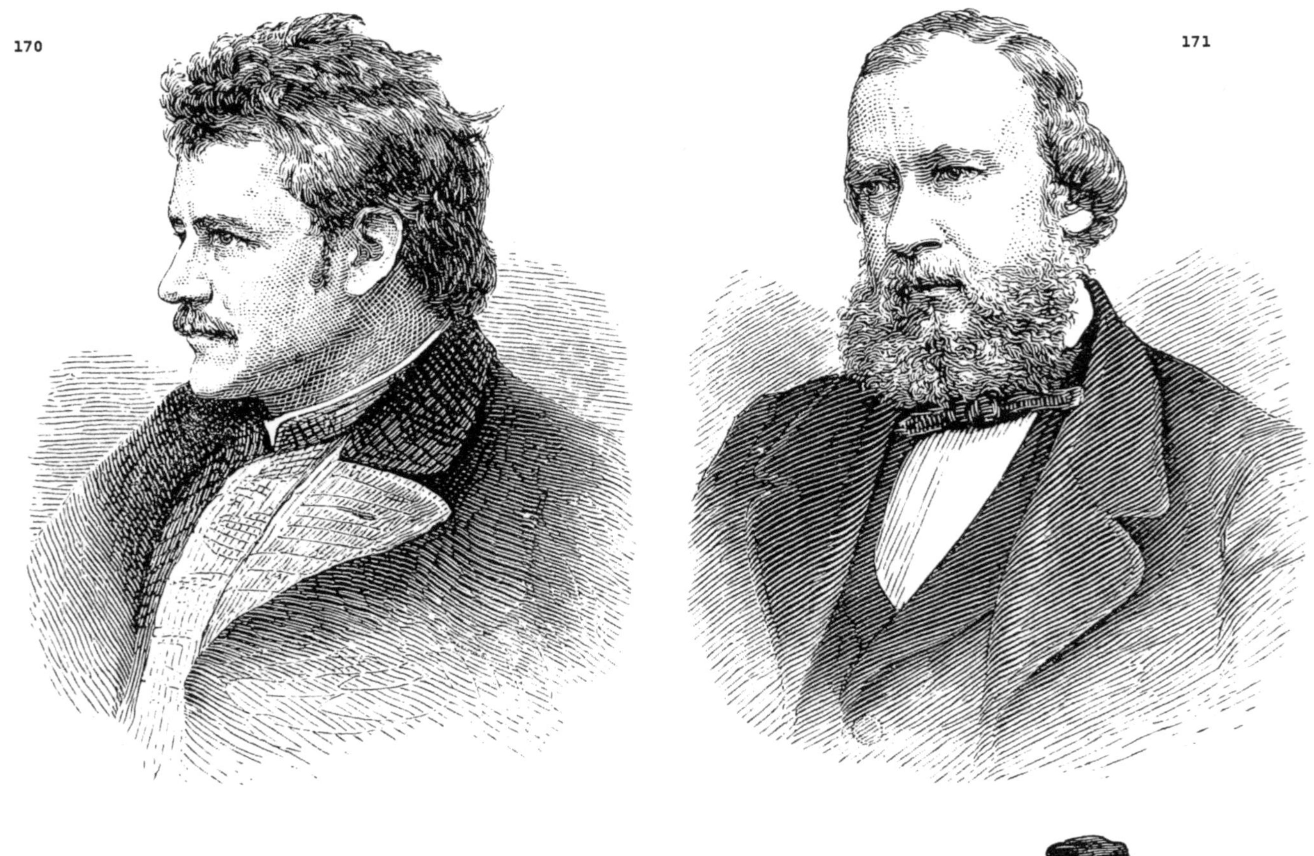

172

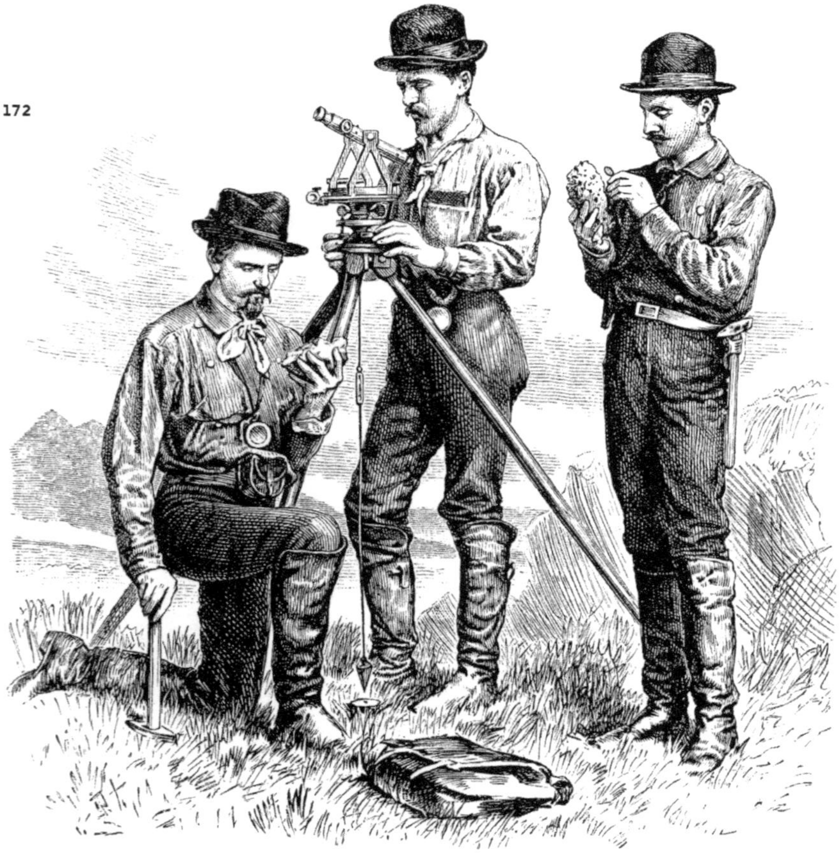

173

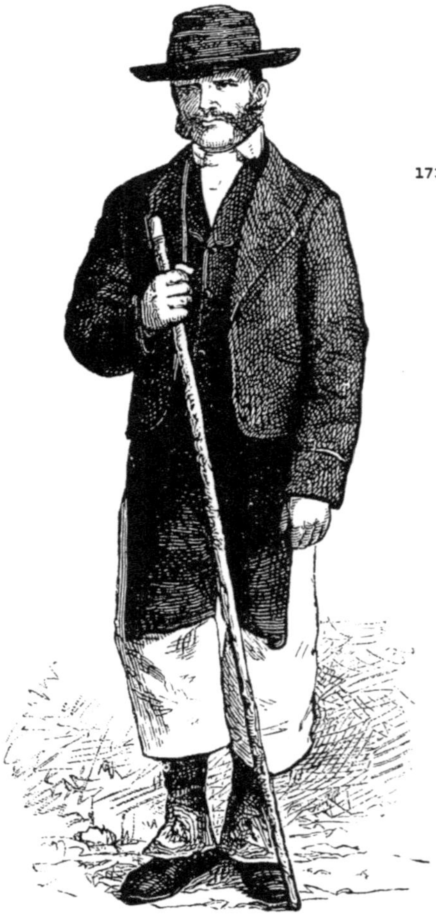

174

175

176

177

178

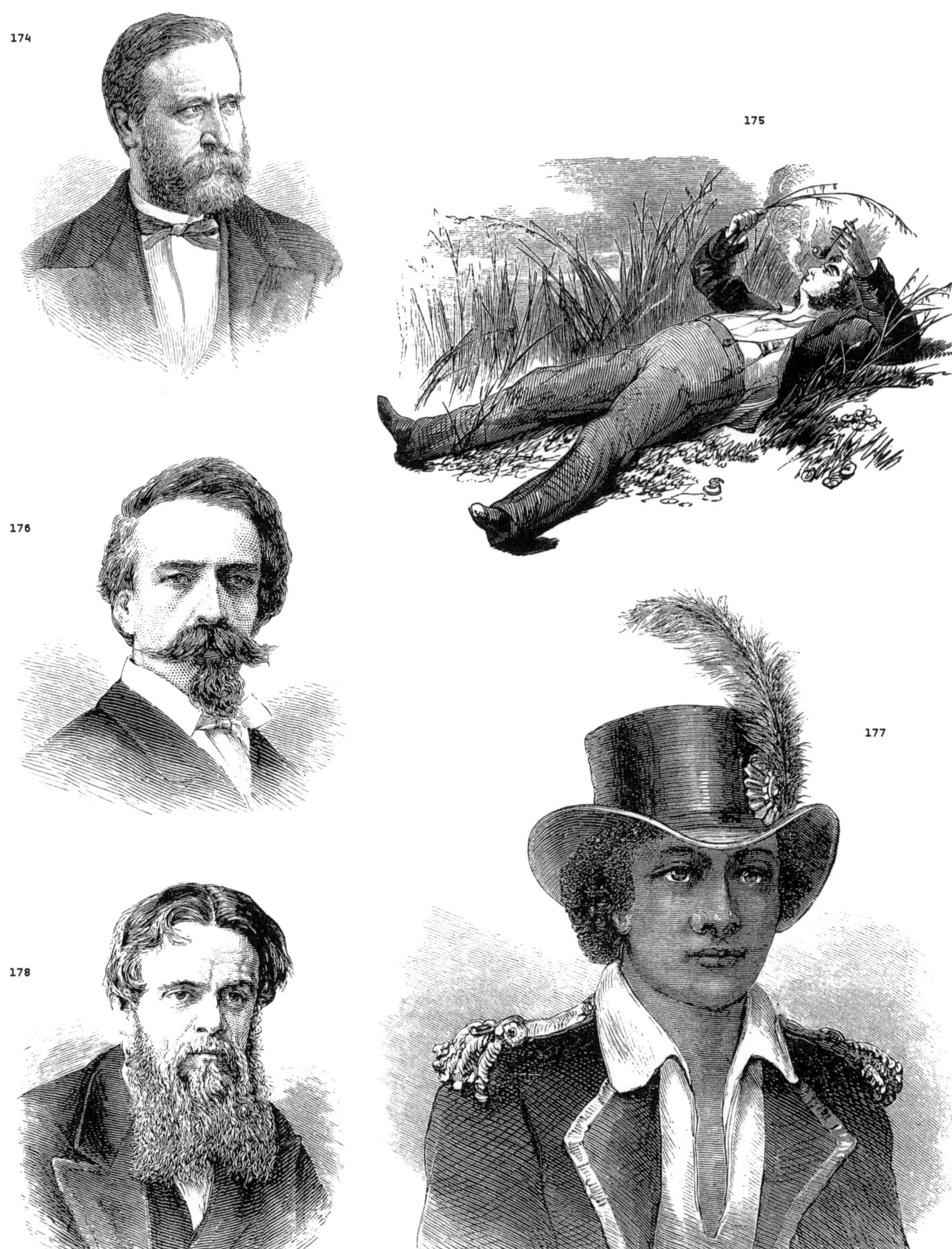

179

180

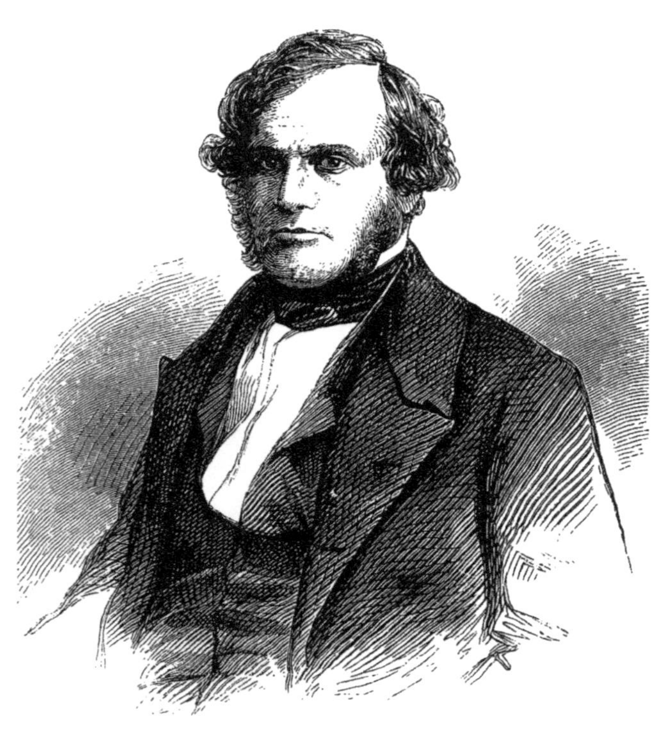

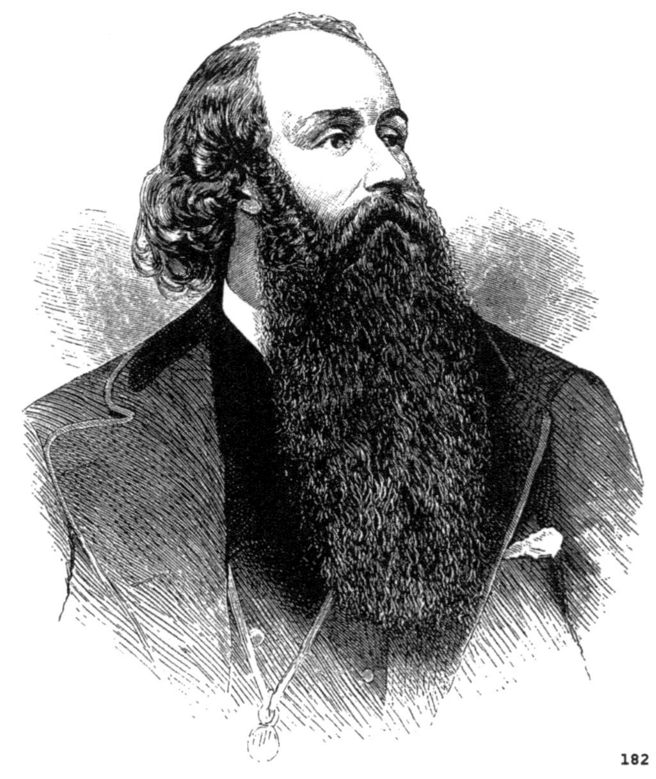

181

182

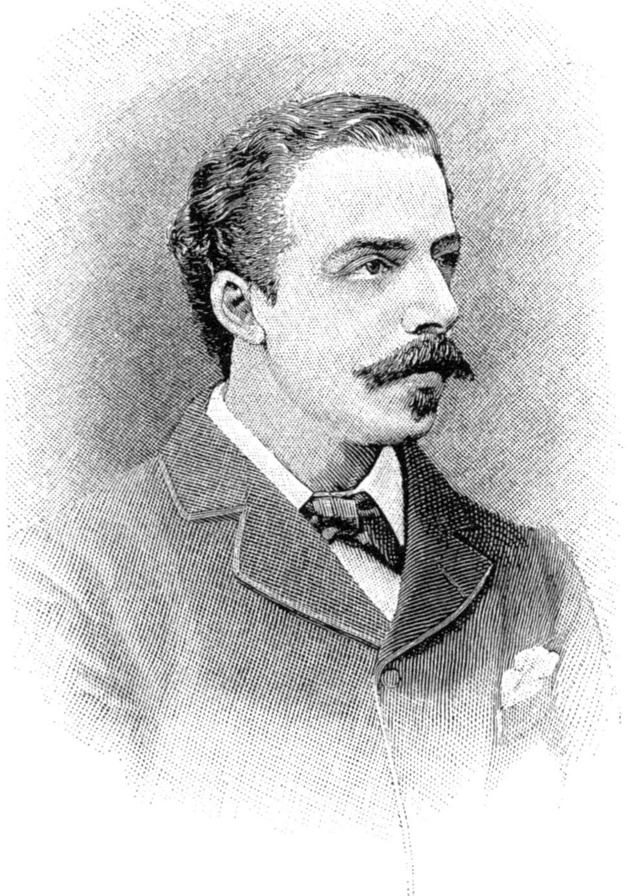

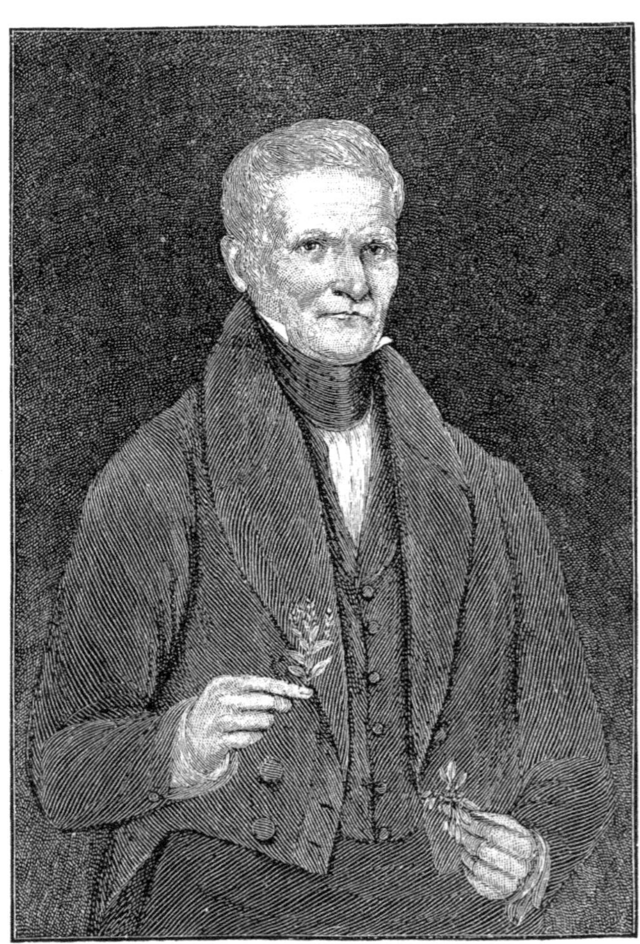

183

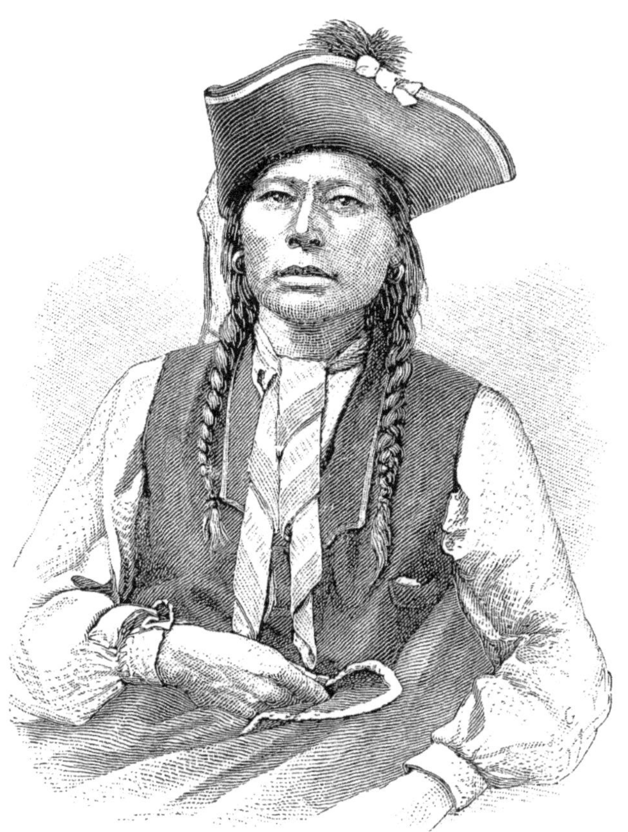

184

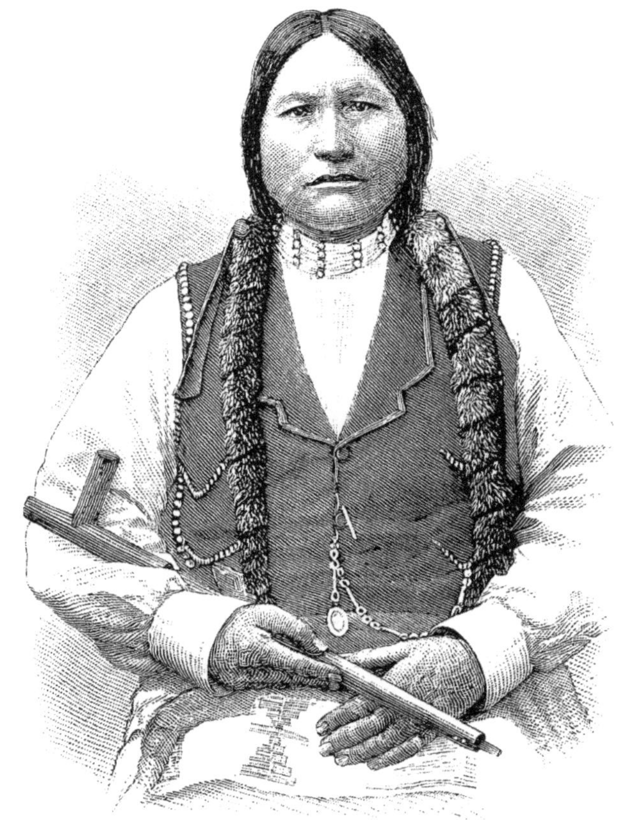

185

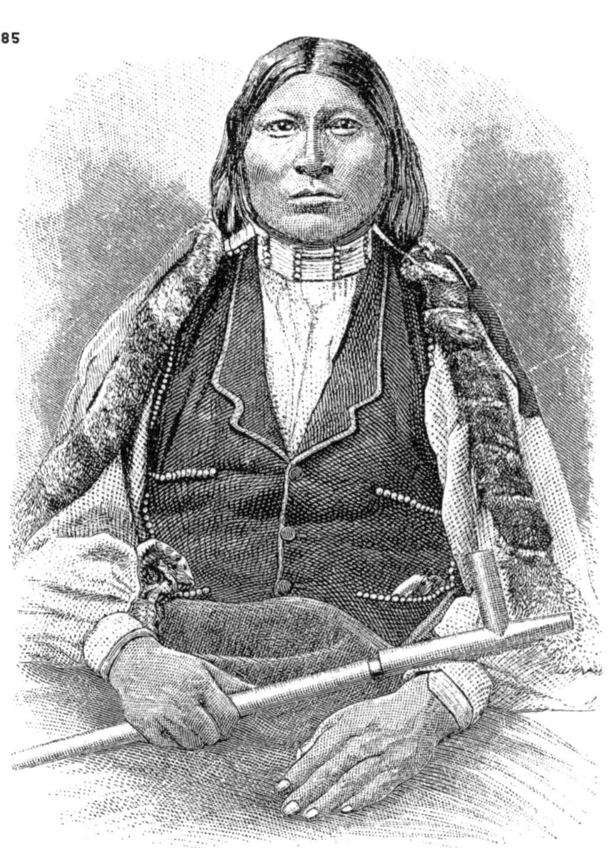

186

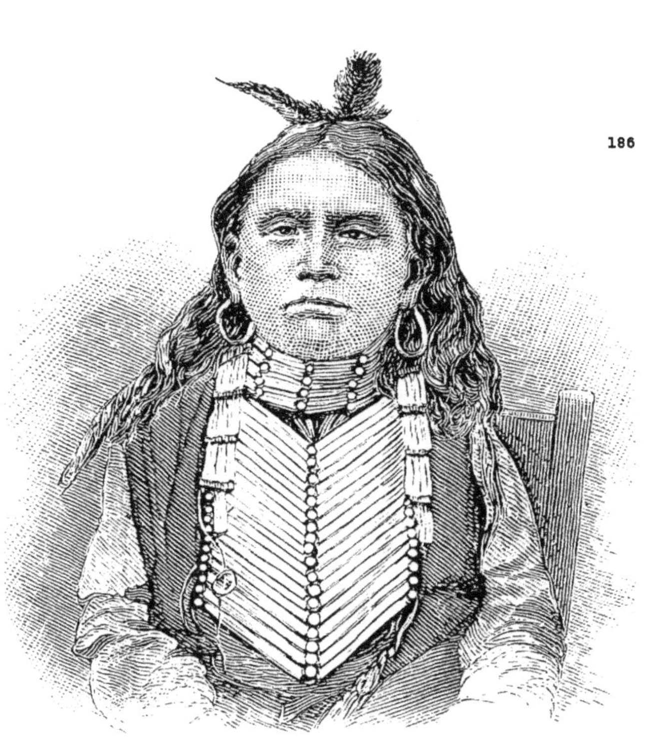

MEN

187

188

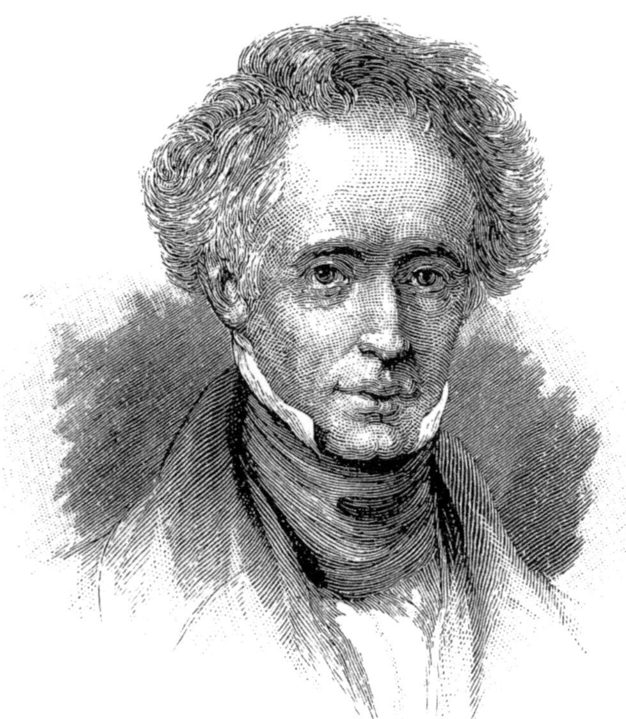

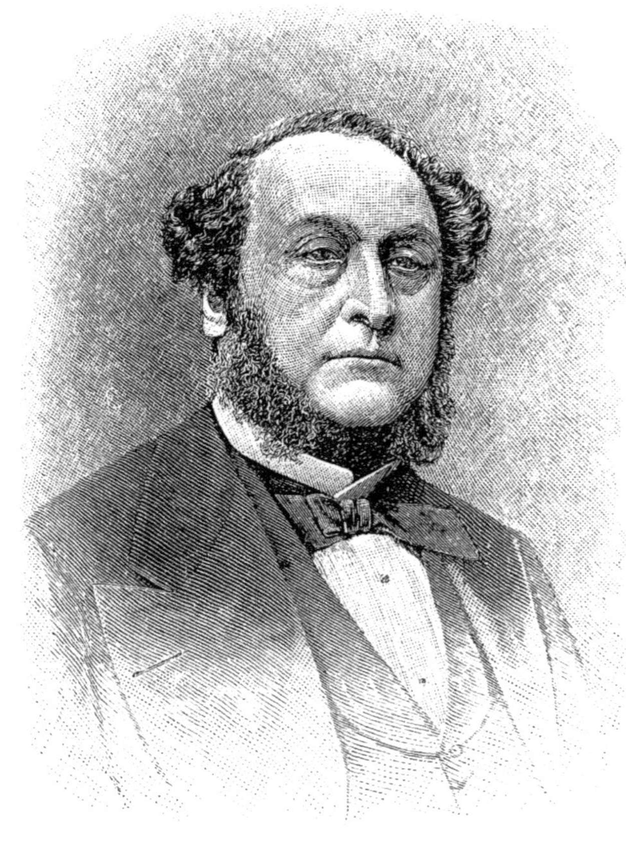

MEN

189

190

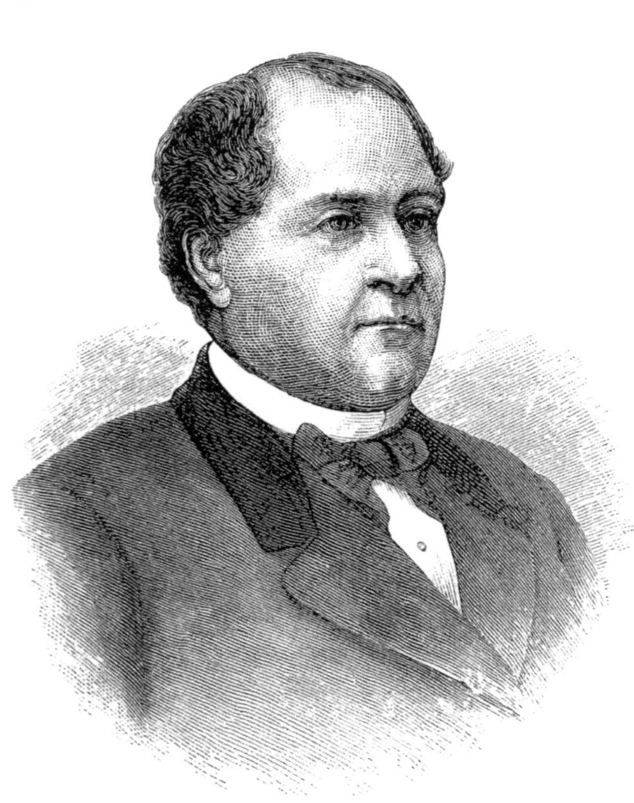

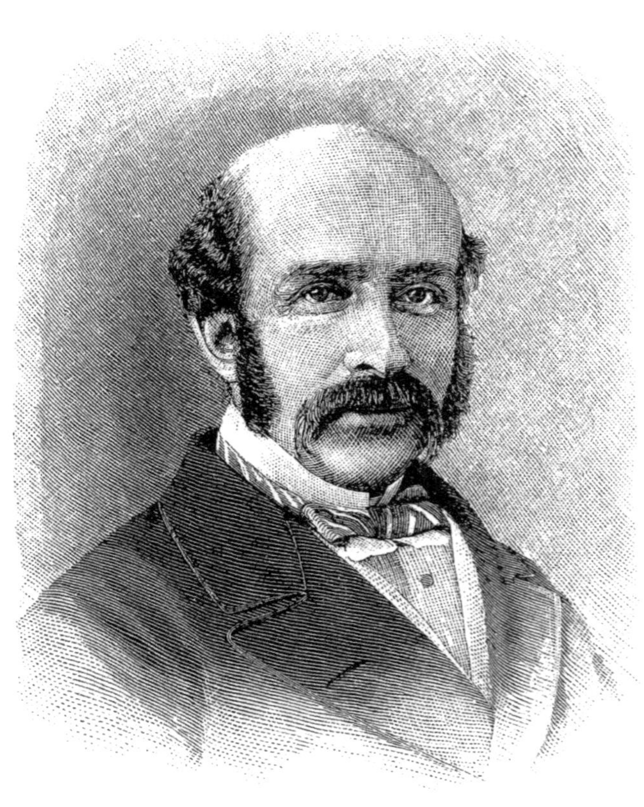

191

192

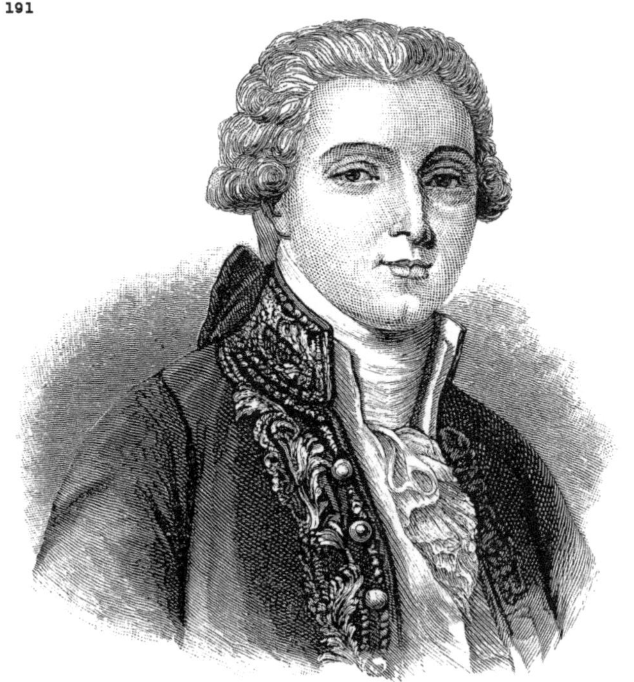

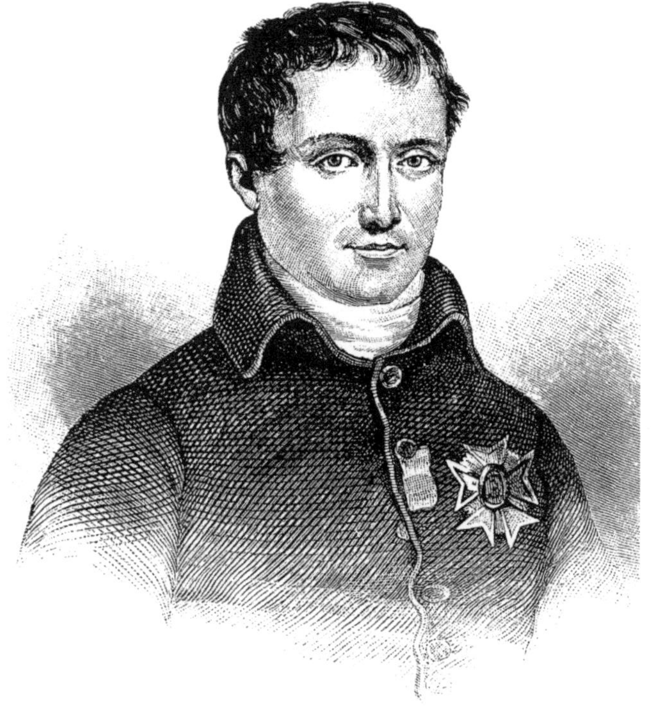

193

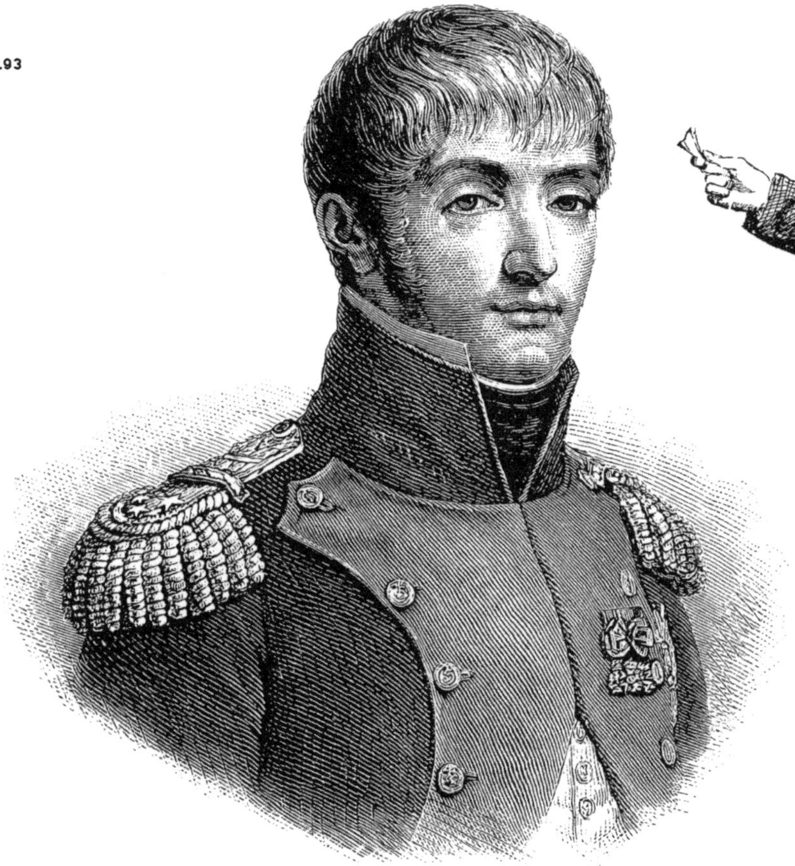

194

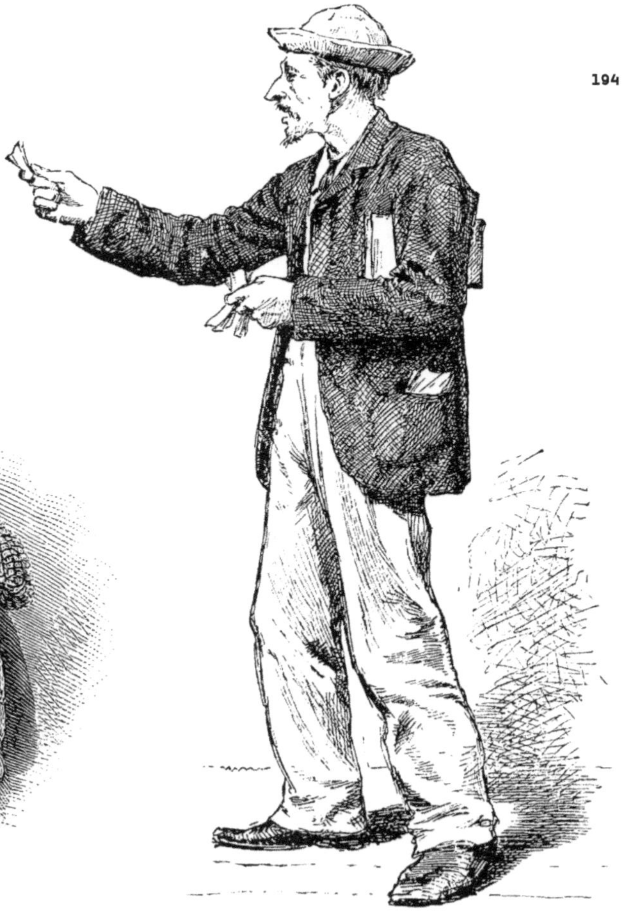

MEN

195

196

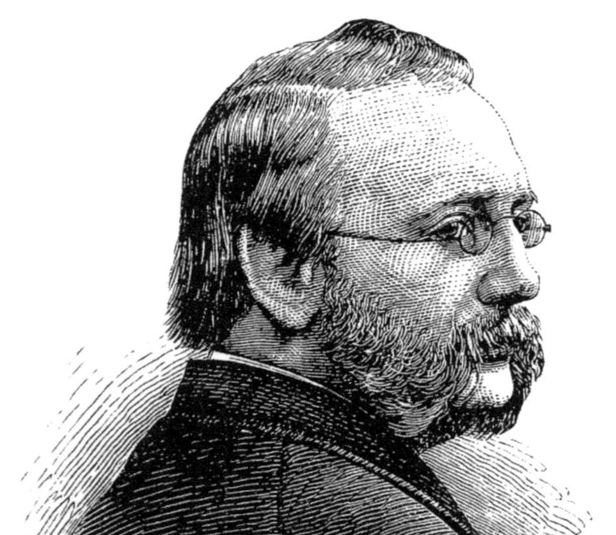

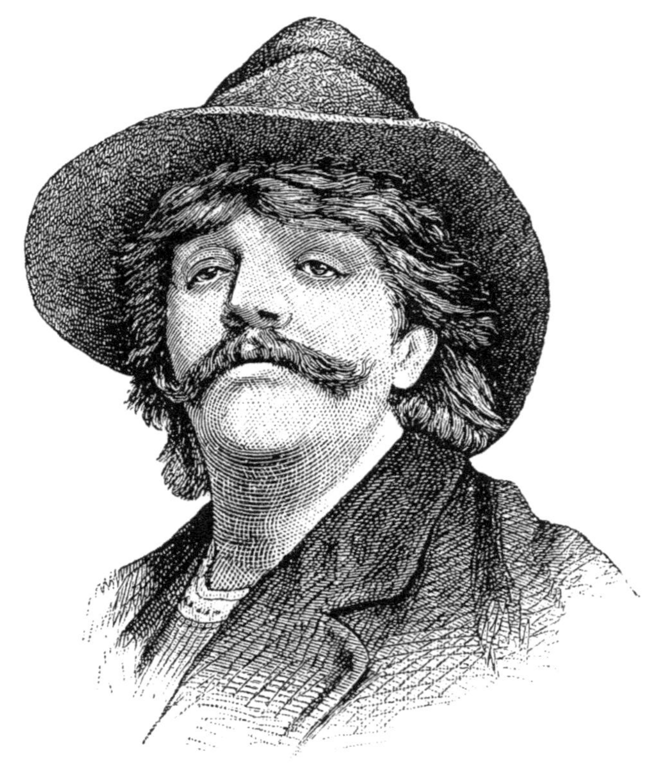

197

198

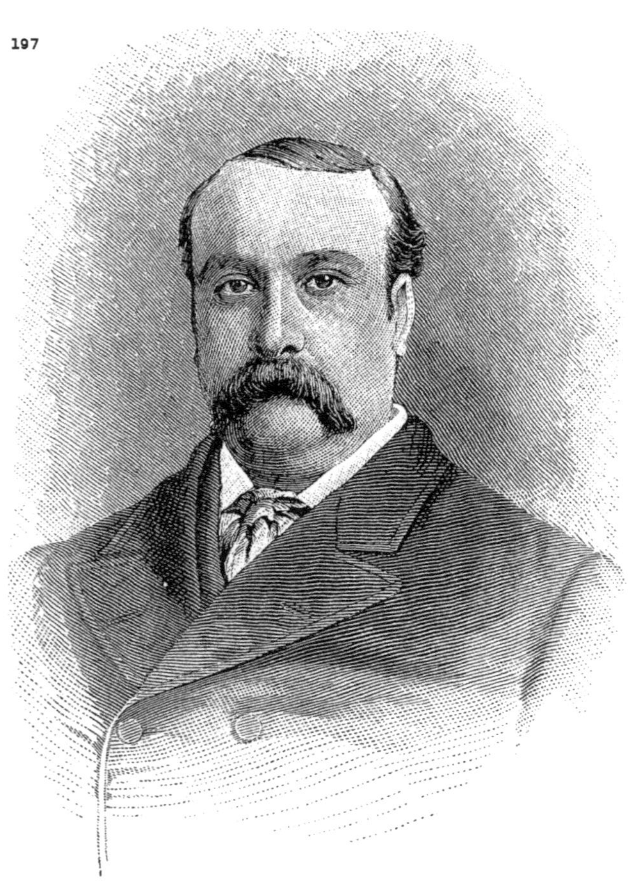

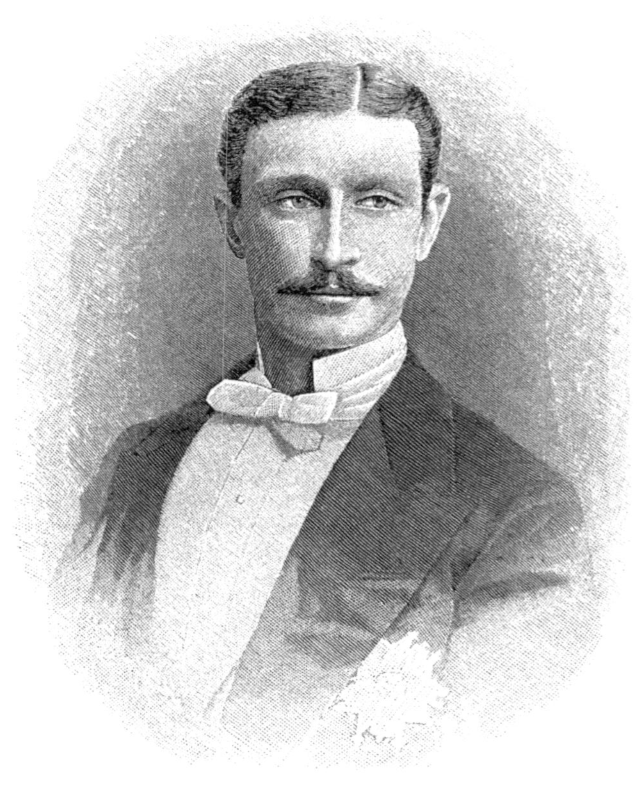

199

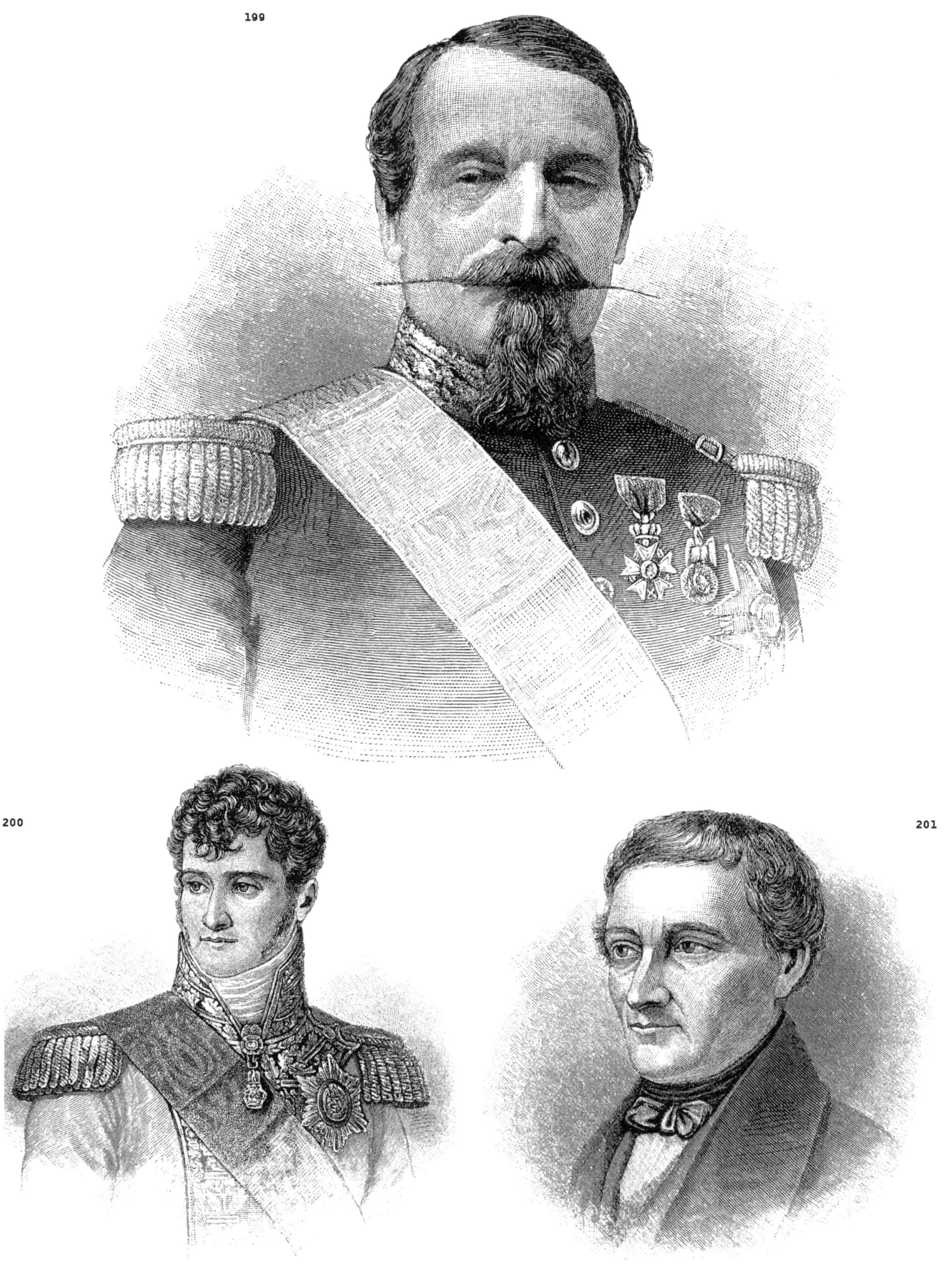

200

201

202

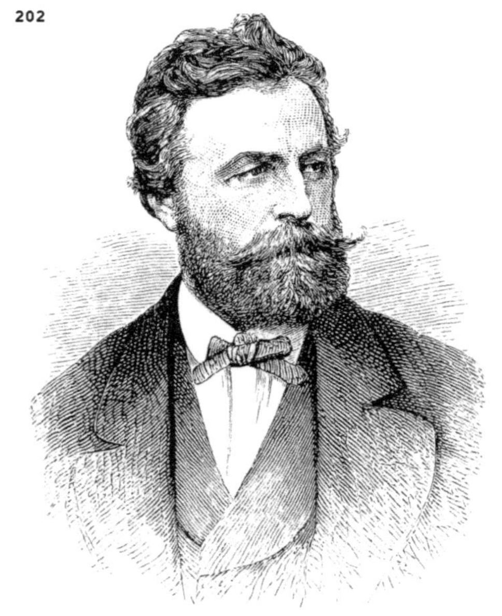

203

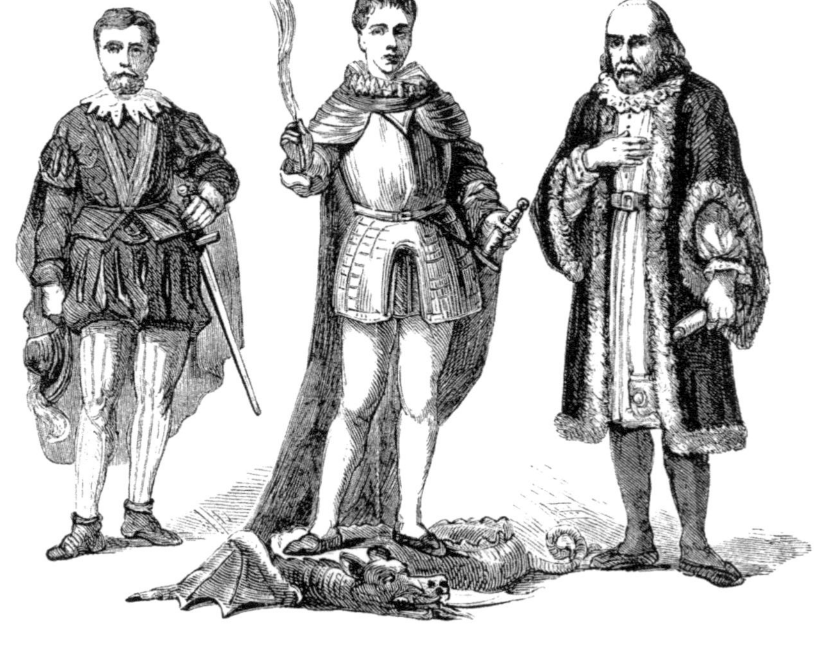

204

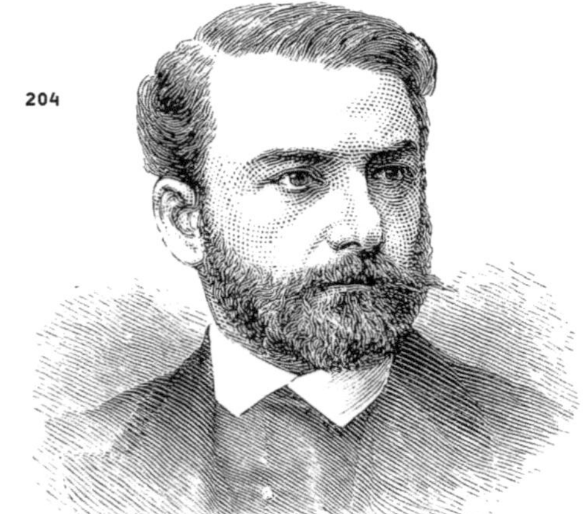

205

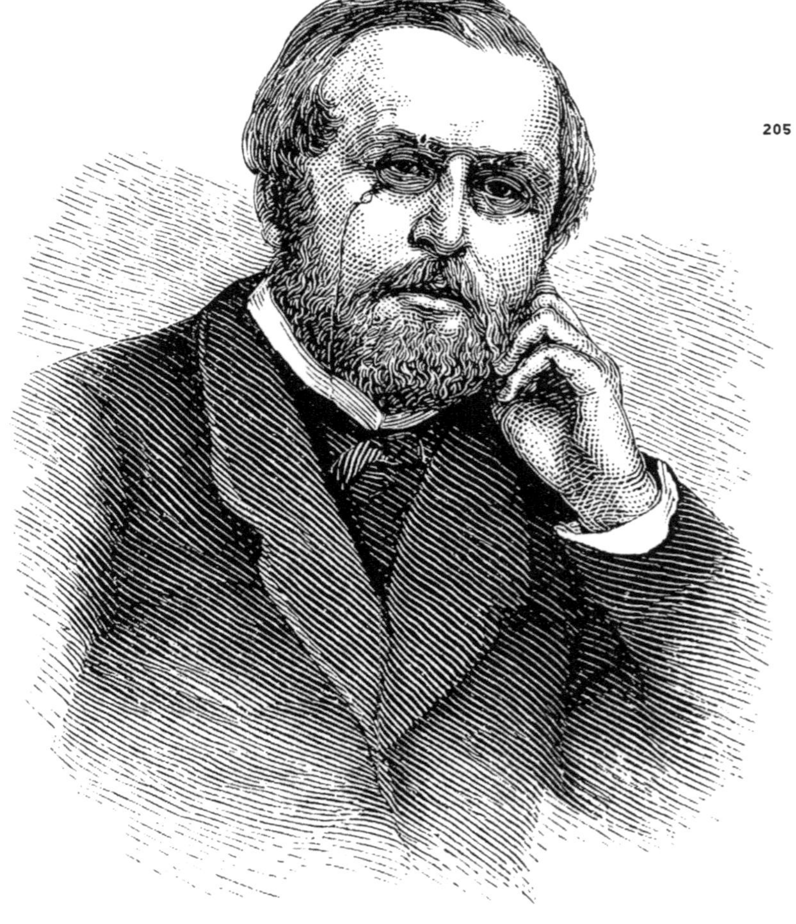

206

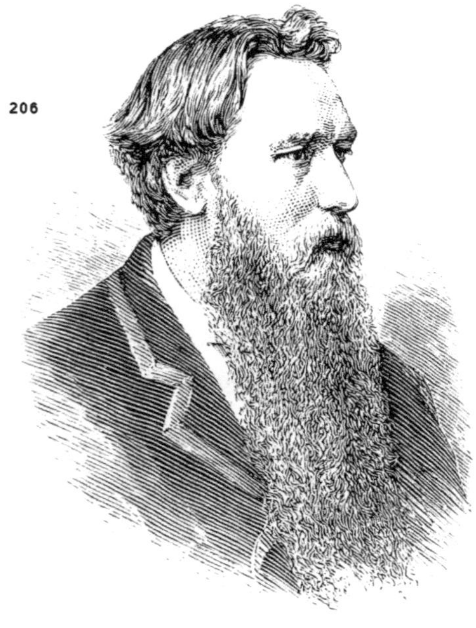

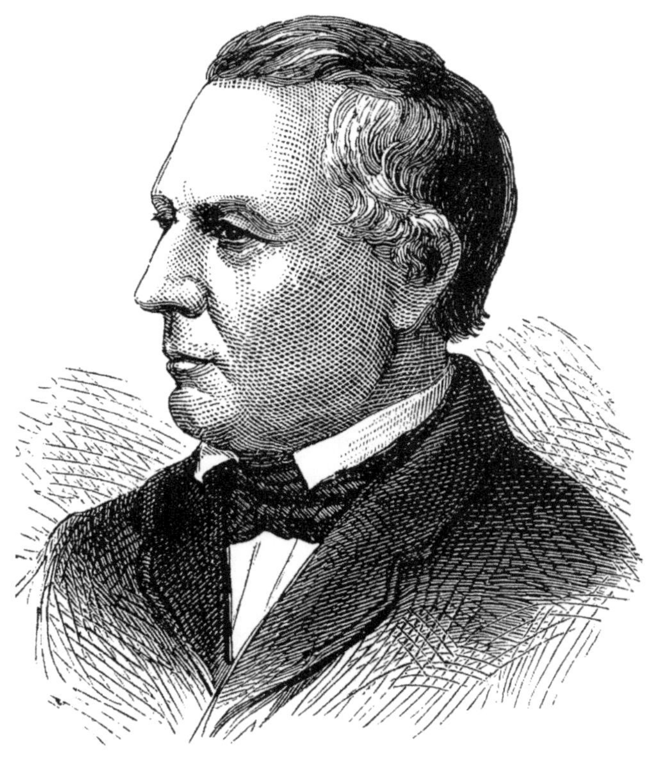

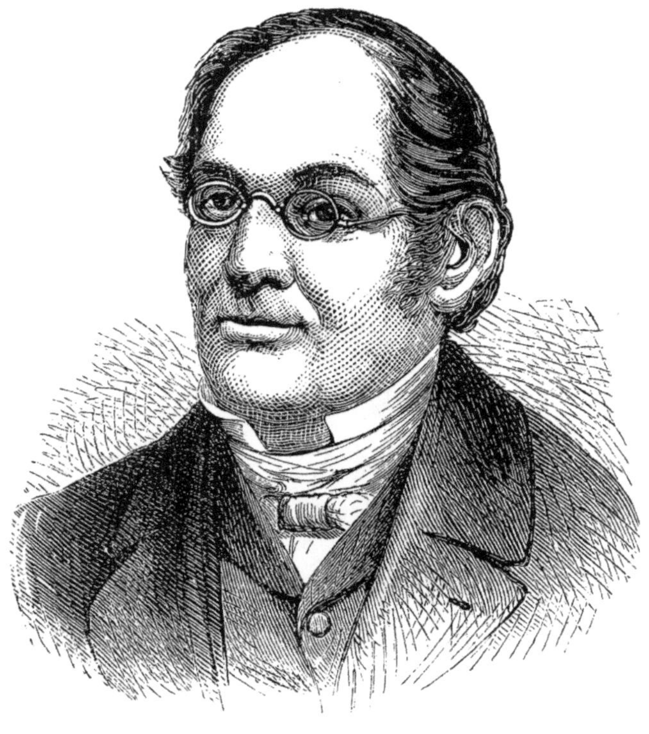

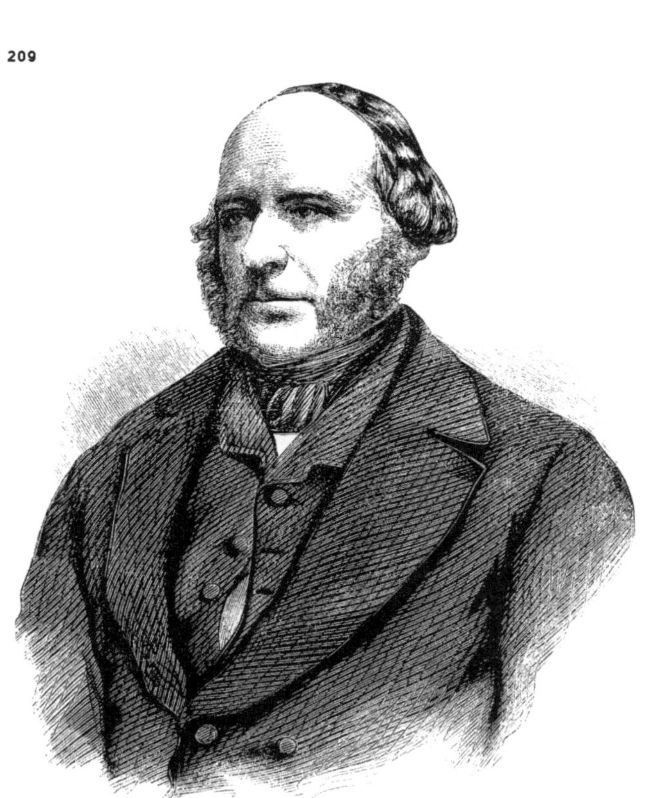

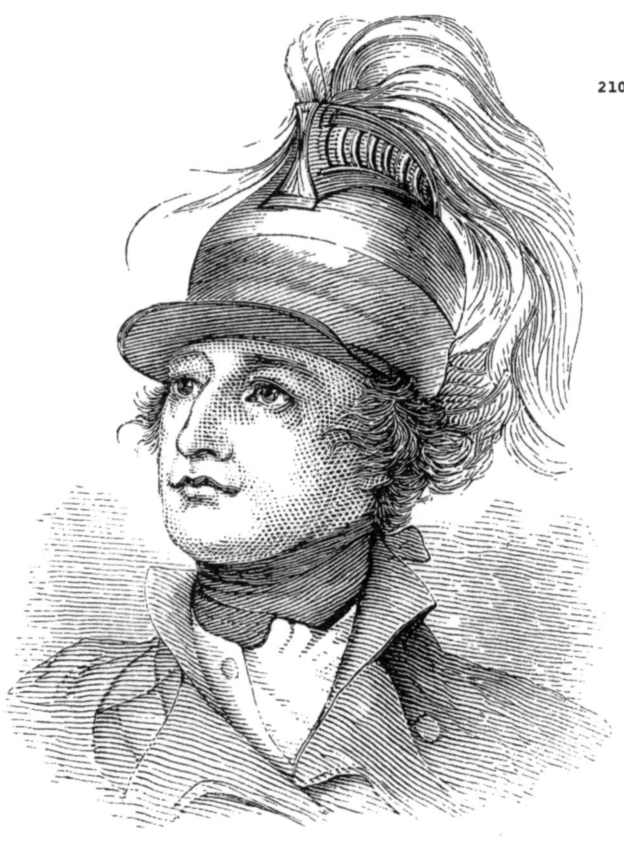

211

212

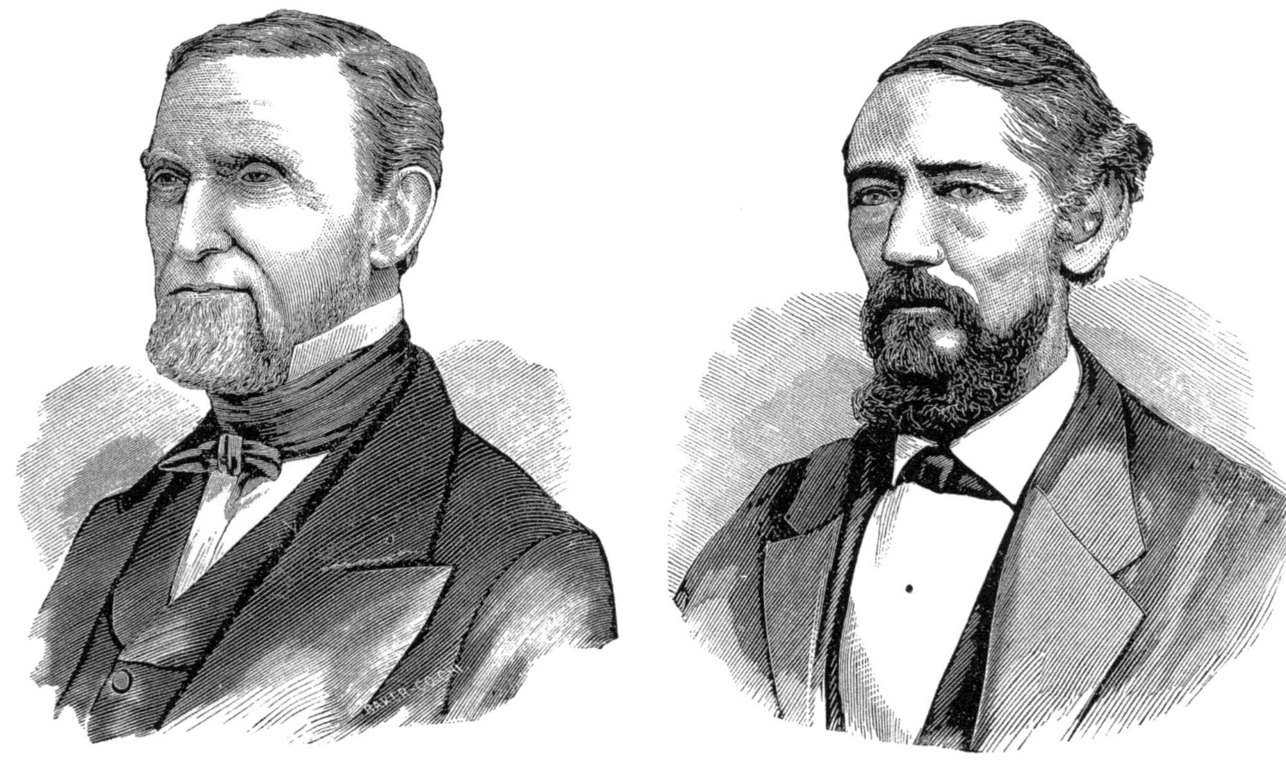

213

214

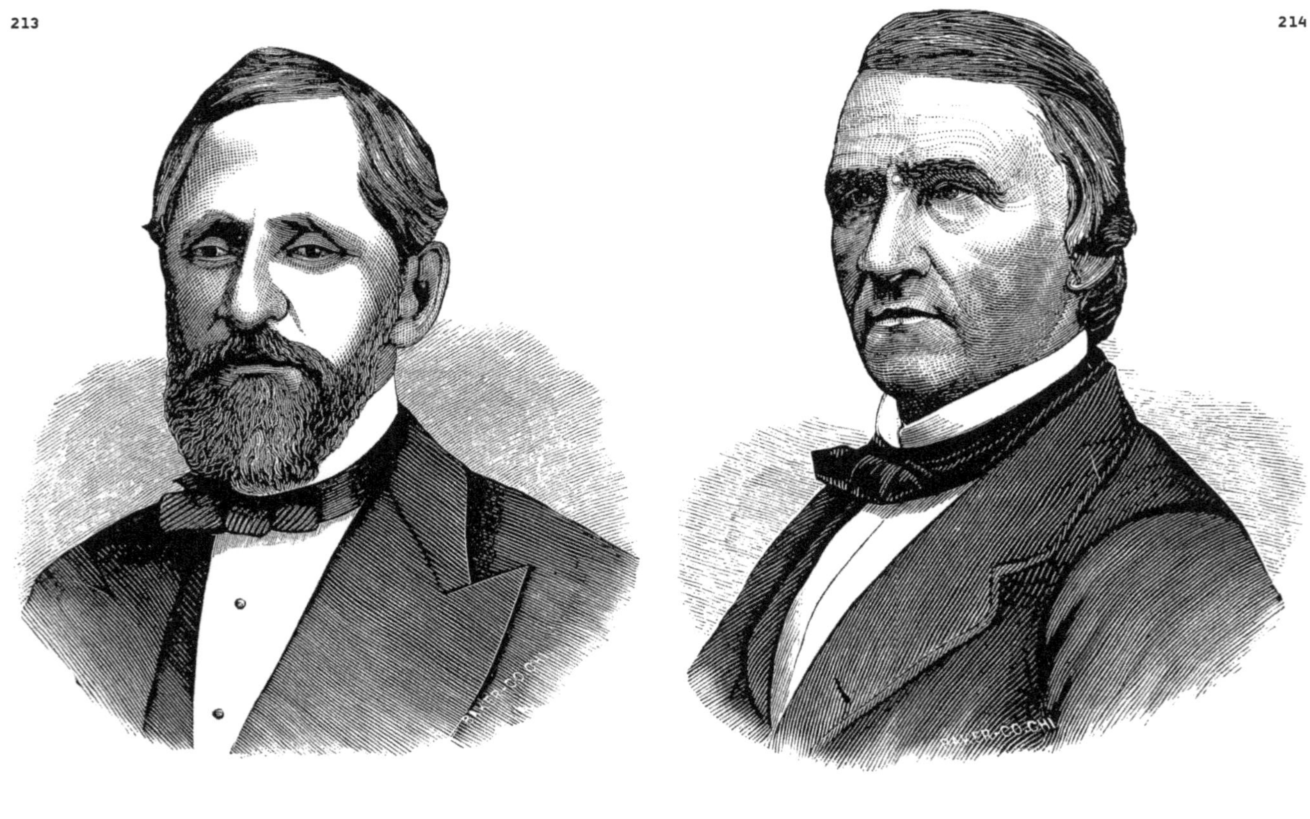

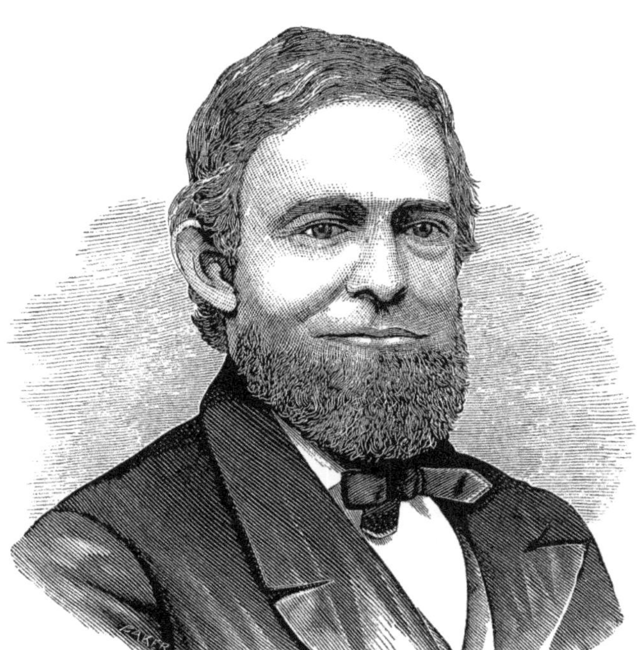

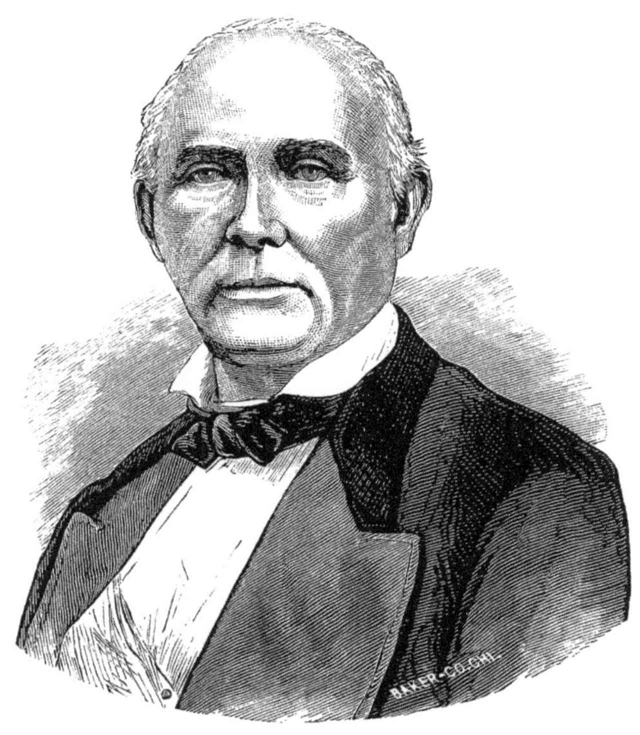

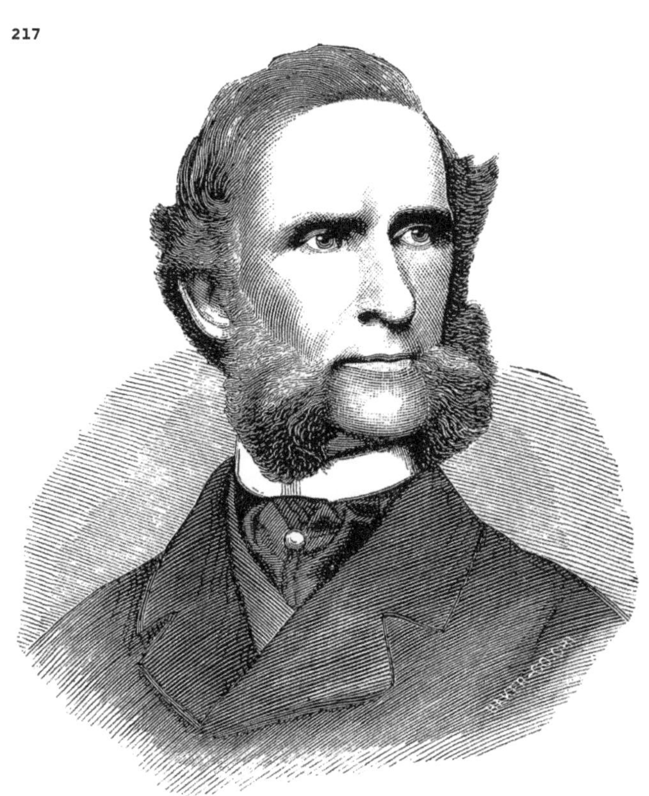

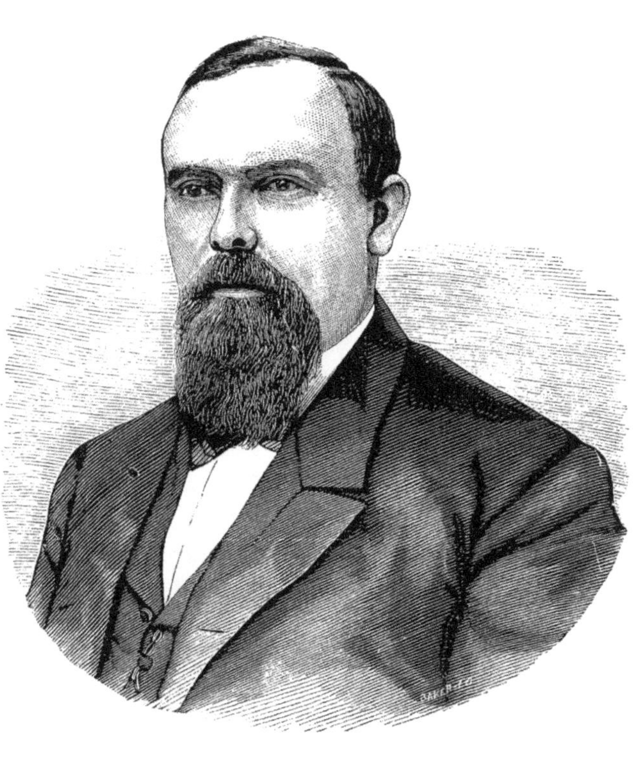

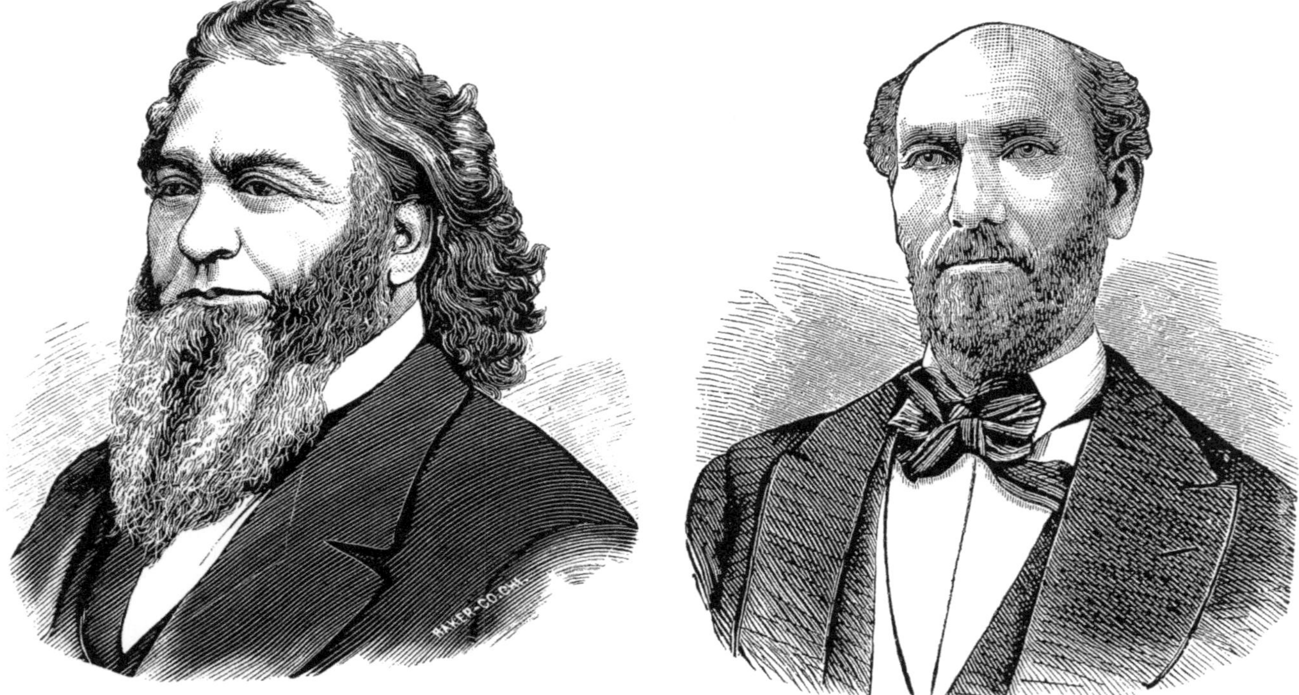

221

222

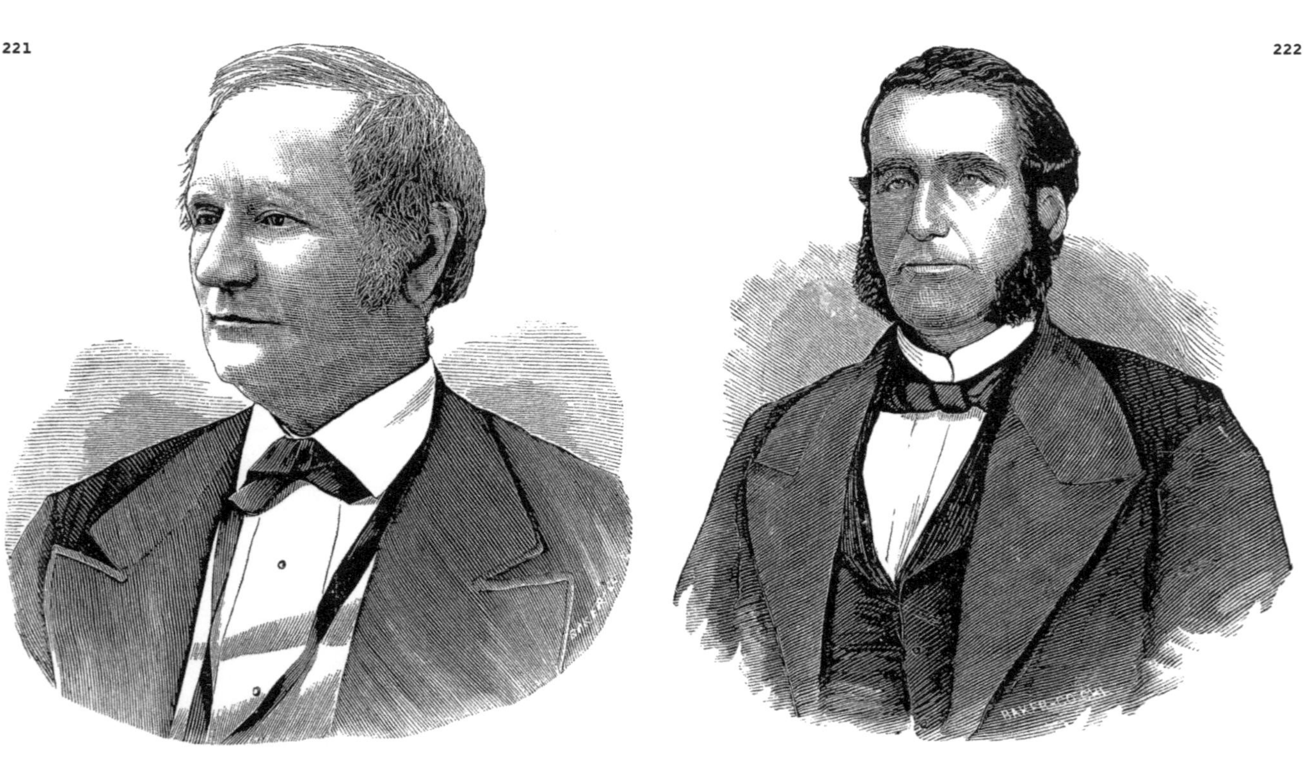

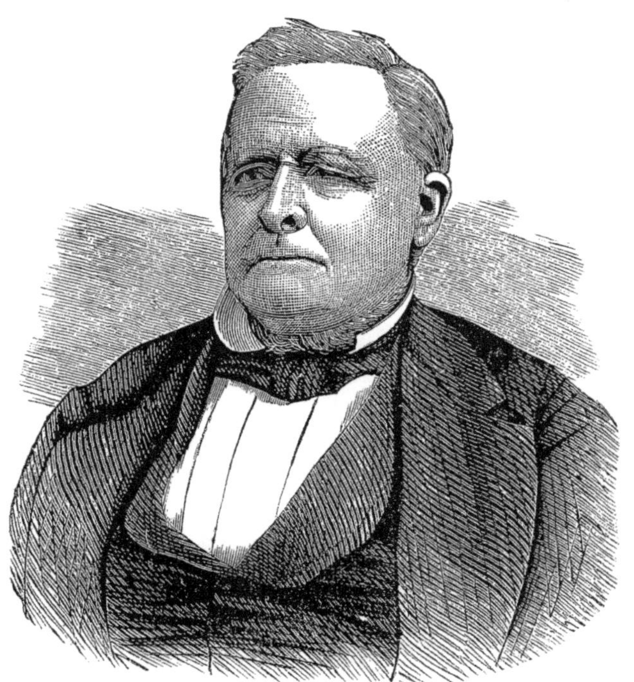

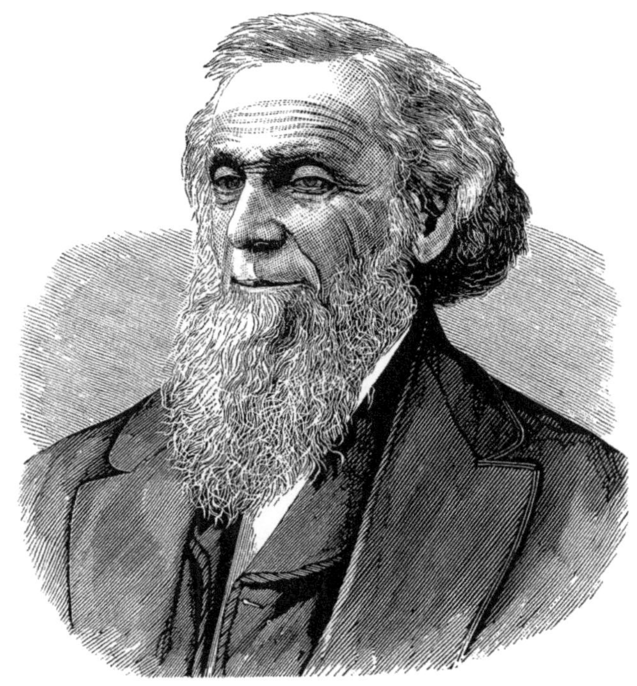

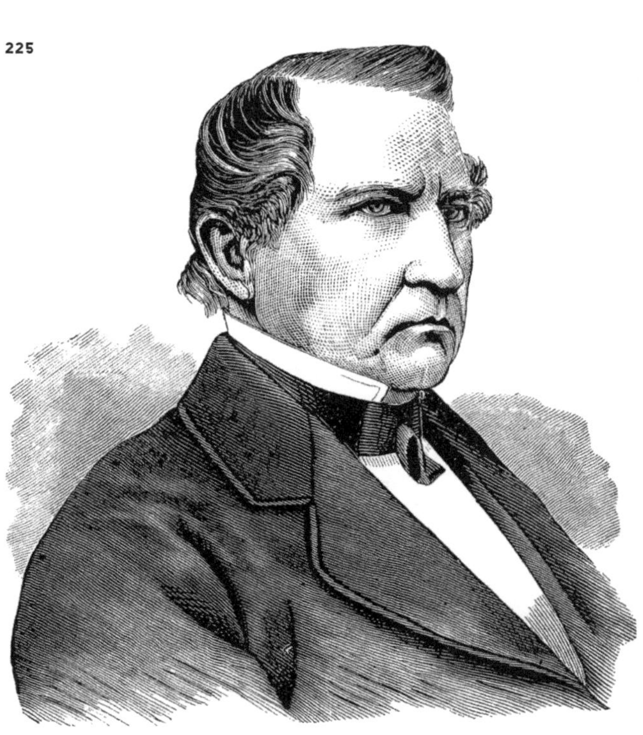

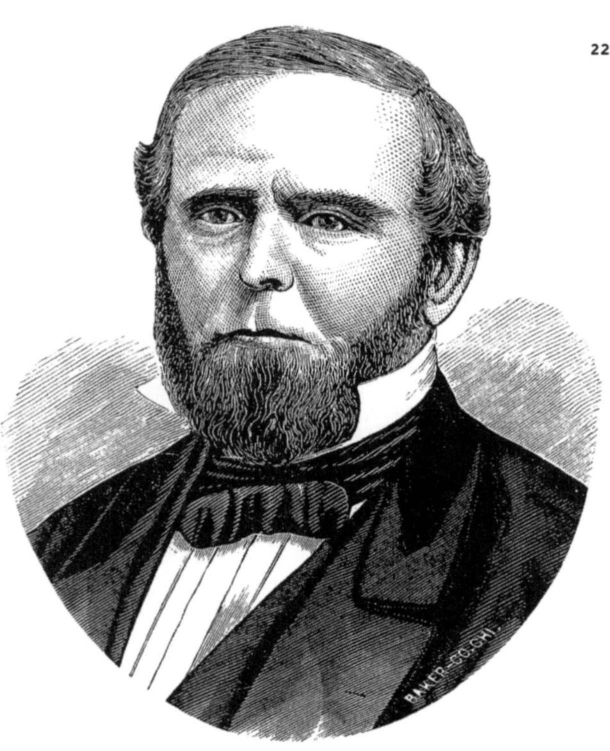

227

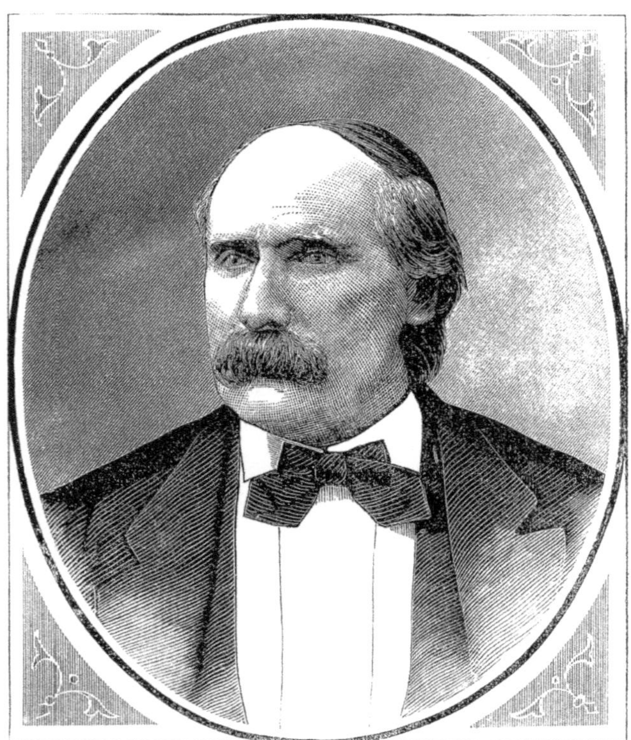

228

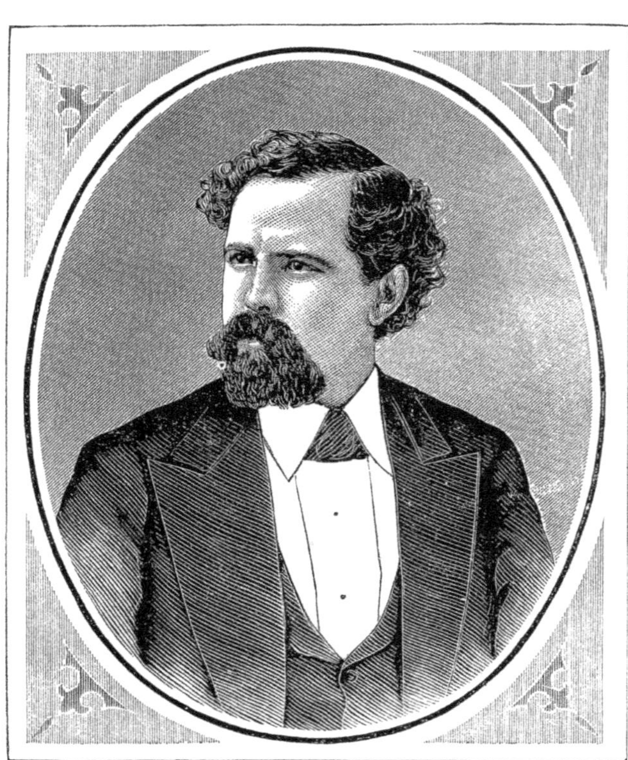

229

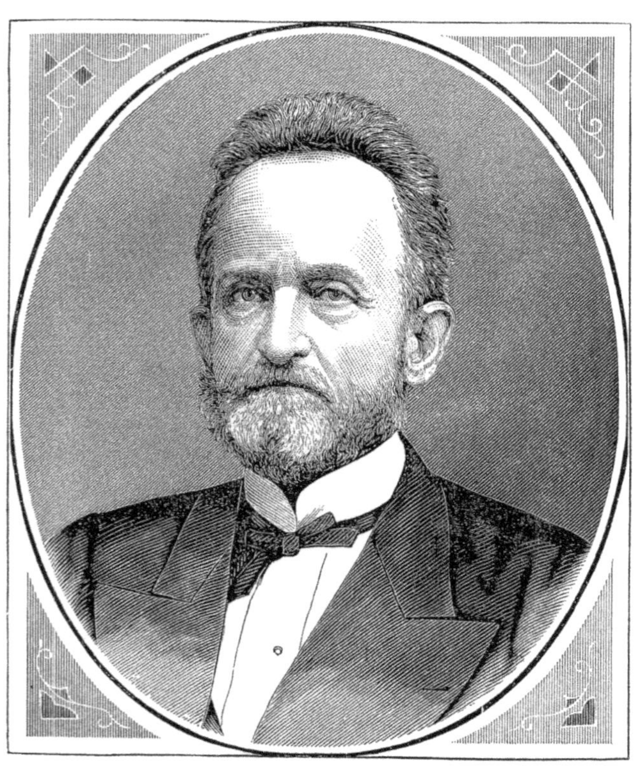

230

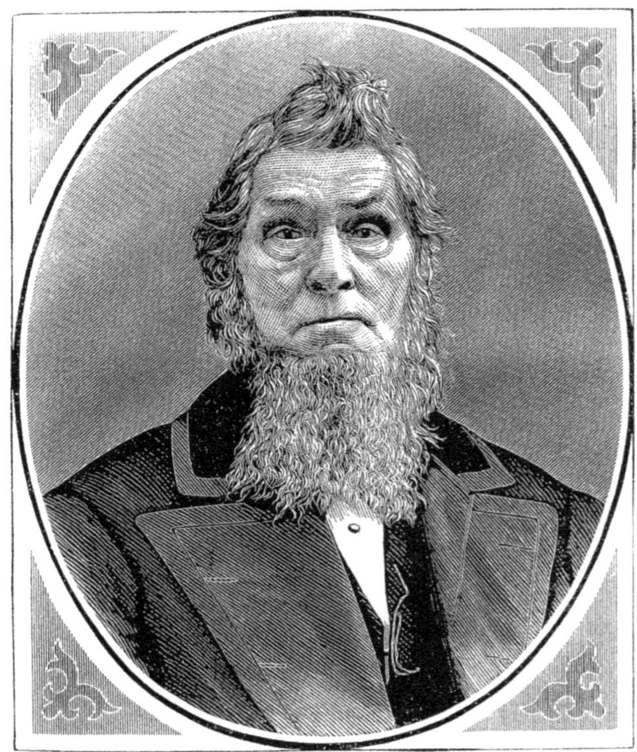

231

232

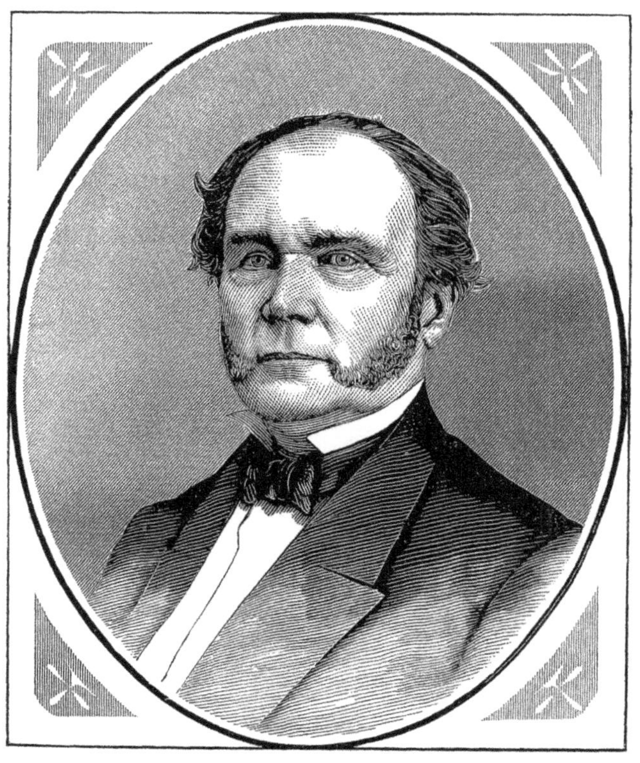

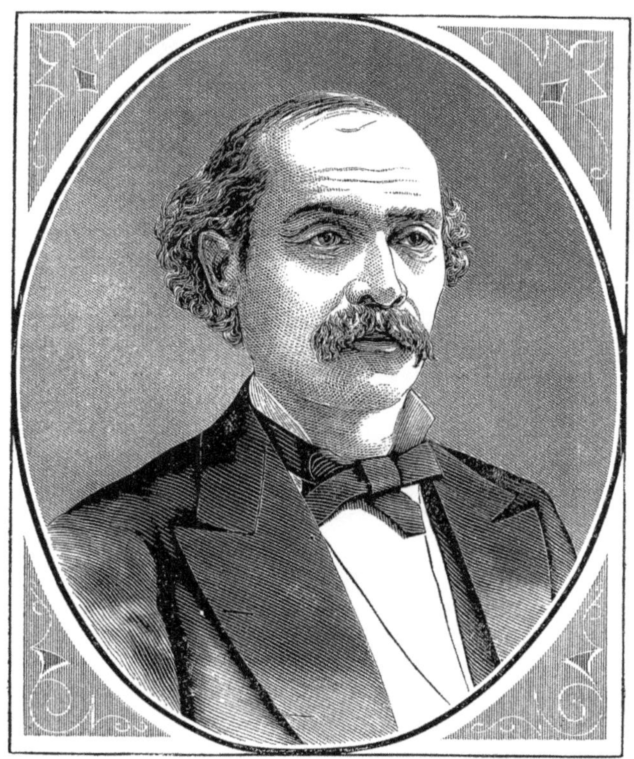

233

234

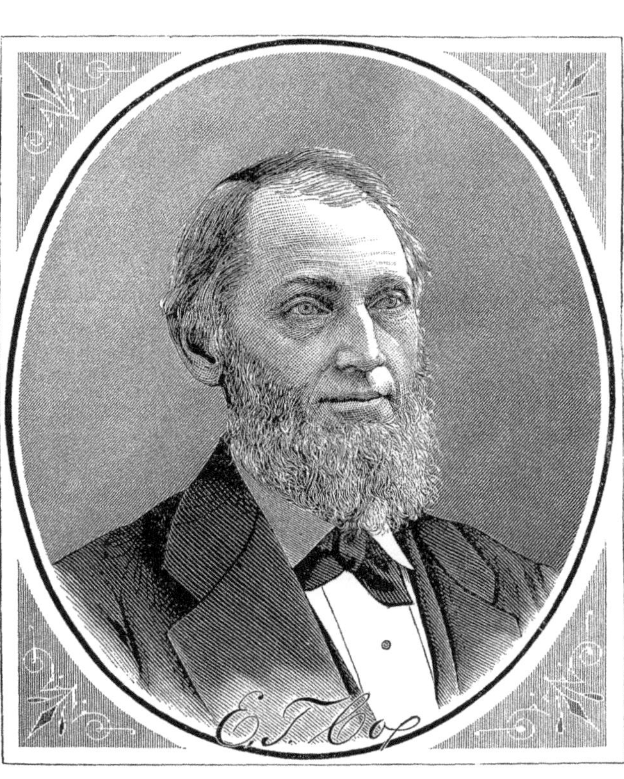

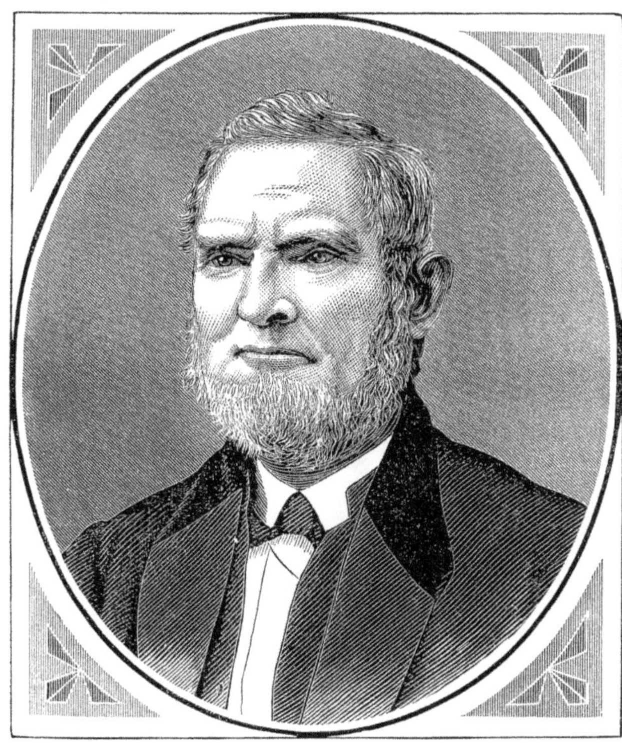

235

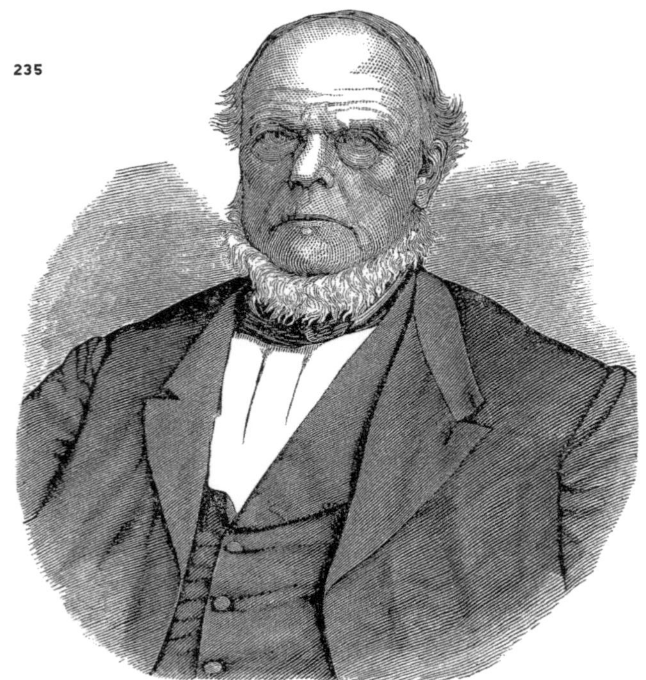

236

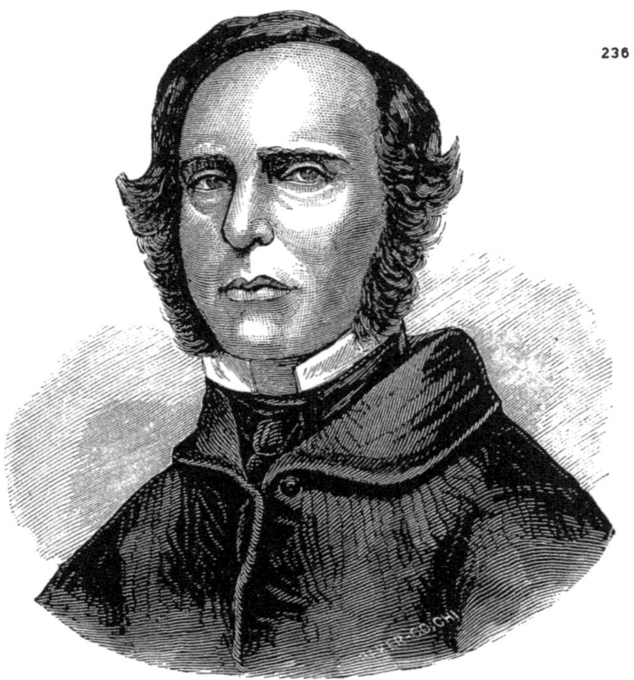

MEN

237

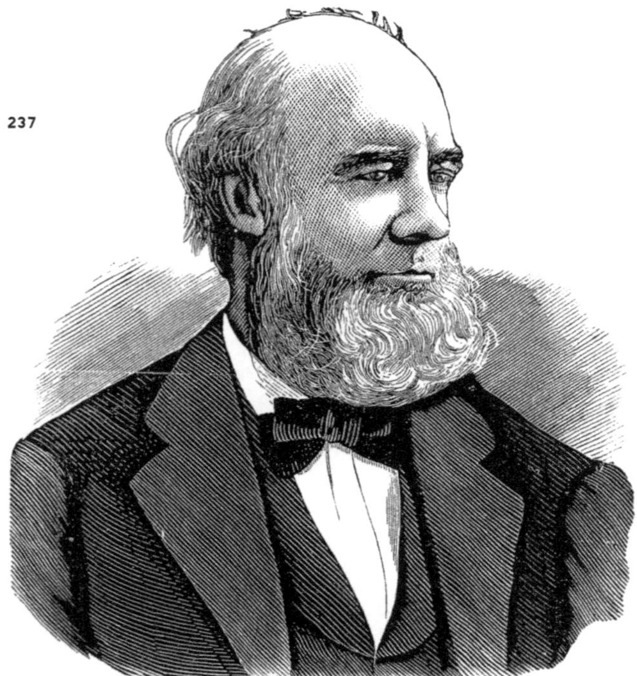

238

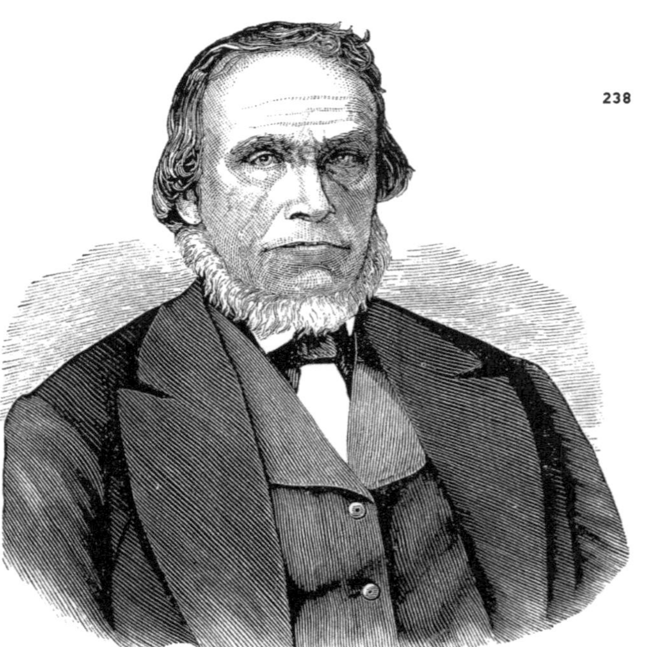

239

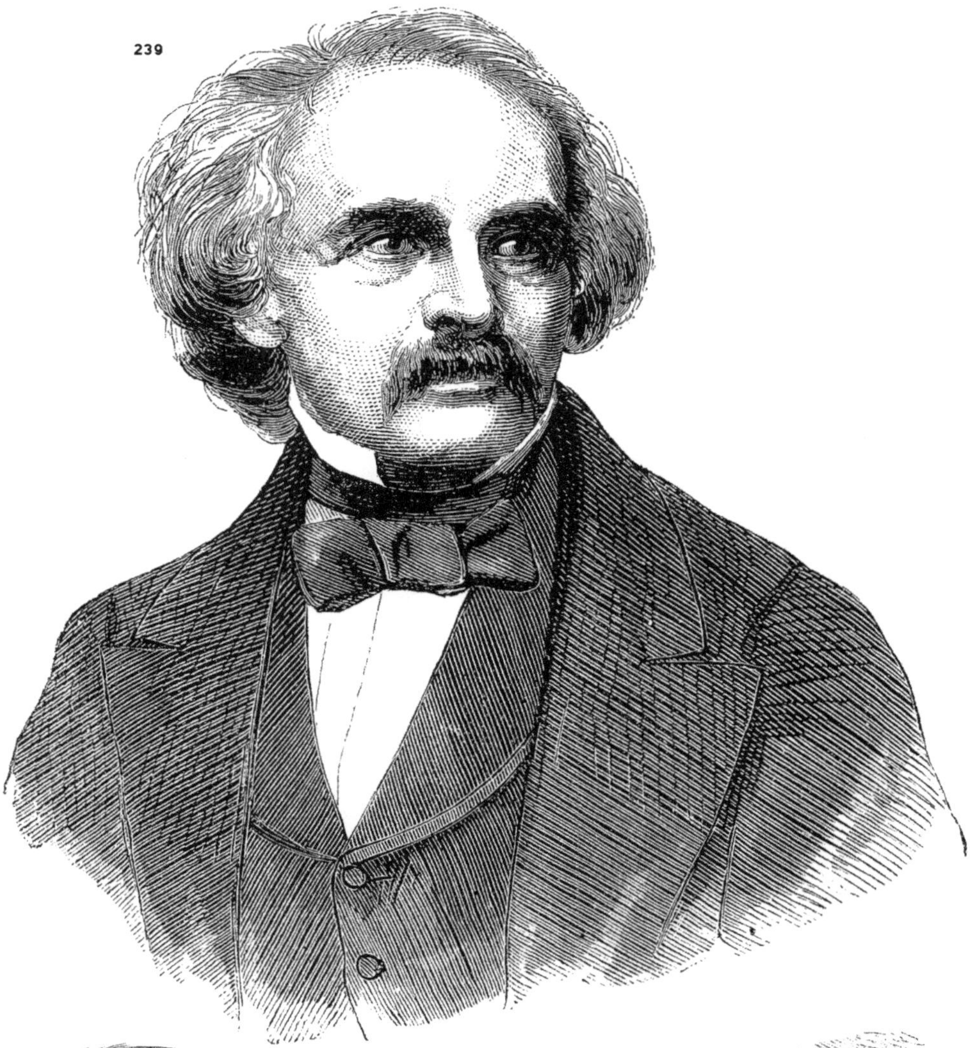

240

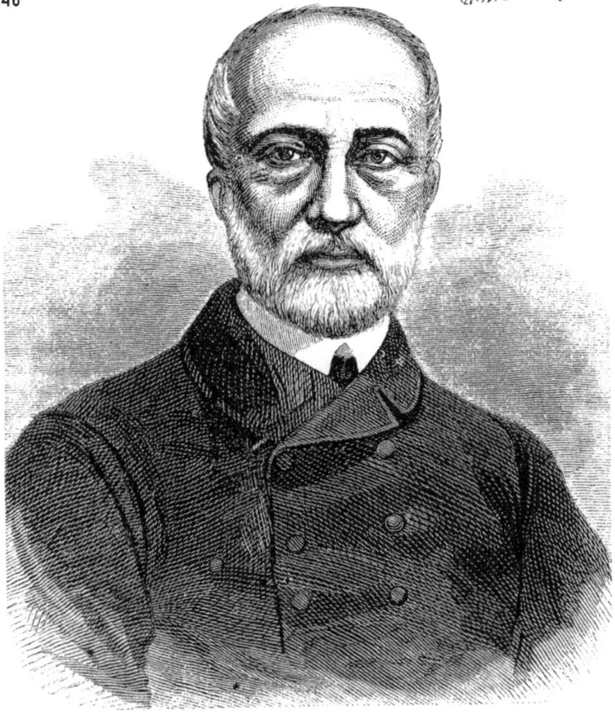

241

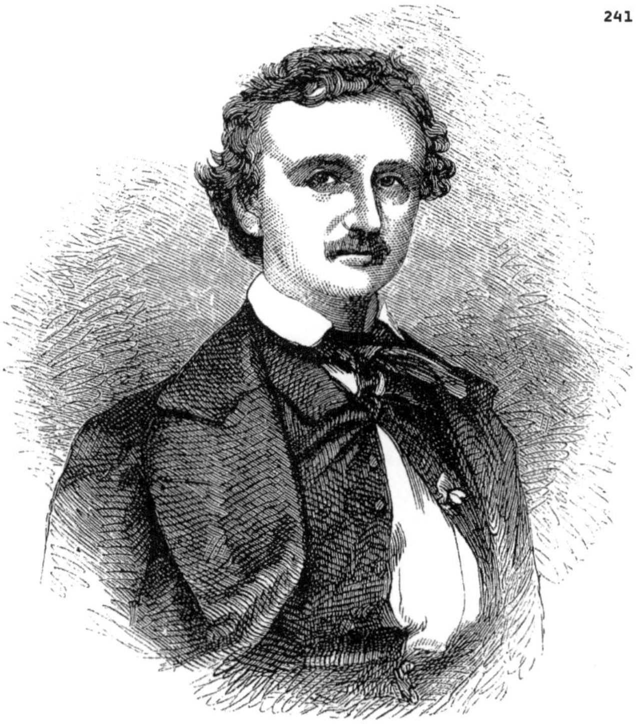

242

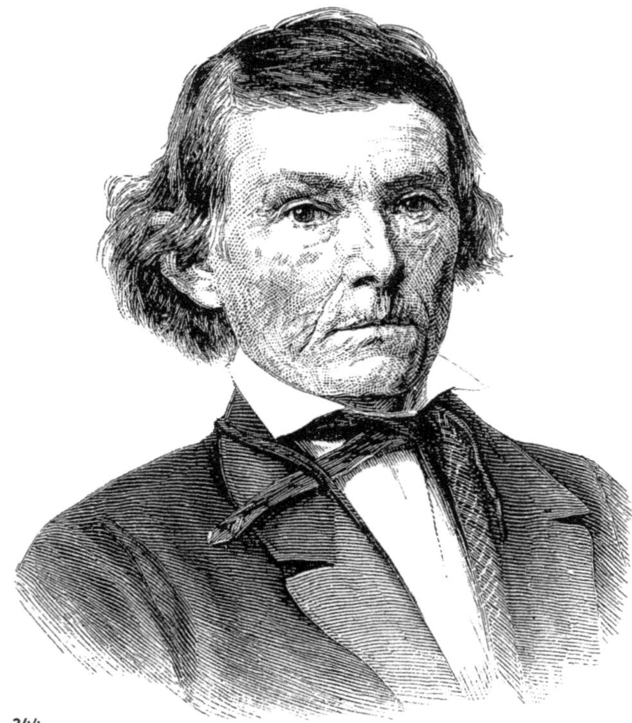

243

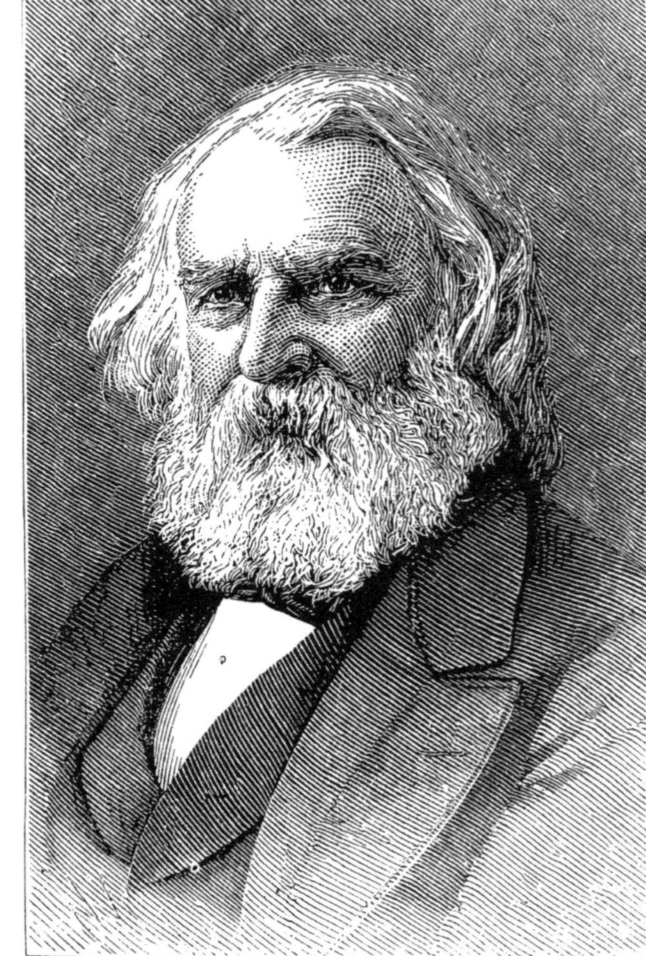

244

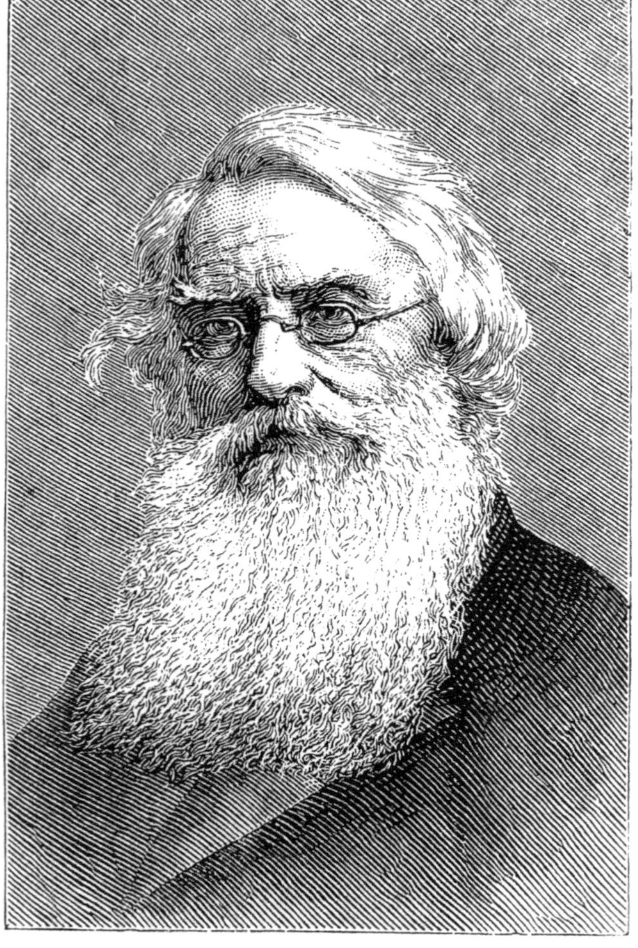

245

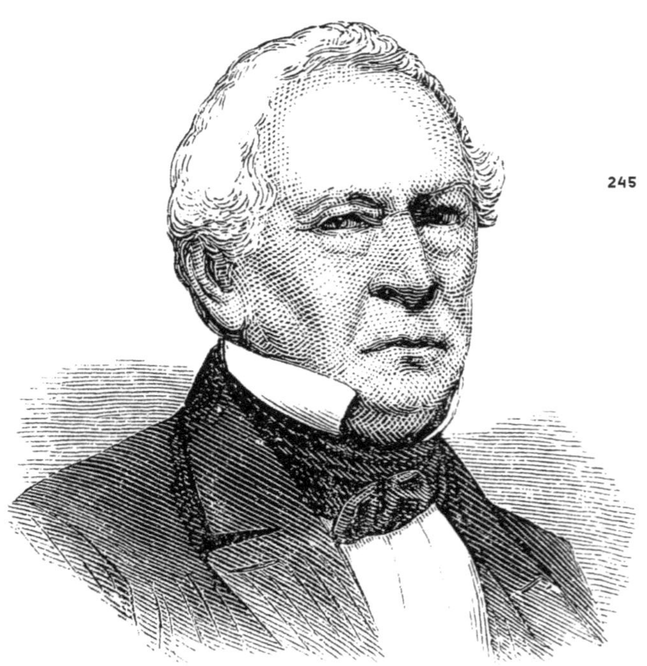

246

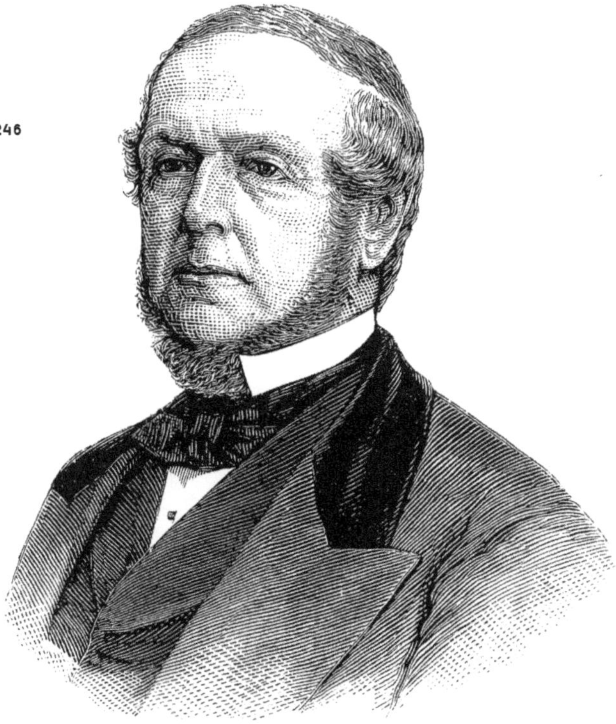

247

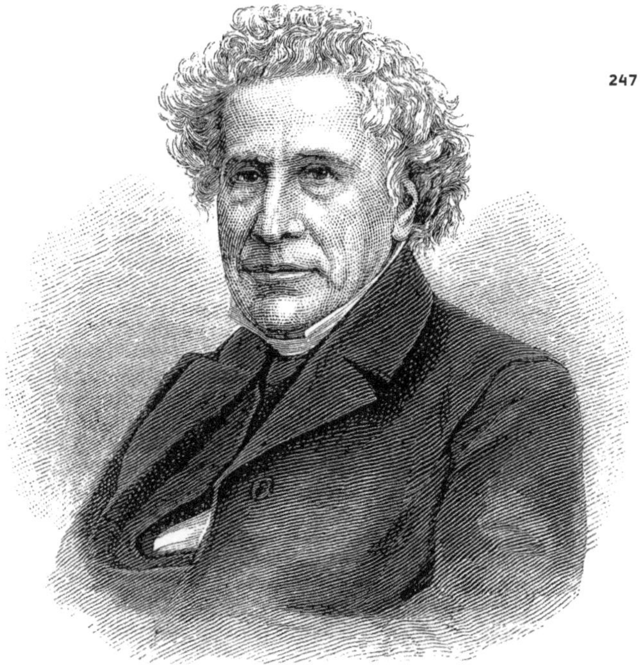

248

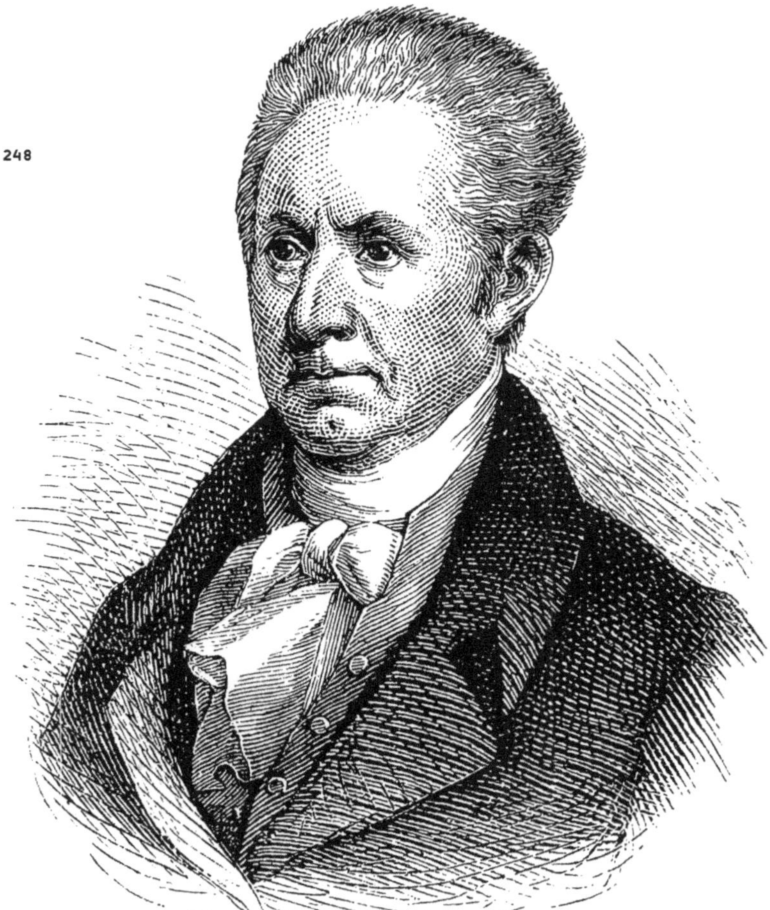

249

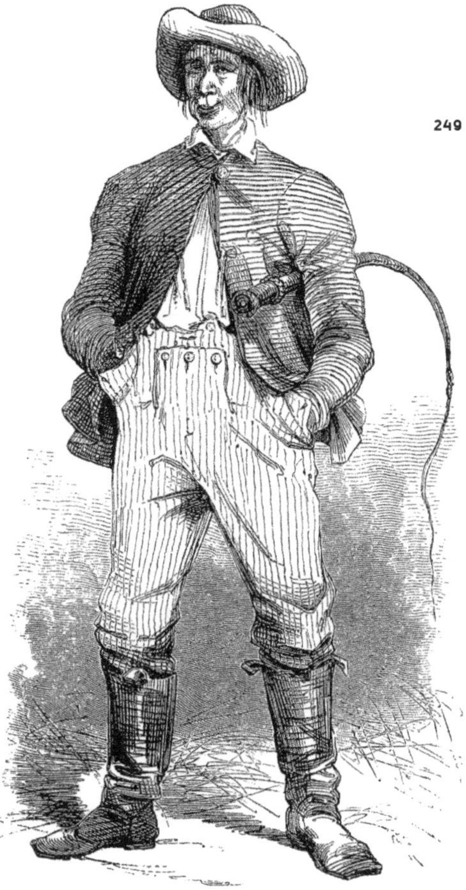

MEN

250

251

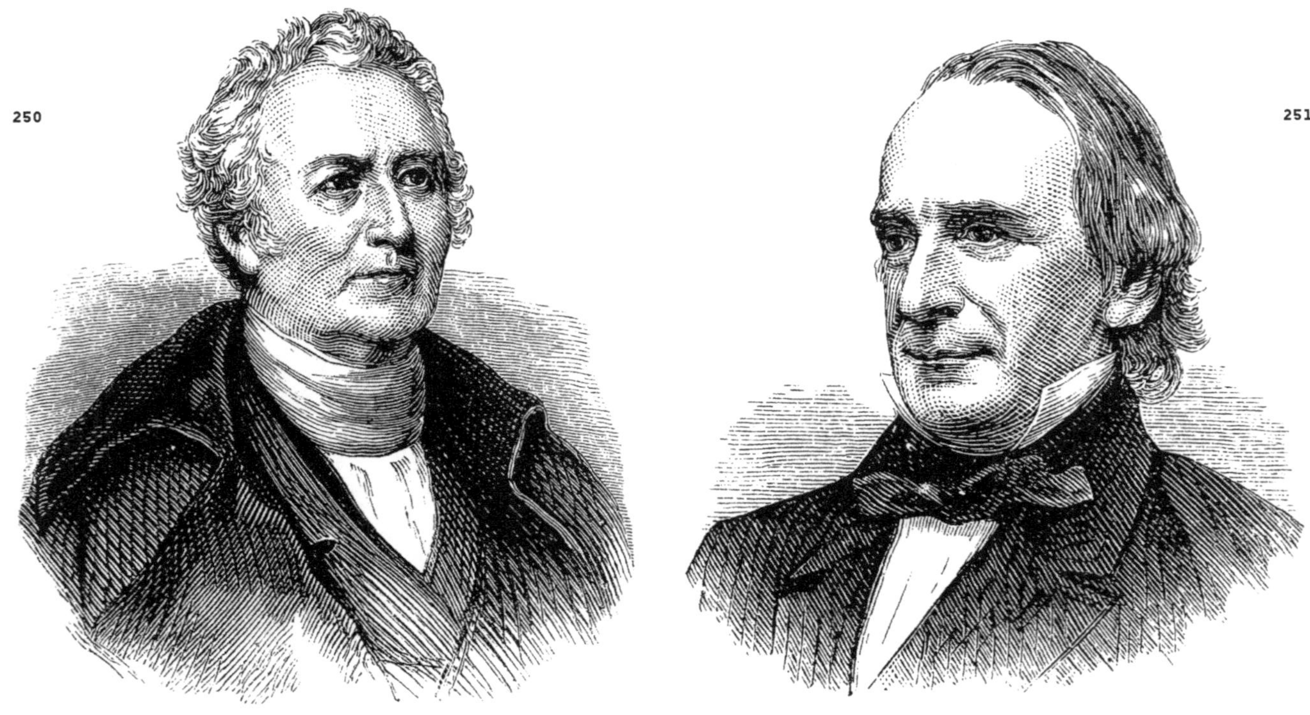

252

253

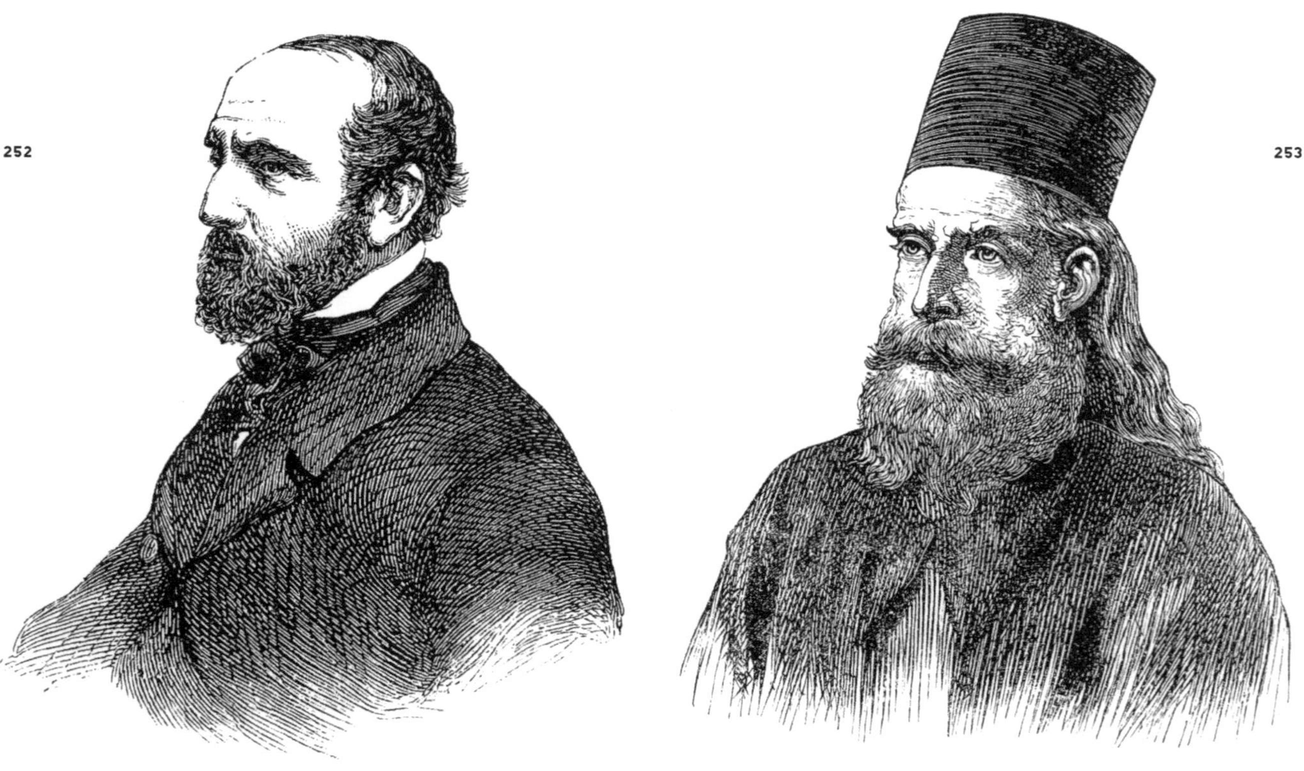

254

255

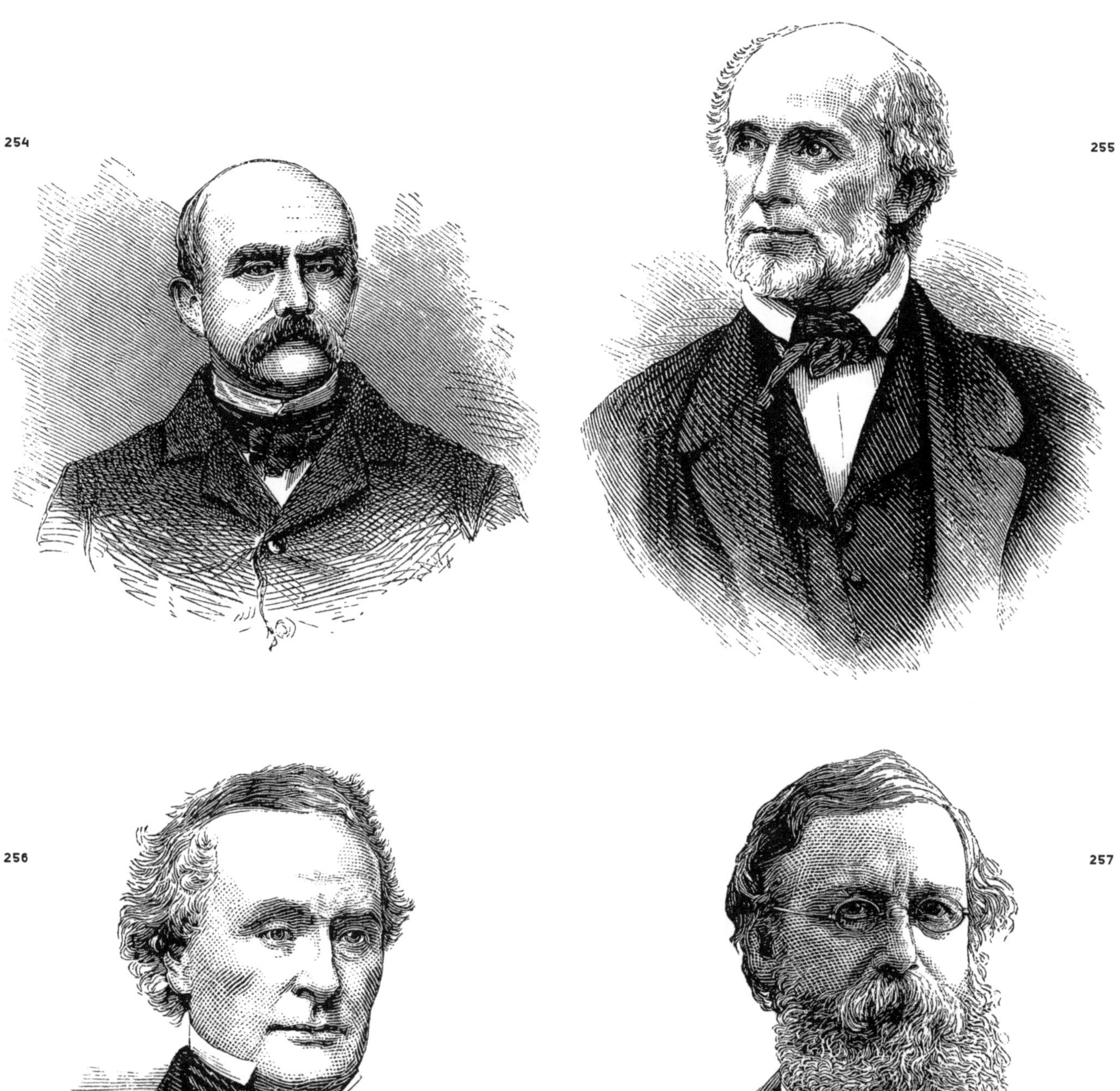

256

257

258

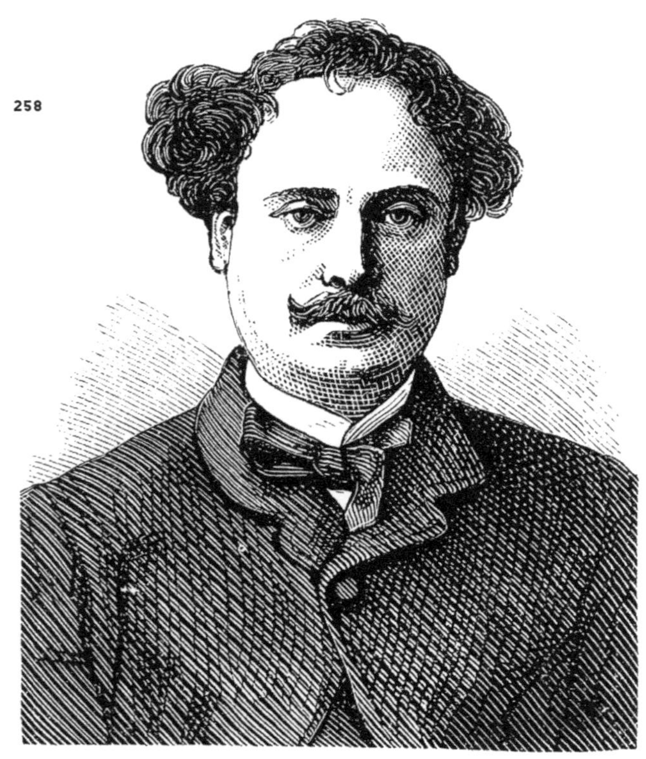

259

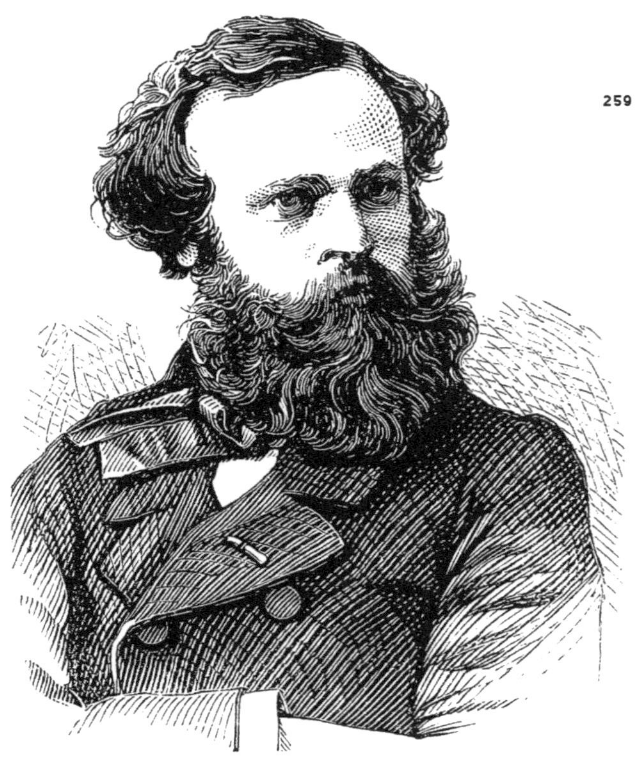

MEN

260

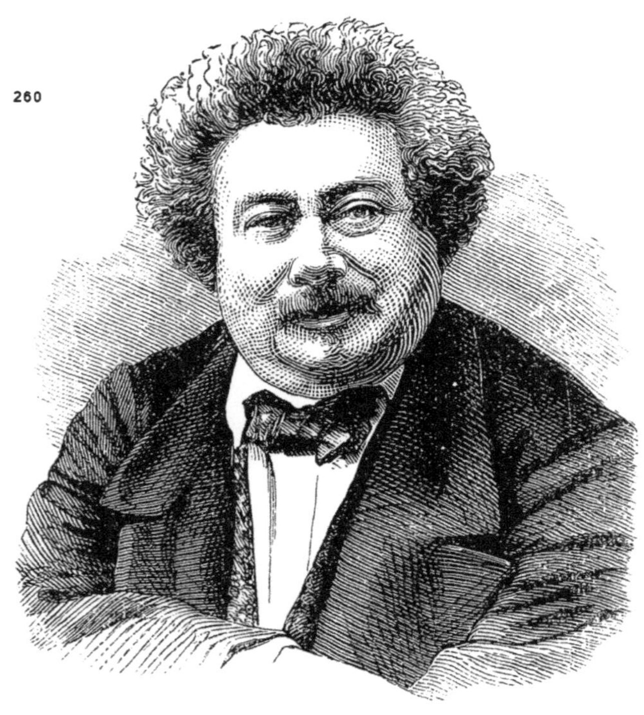

261

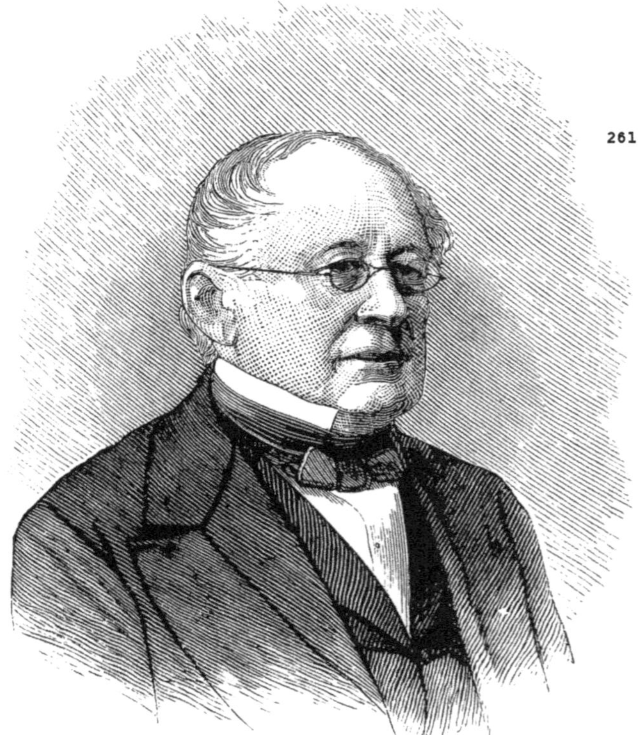

262

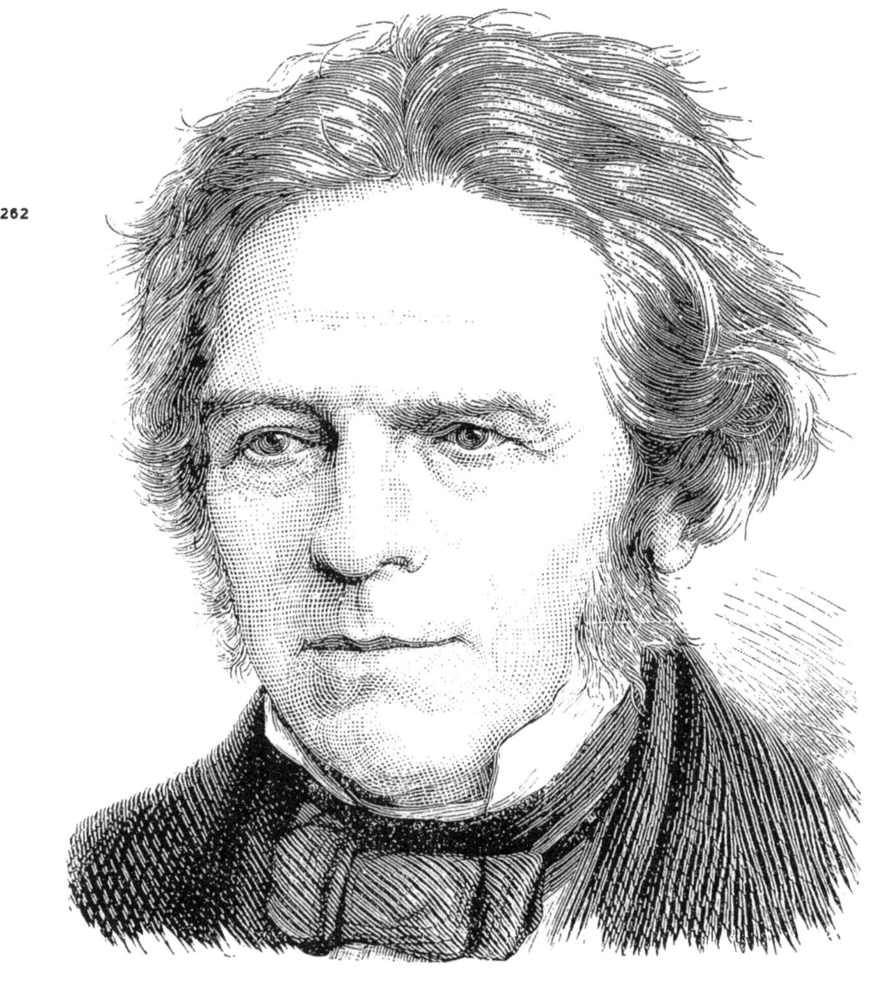

263

264

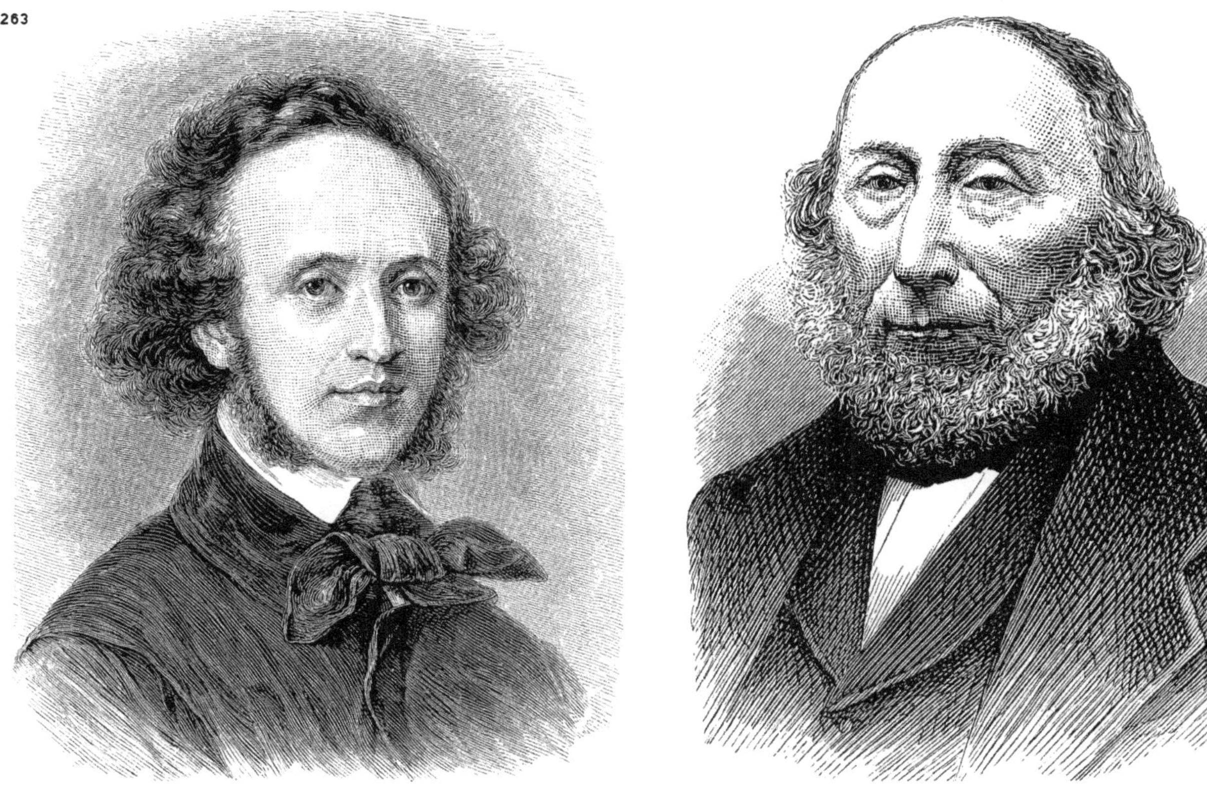

265

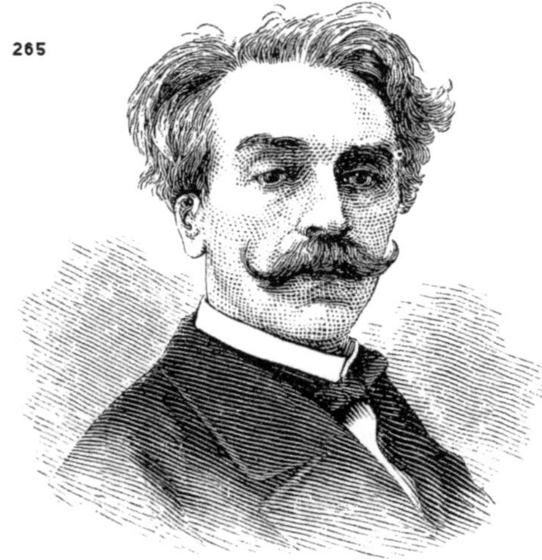

266

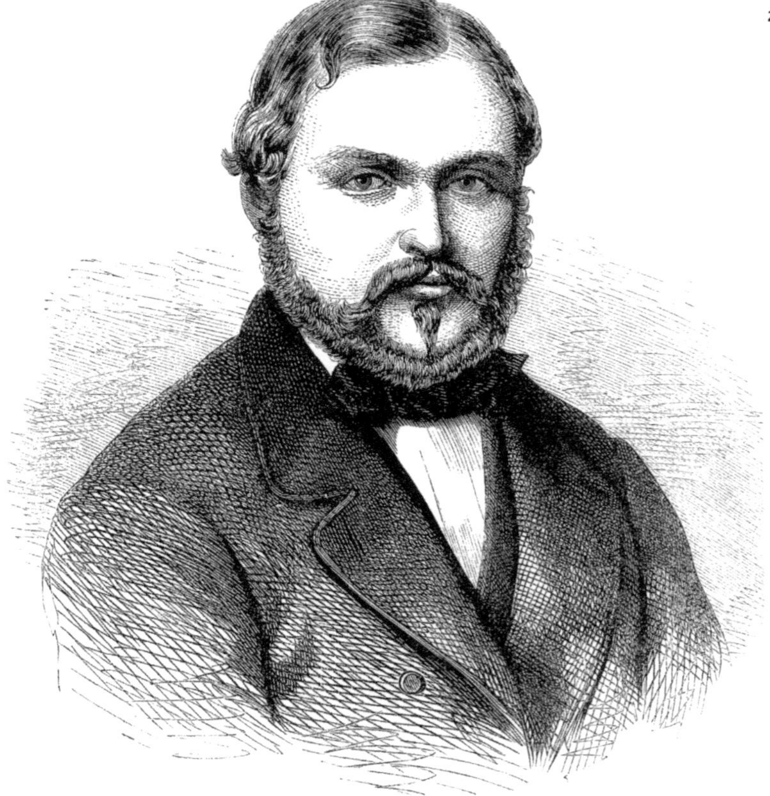

MEN

267

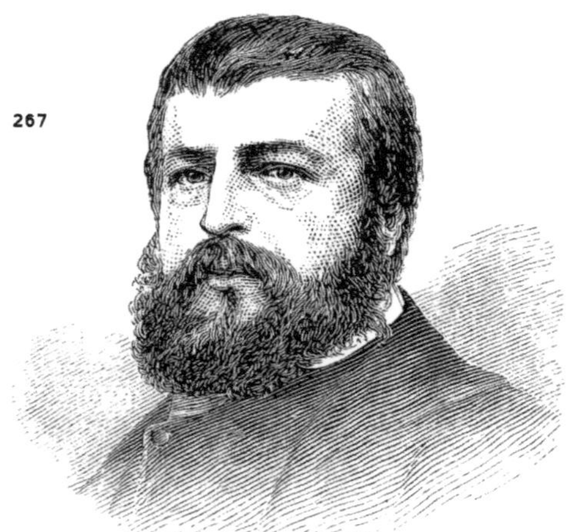

268

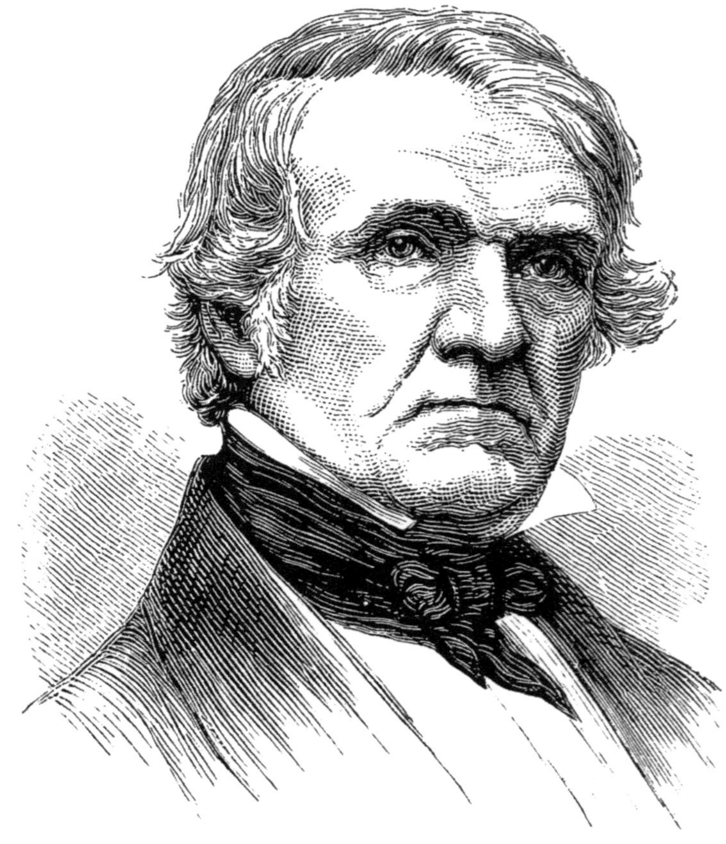

269

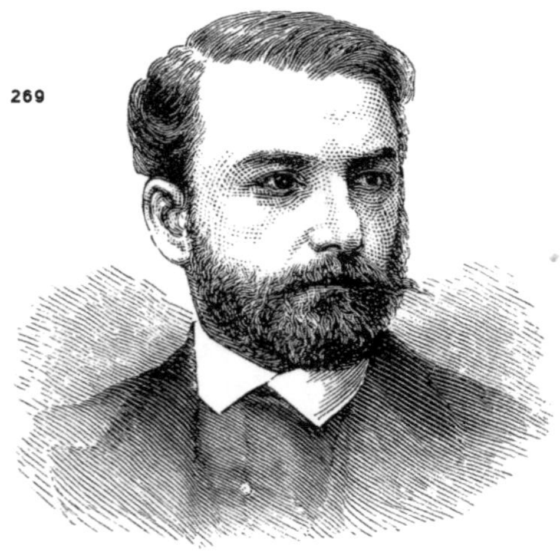

270

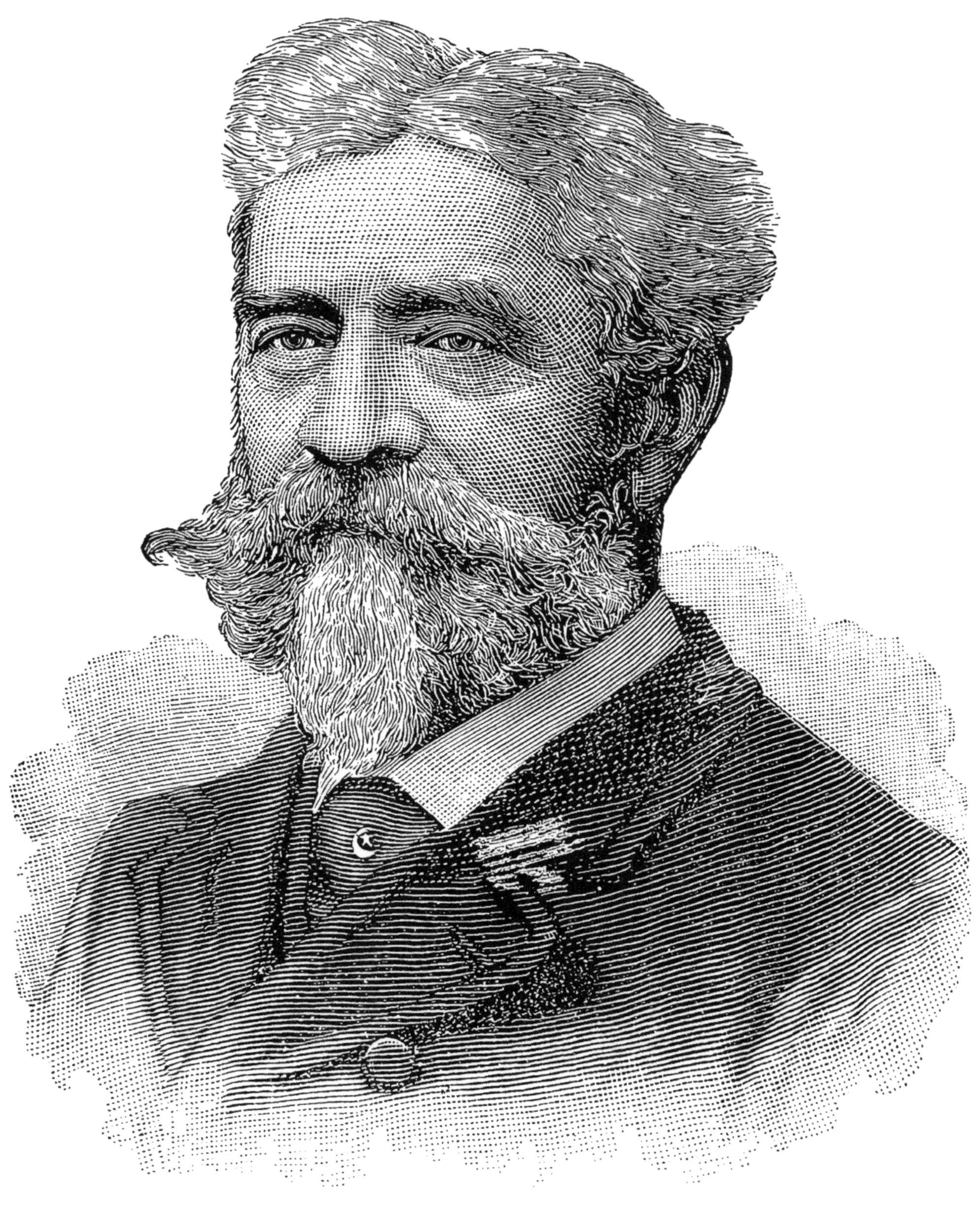

MEN

271

272

273

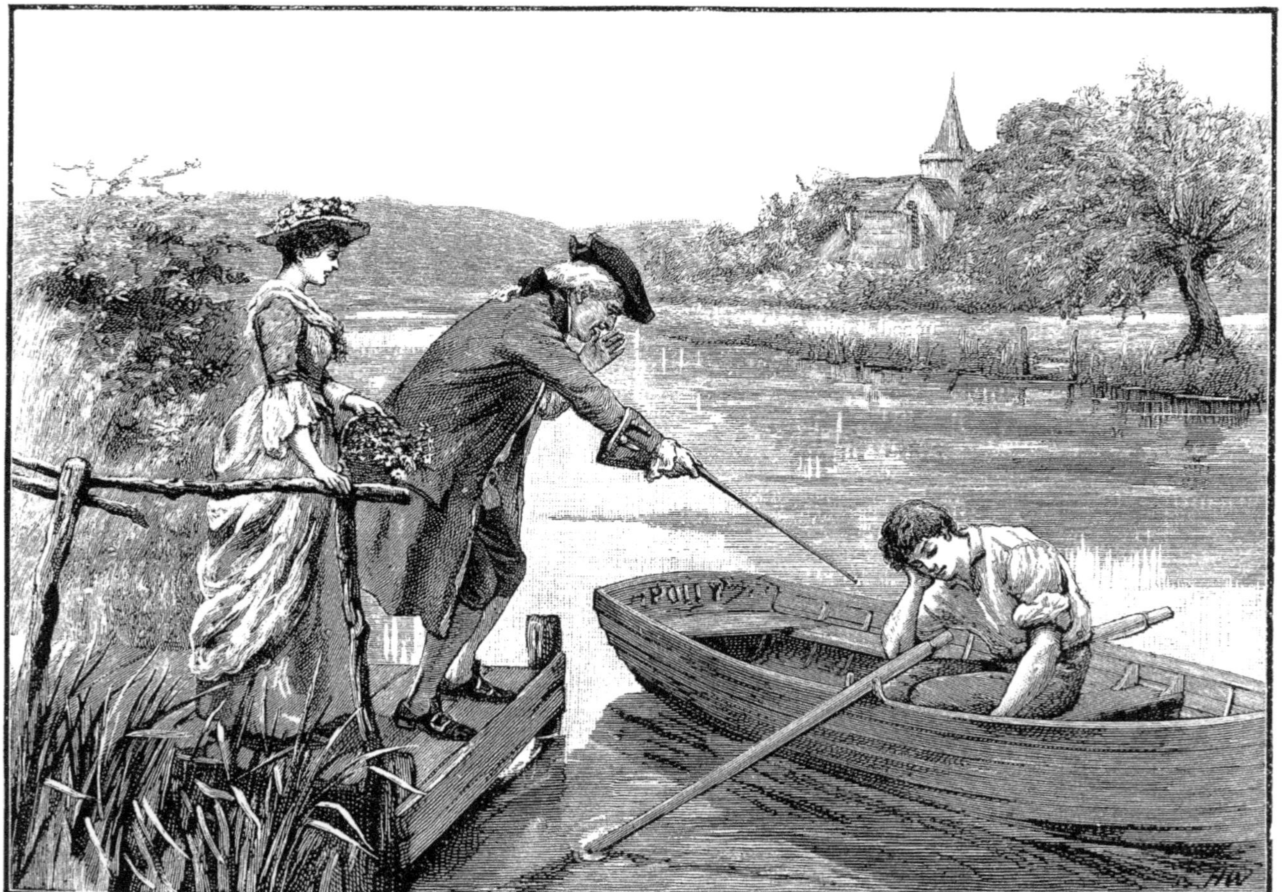

MEN

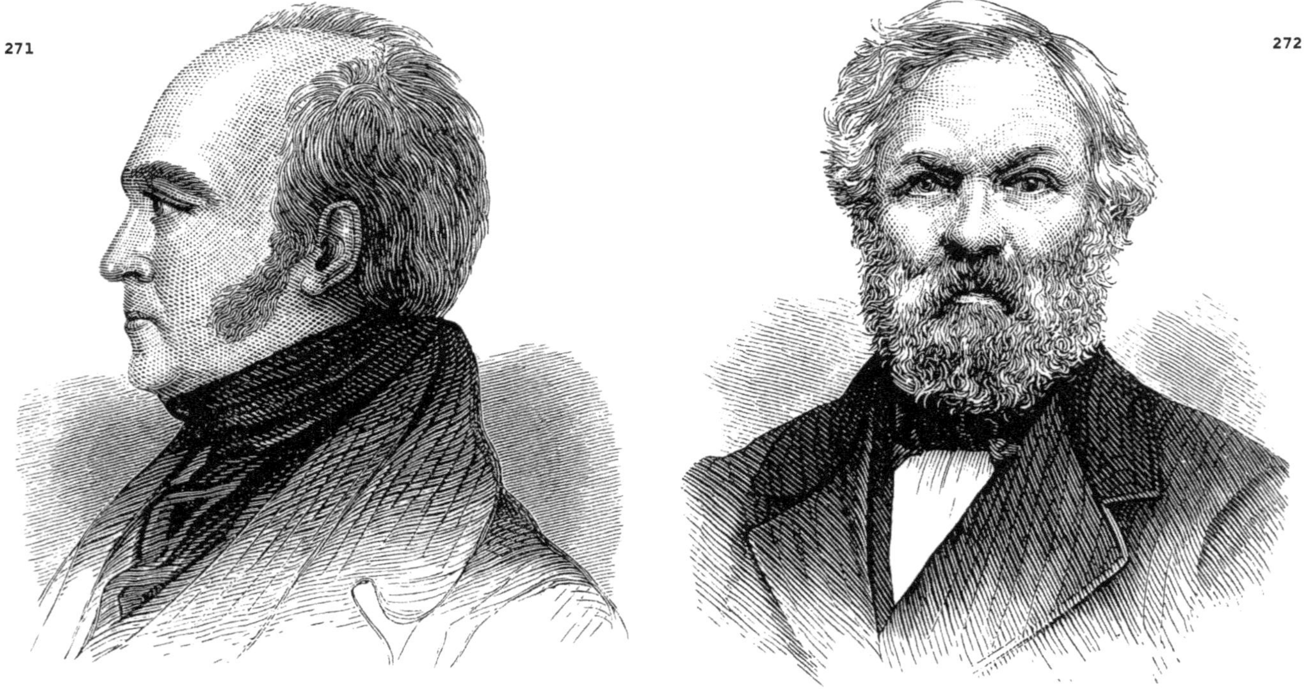

274

275

276

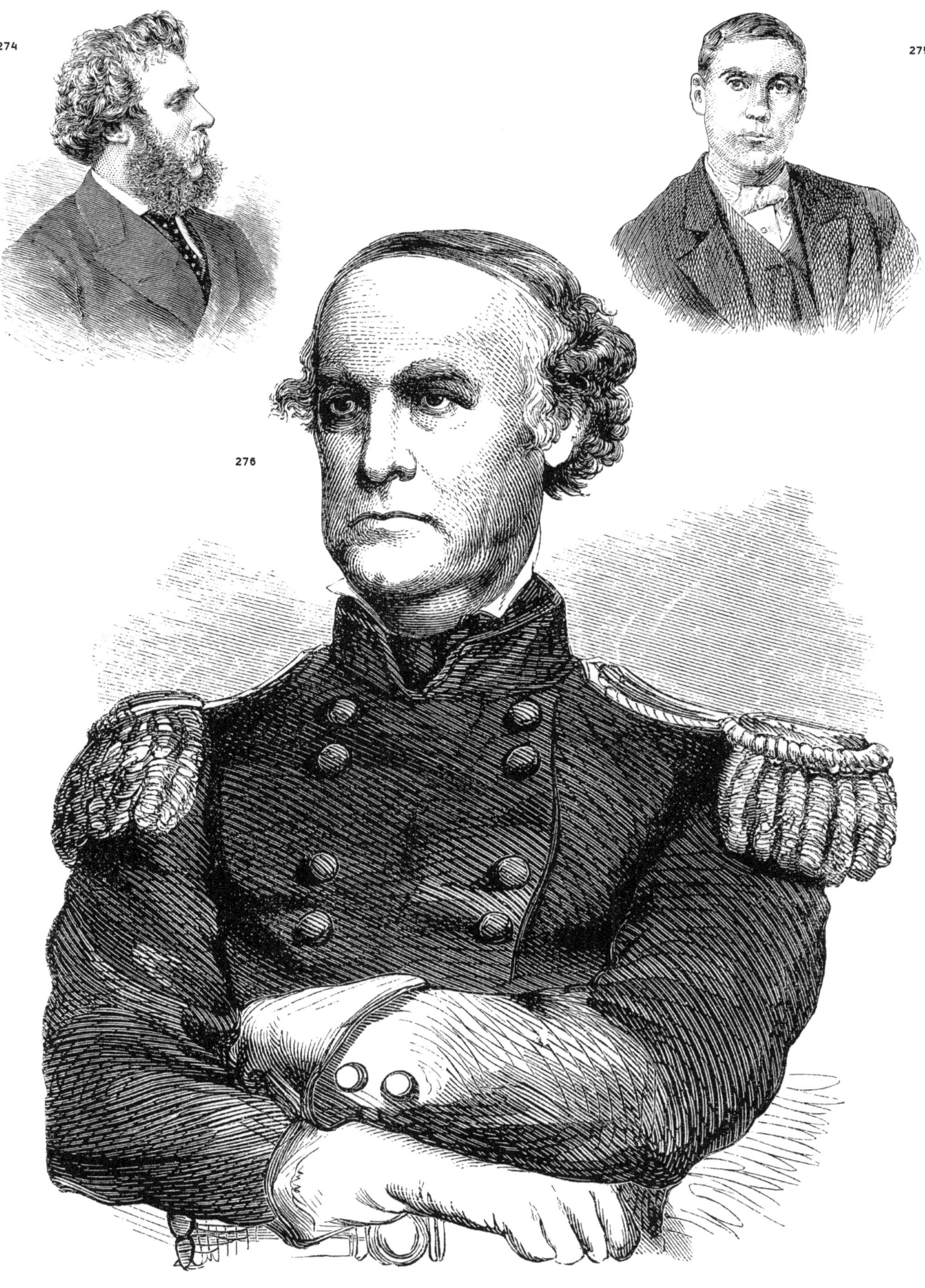

277

278

MEN

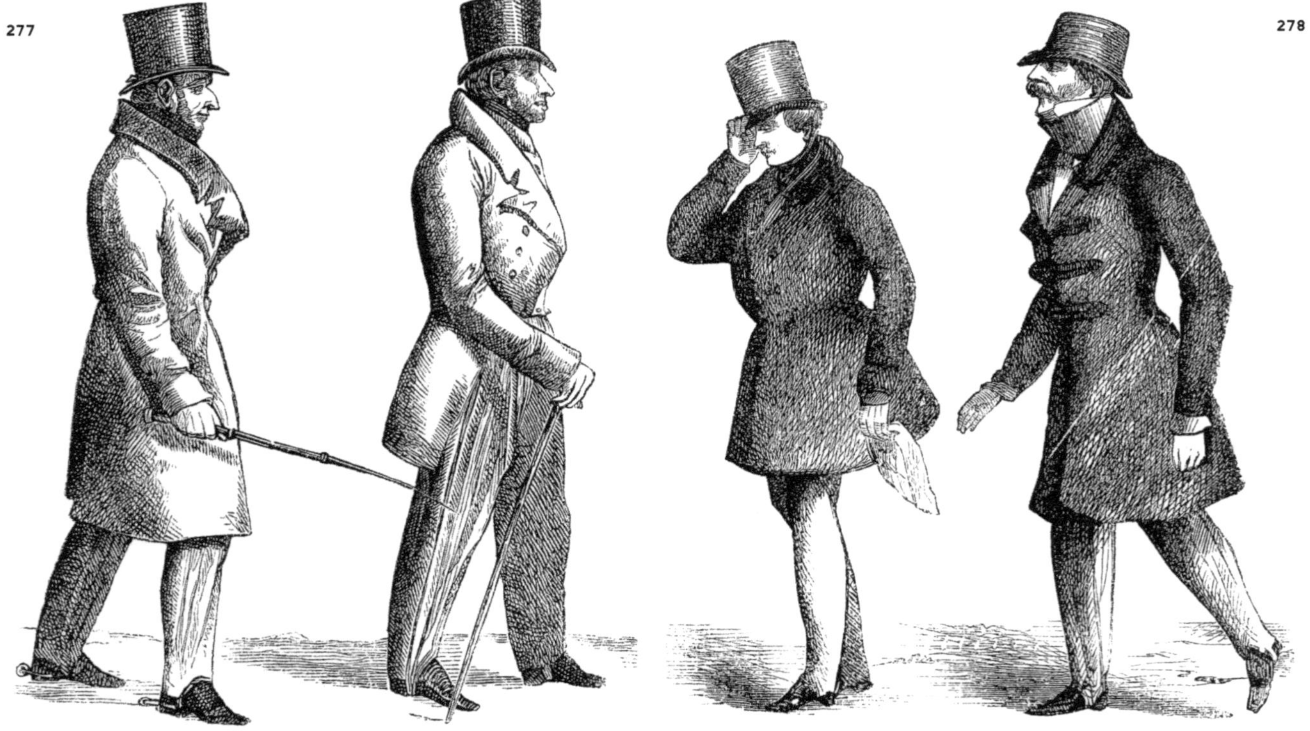

279

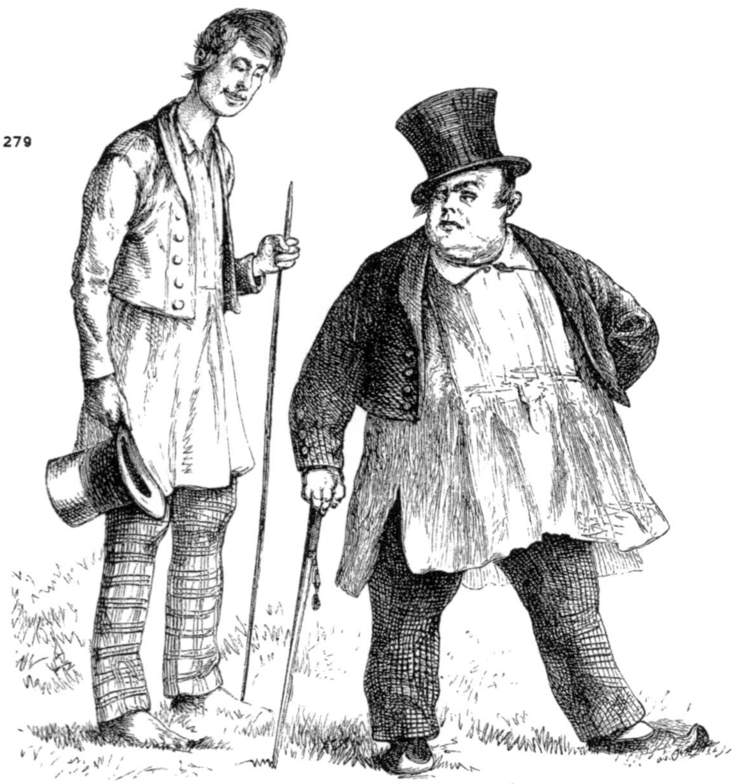

280

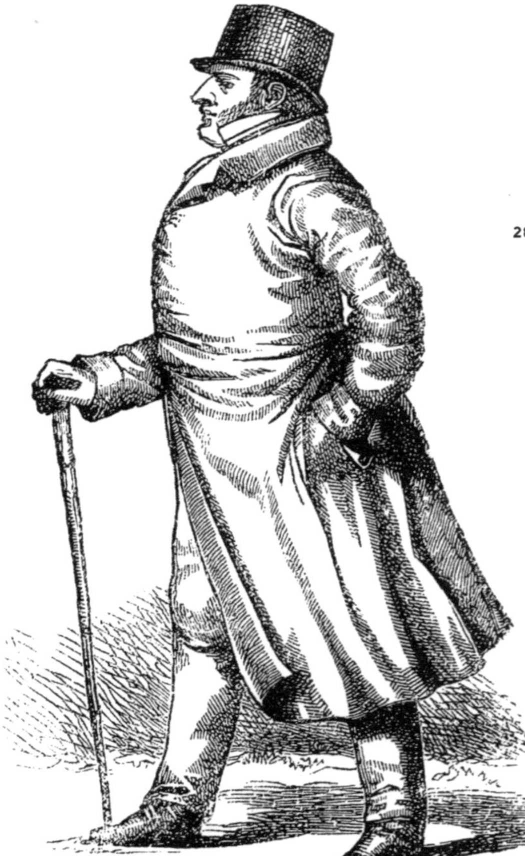

281

282

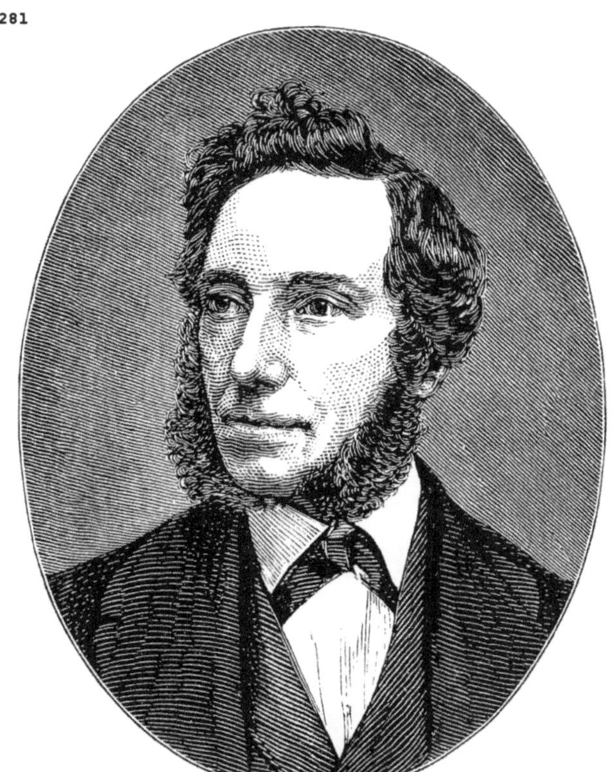

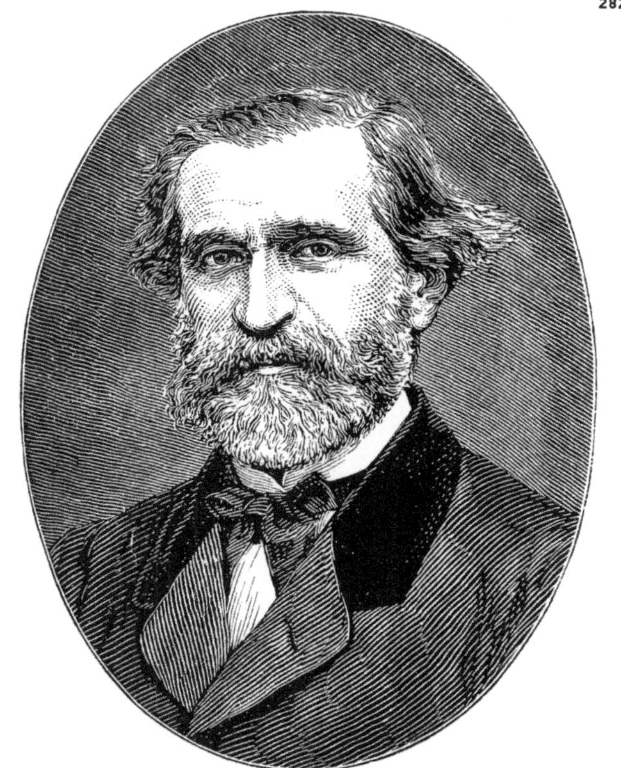

MEN

283

284

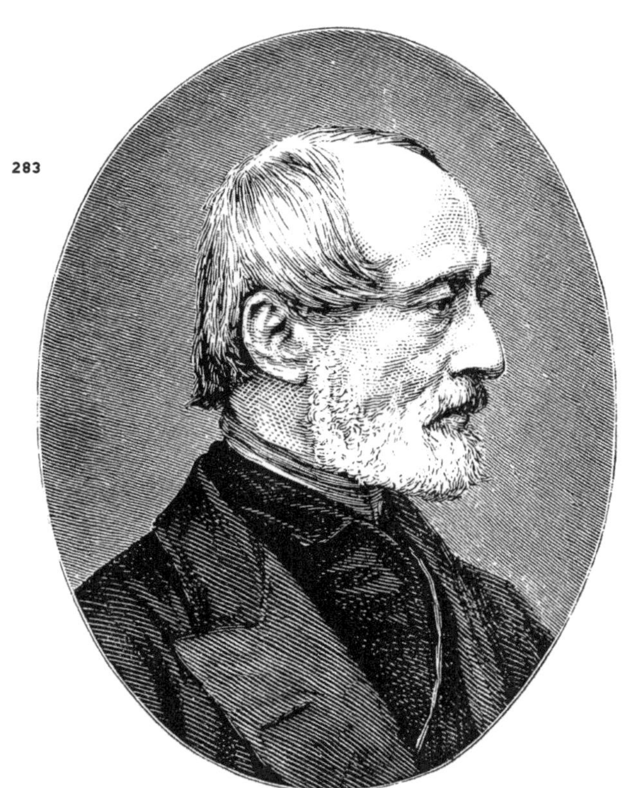

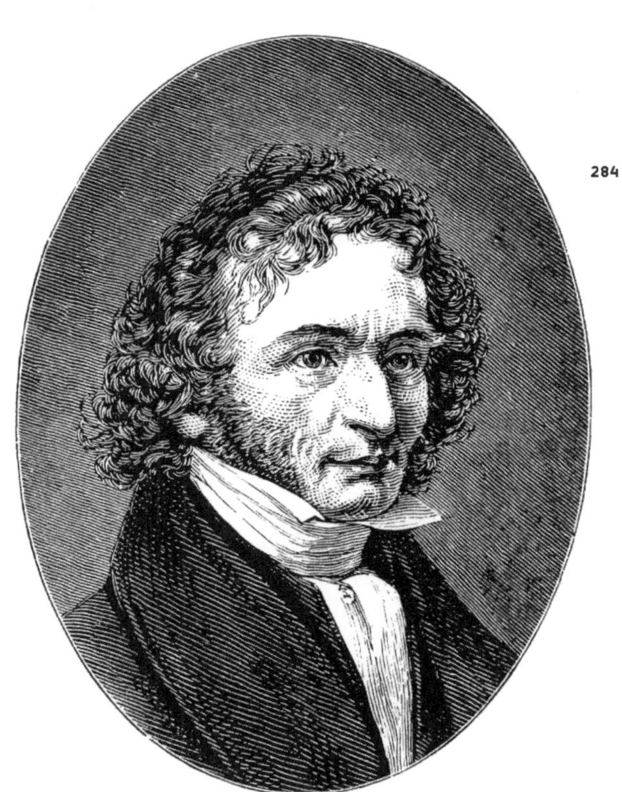

285

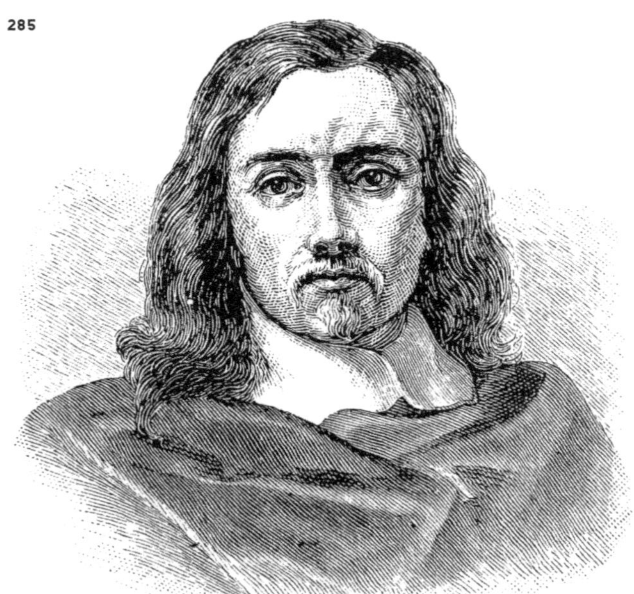

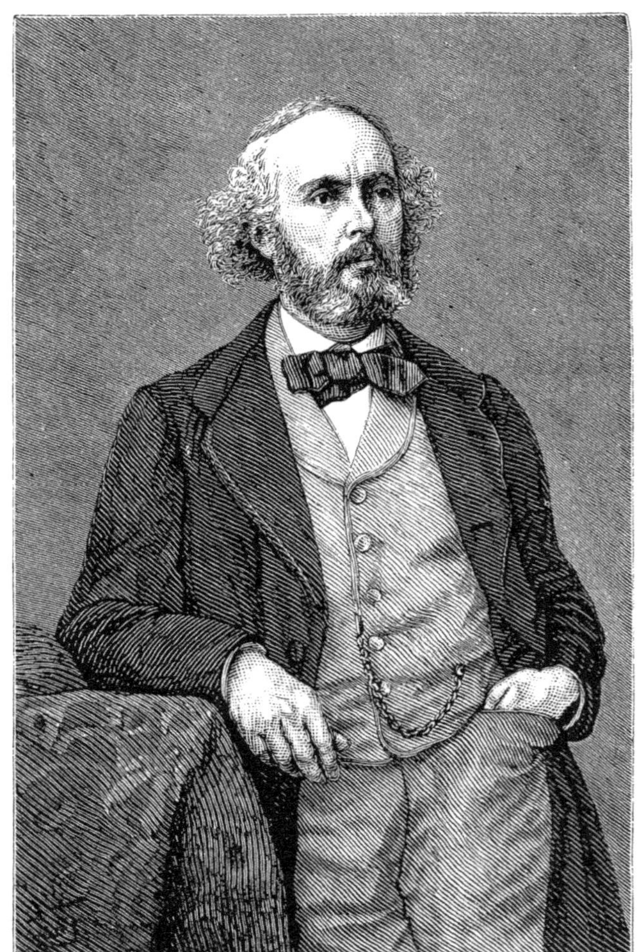

287

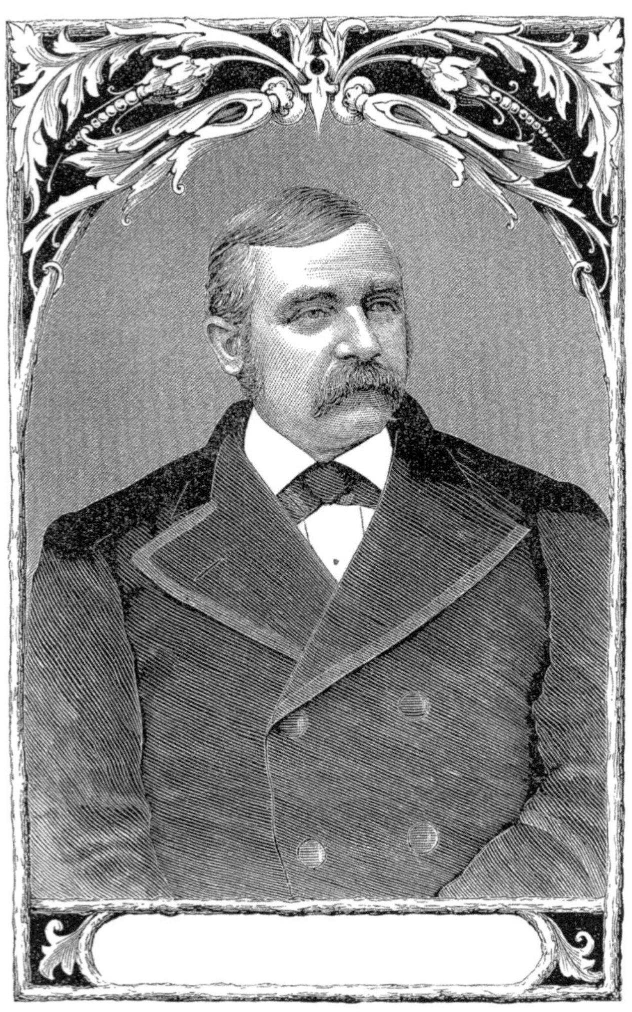

288

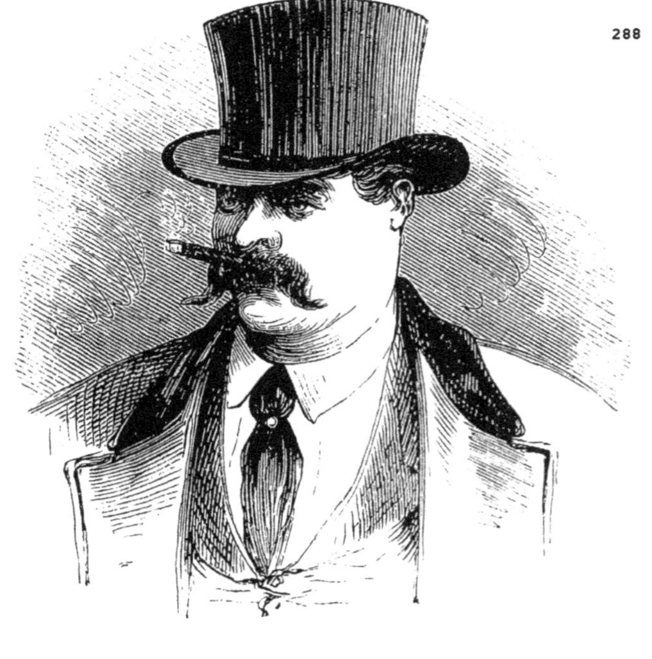

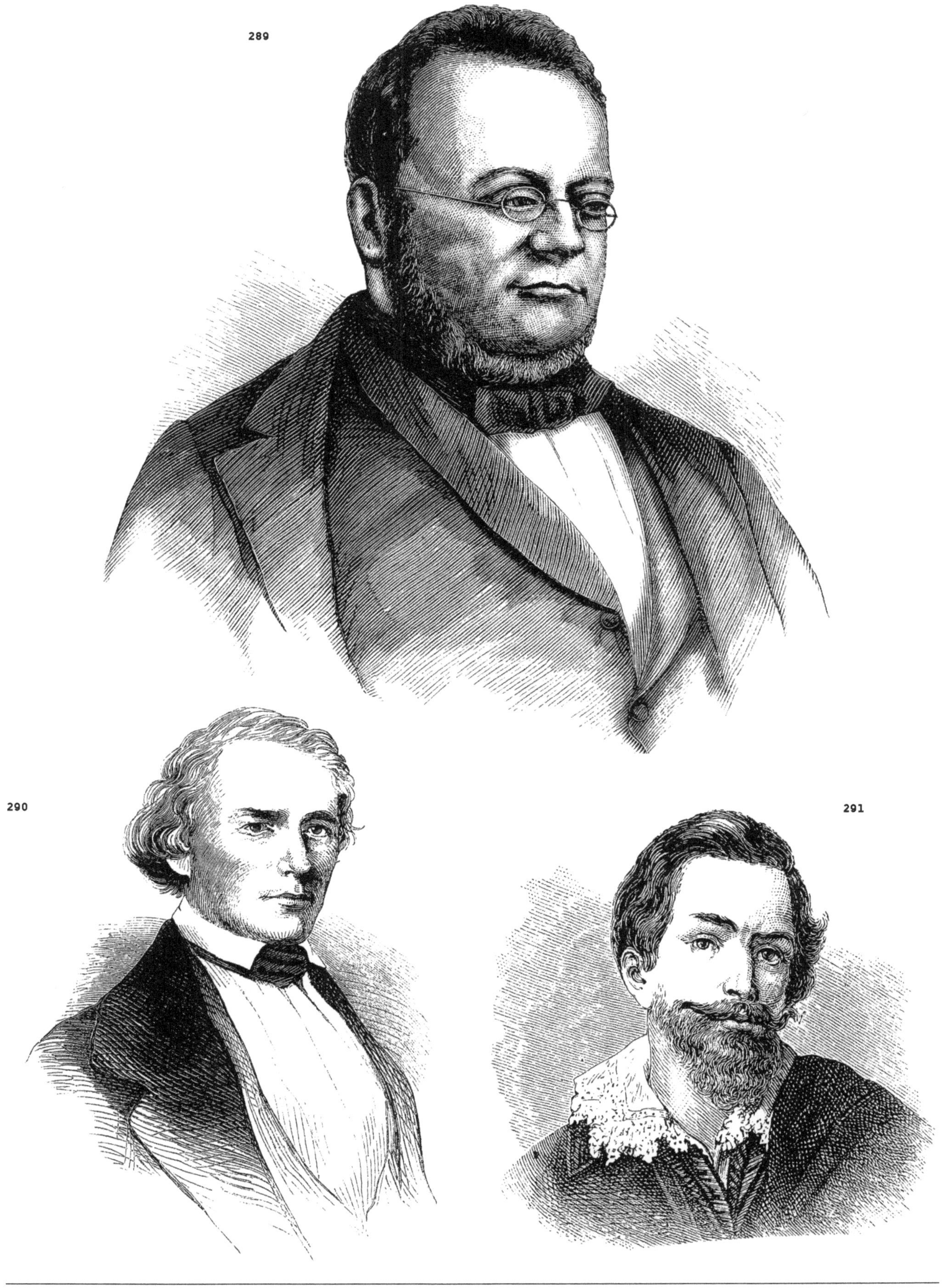

289

290

291

292

293

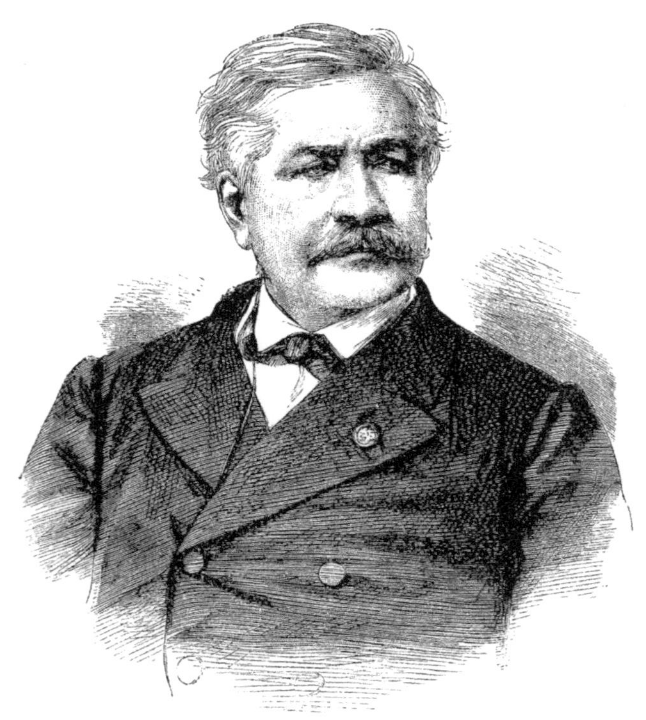

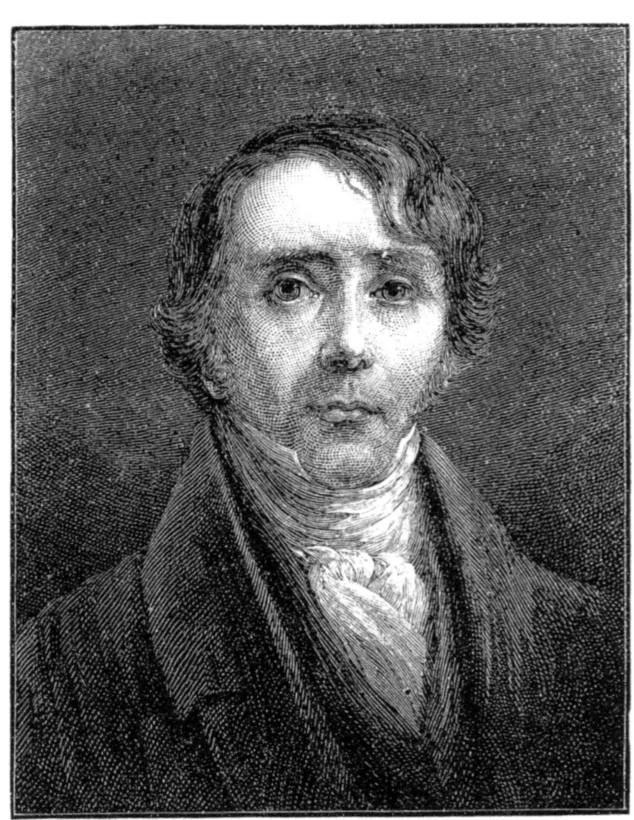

294

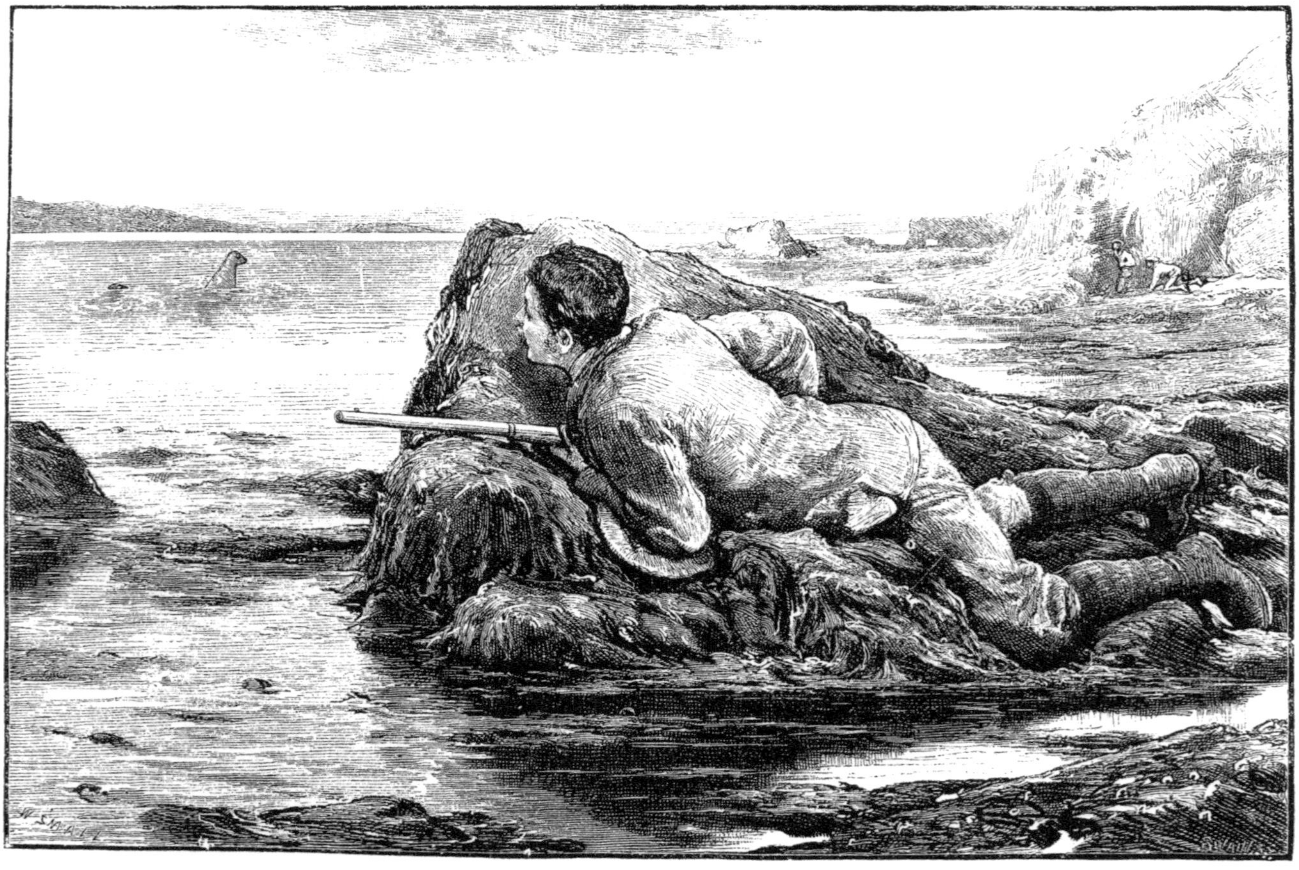

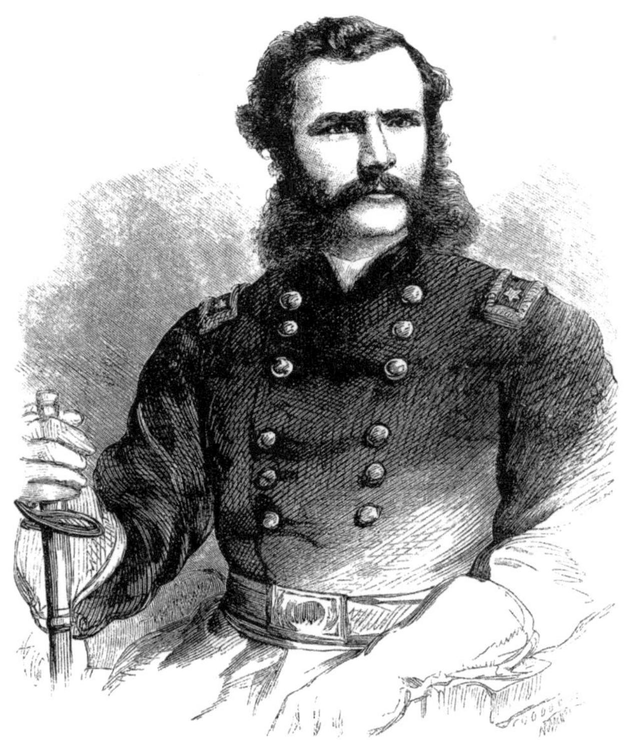

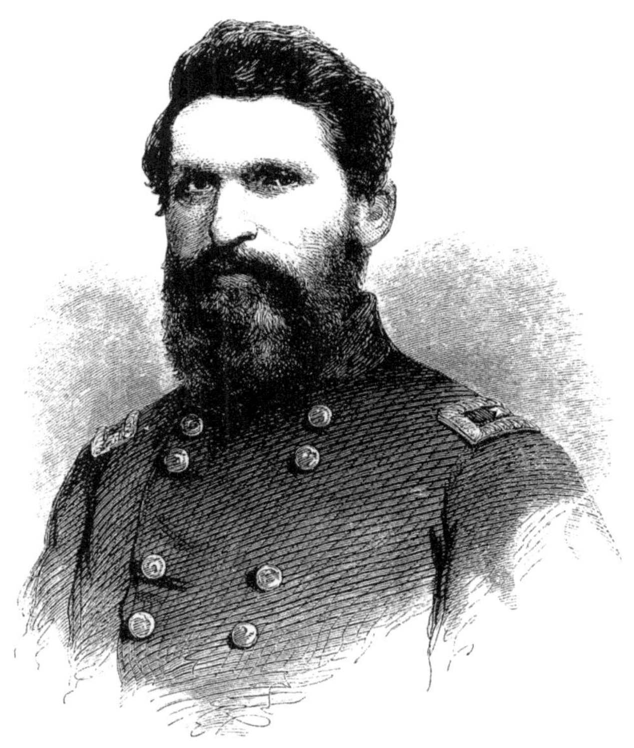

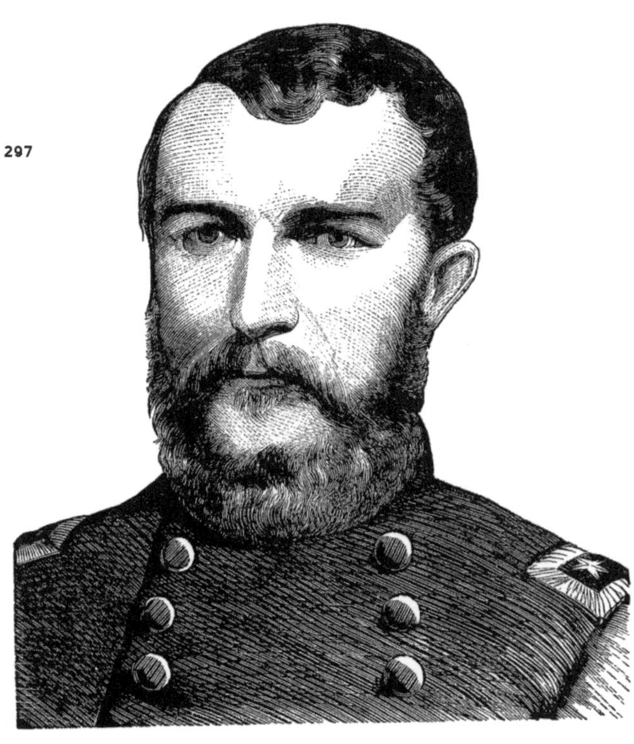

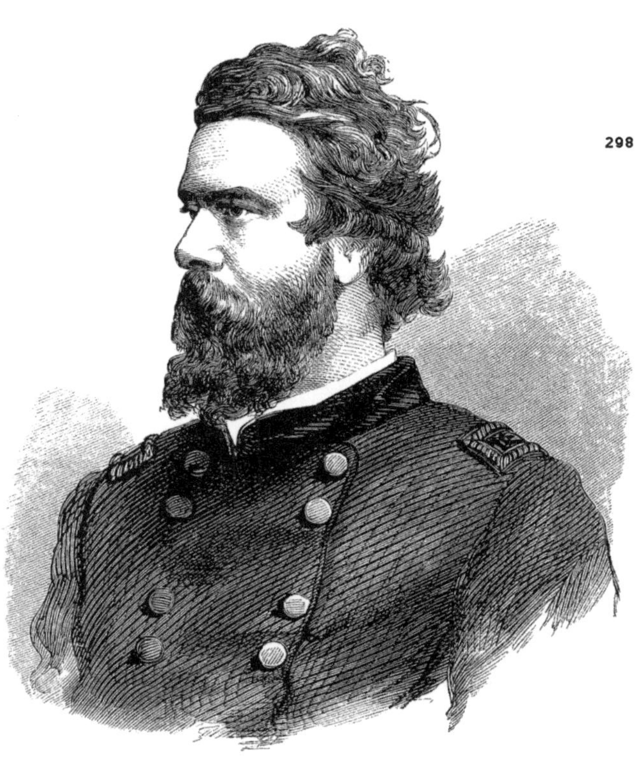

MEN

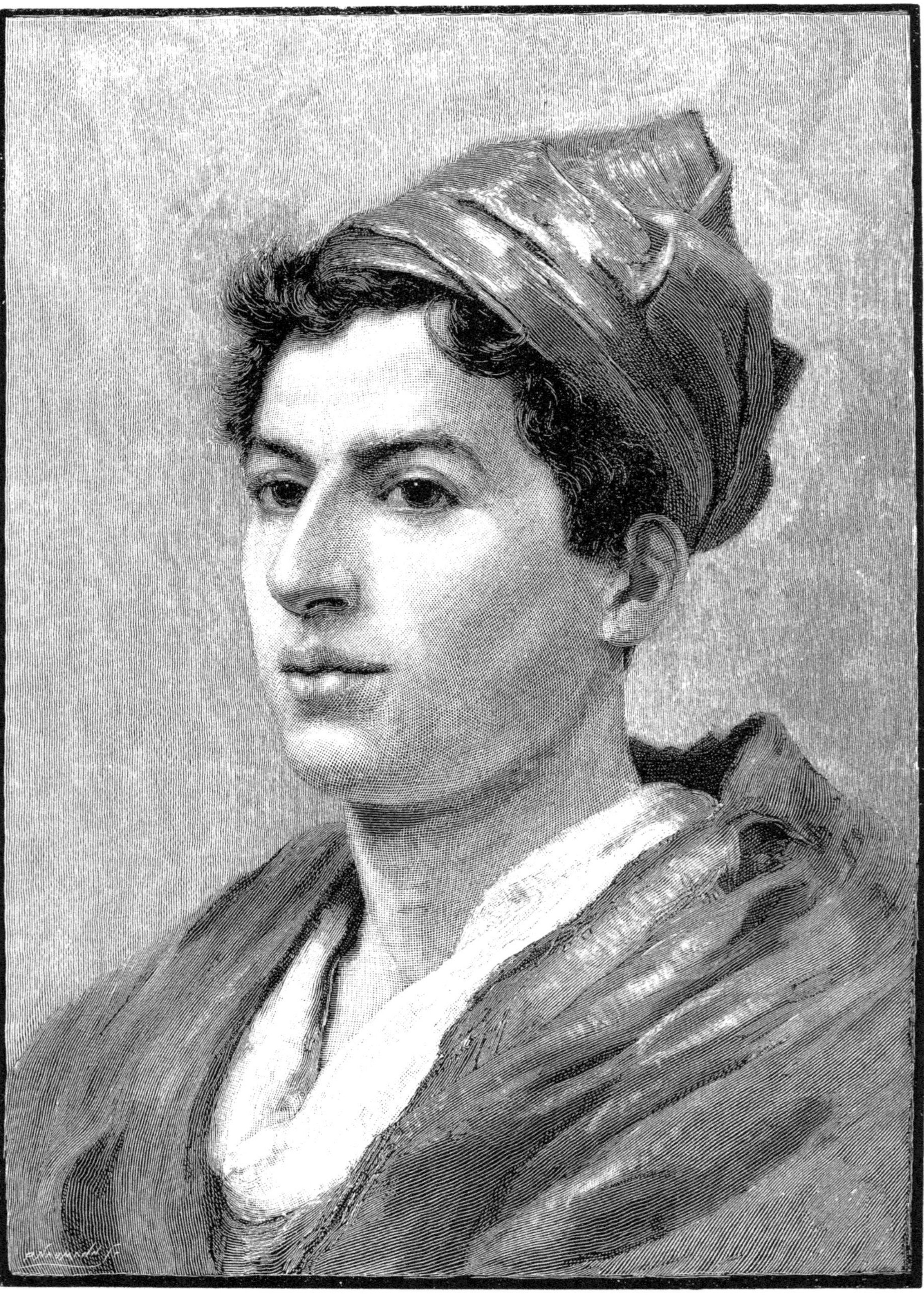

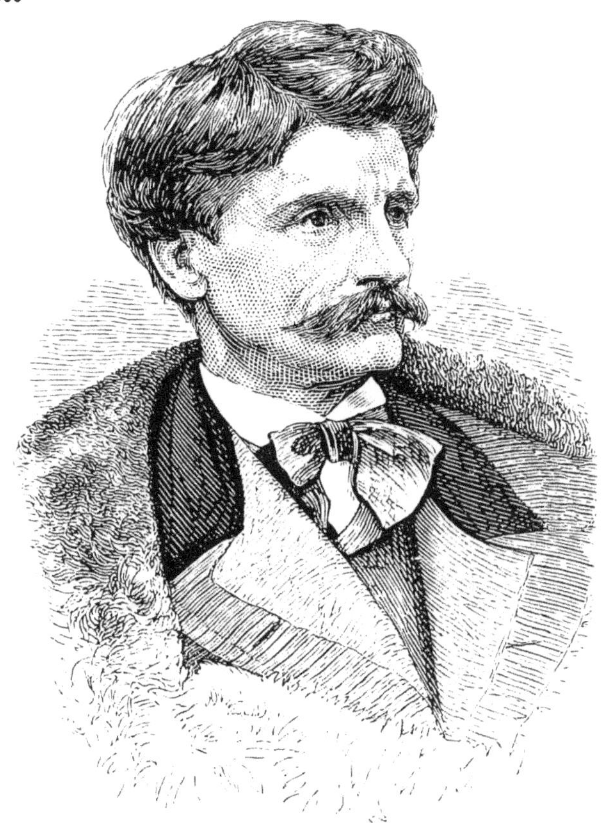

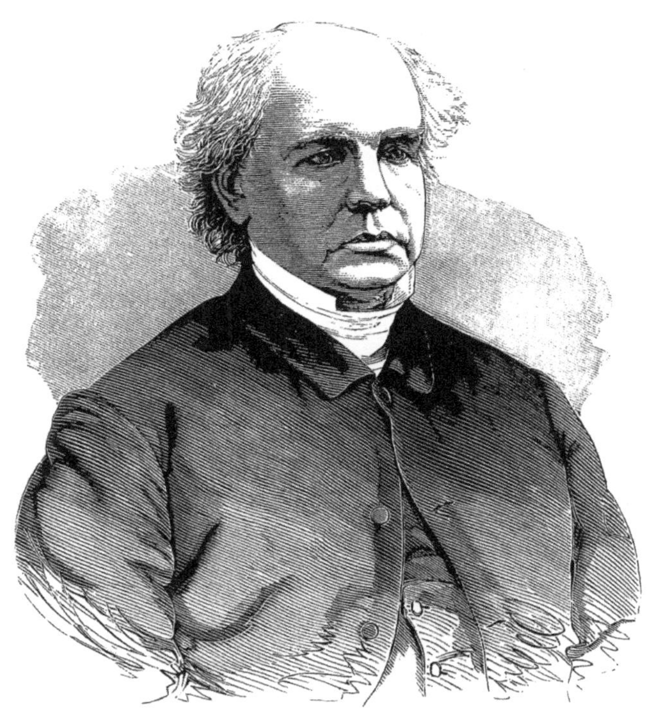

MEN

302   303

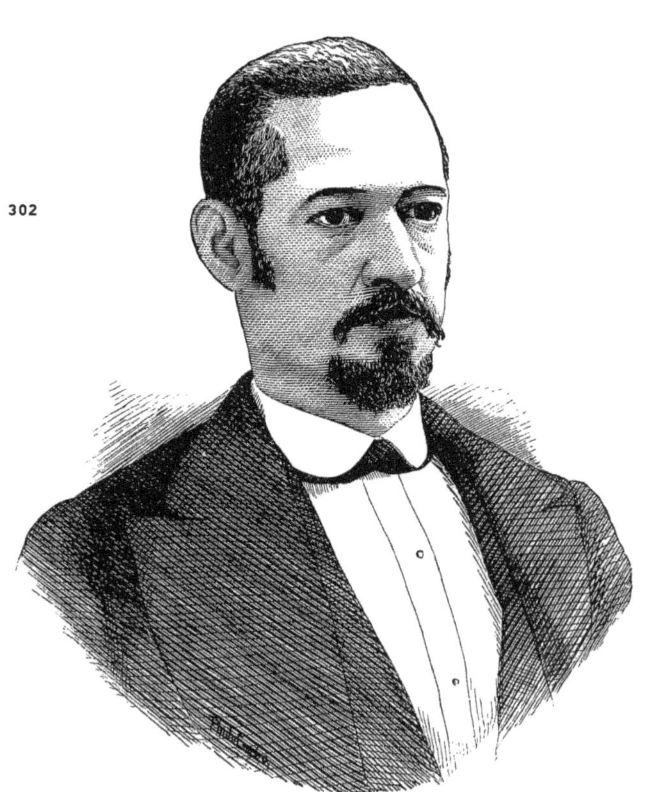

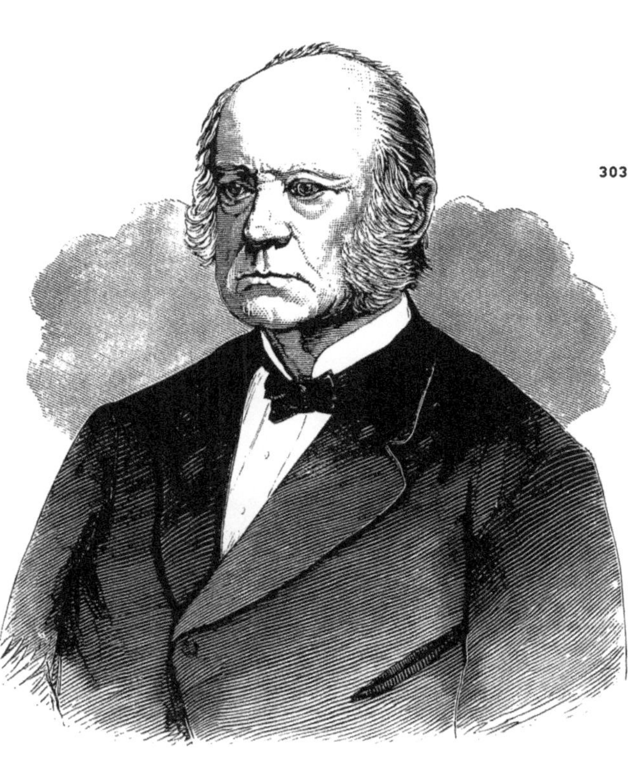

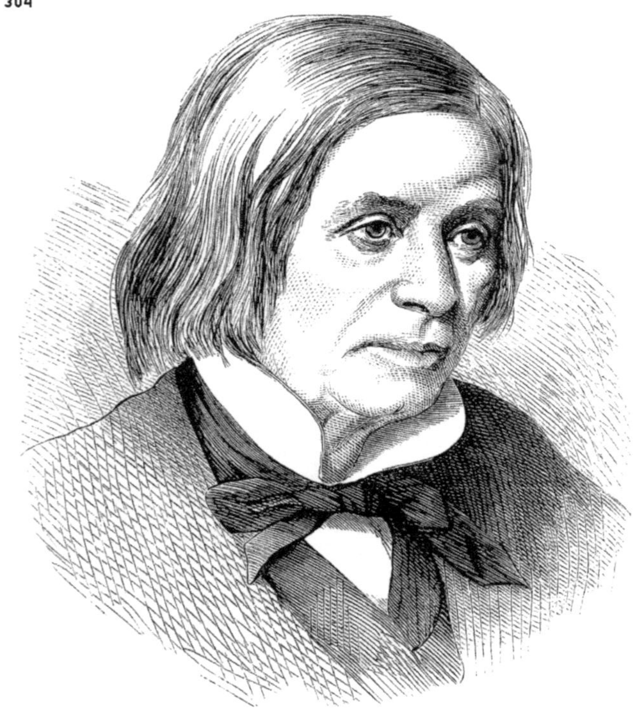

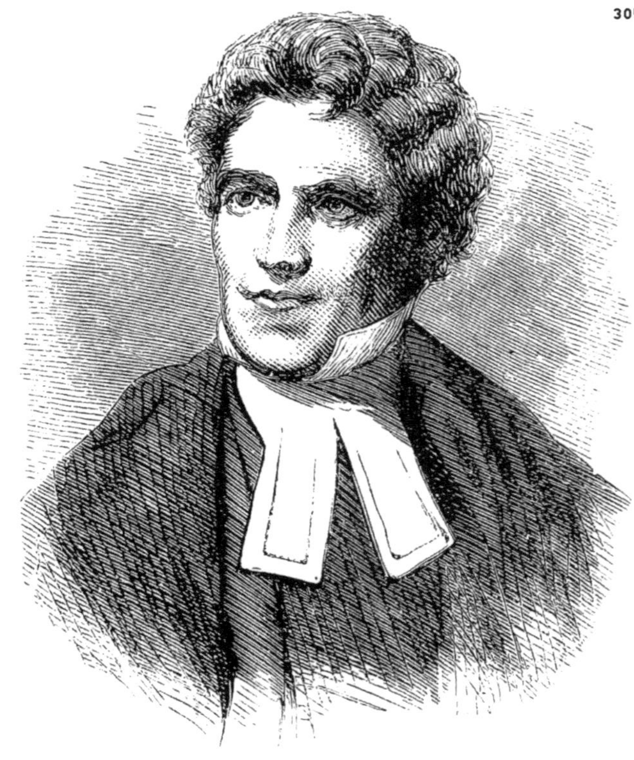

306

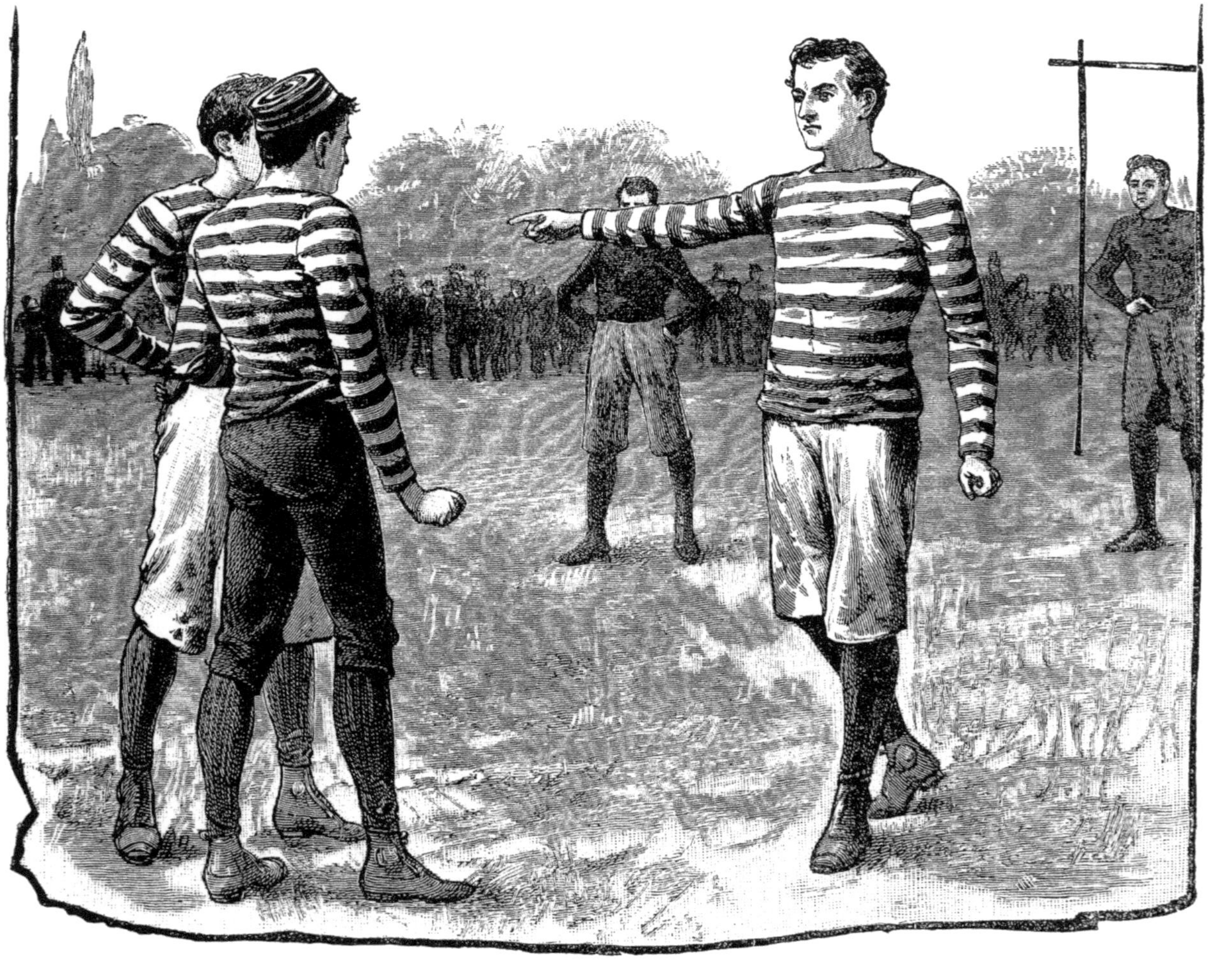

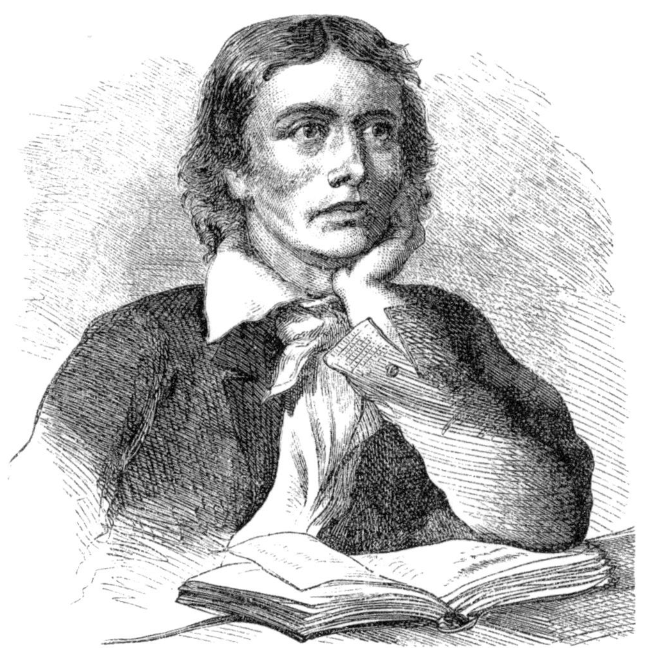

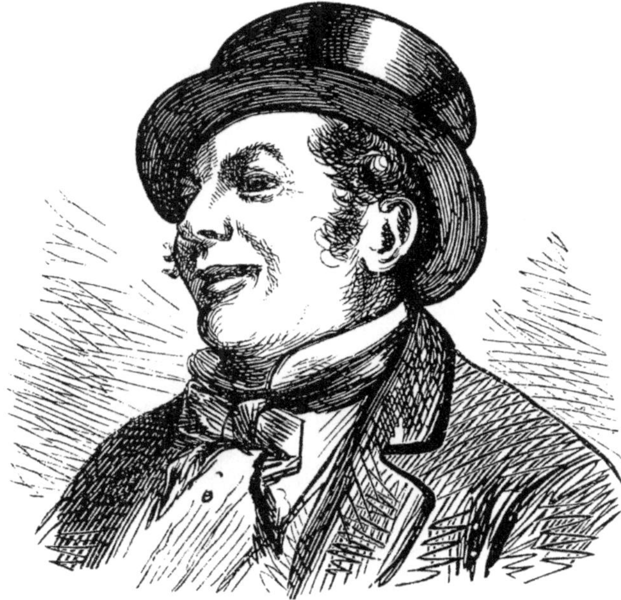

309

MEN

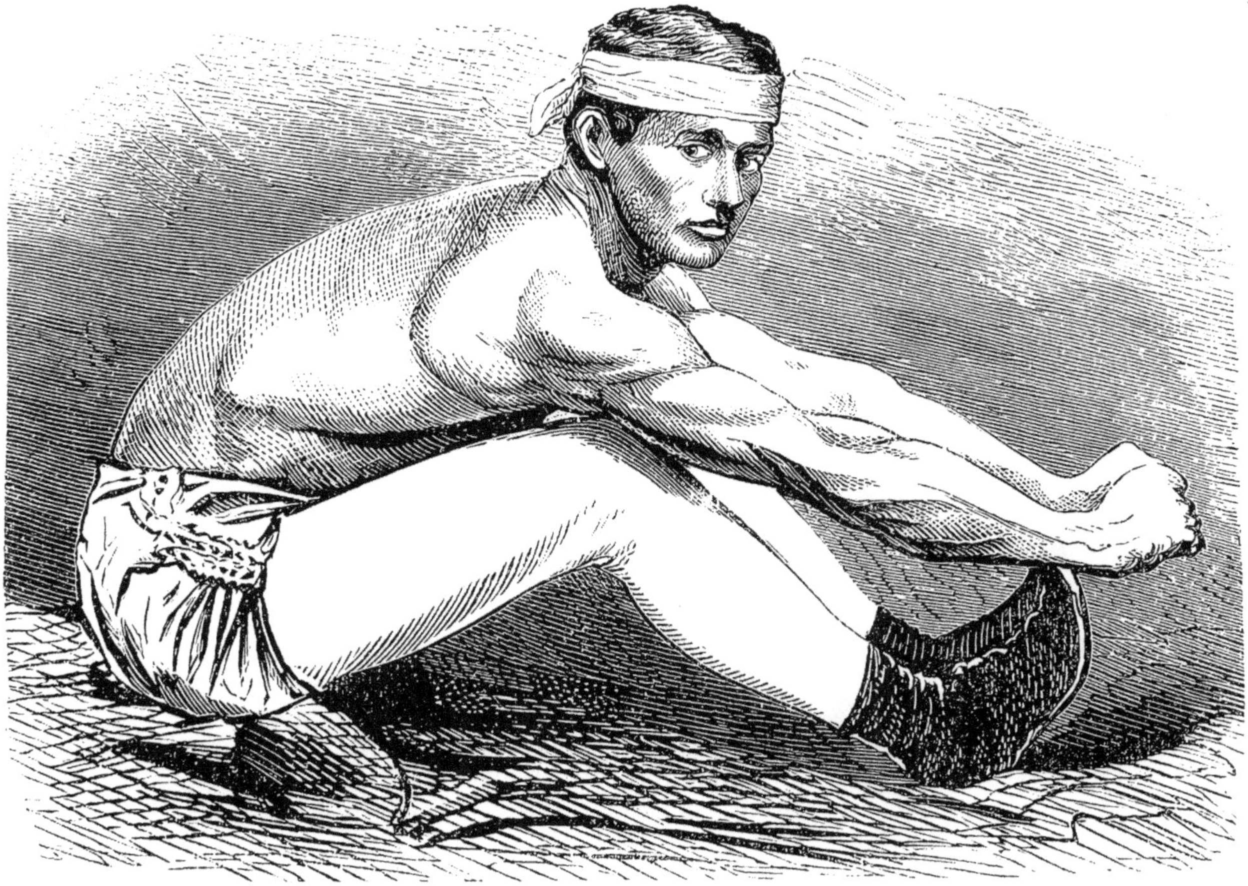

310

311

312

313

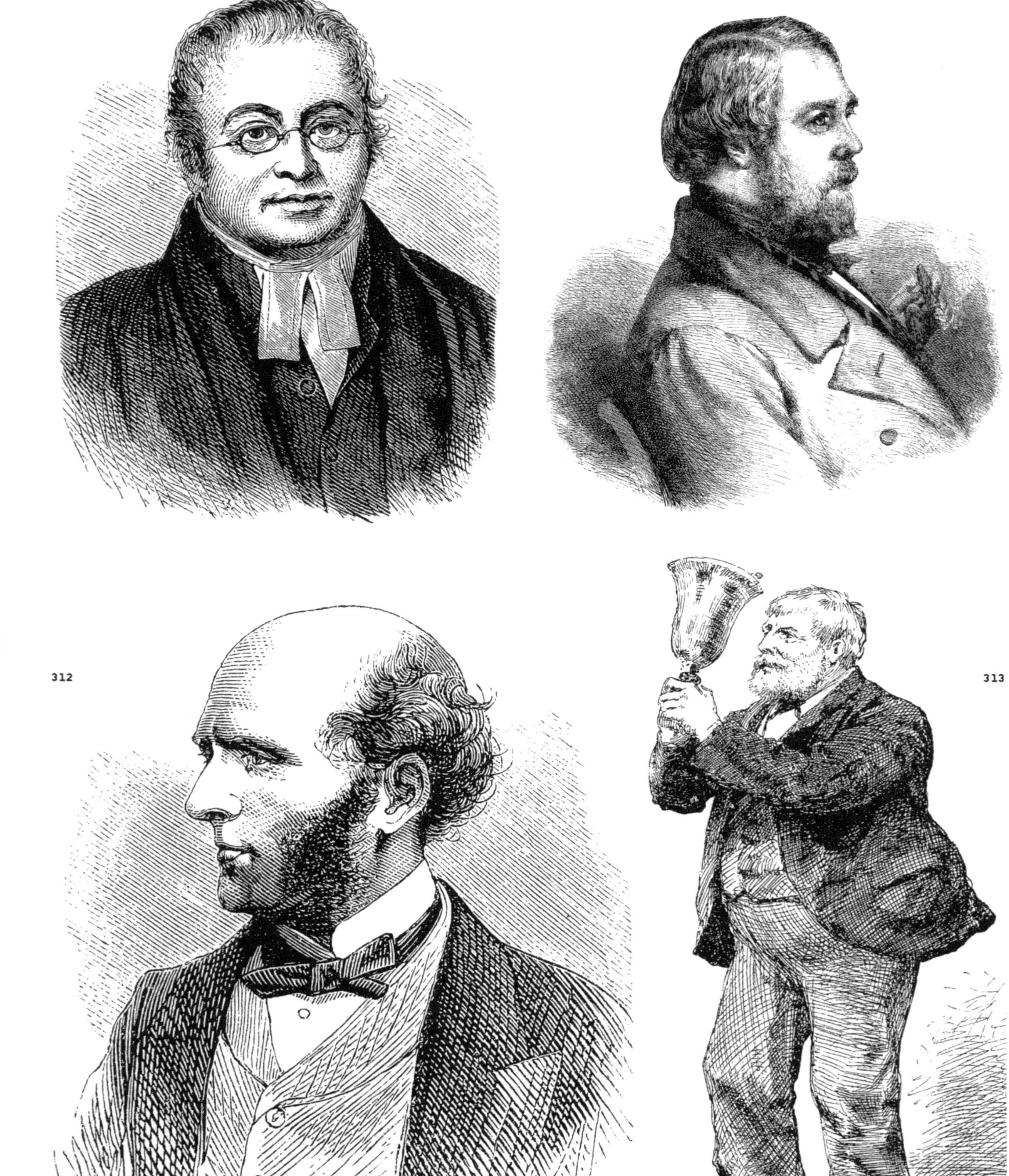

314

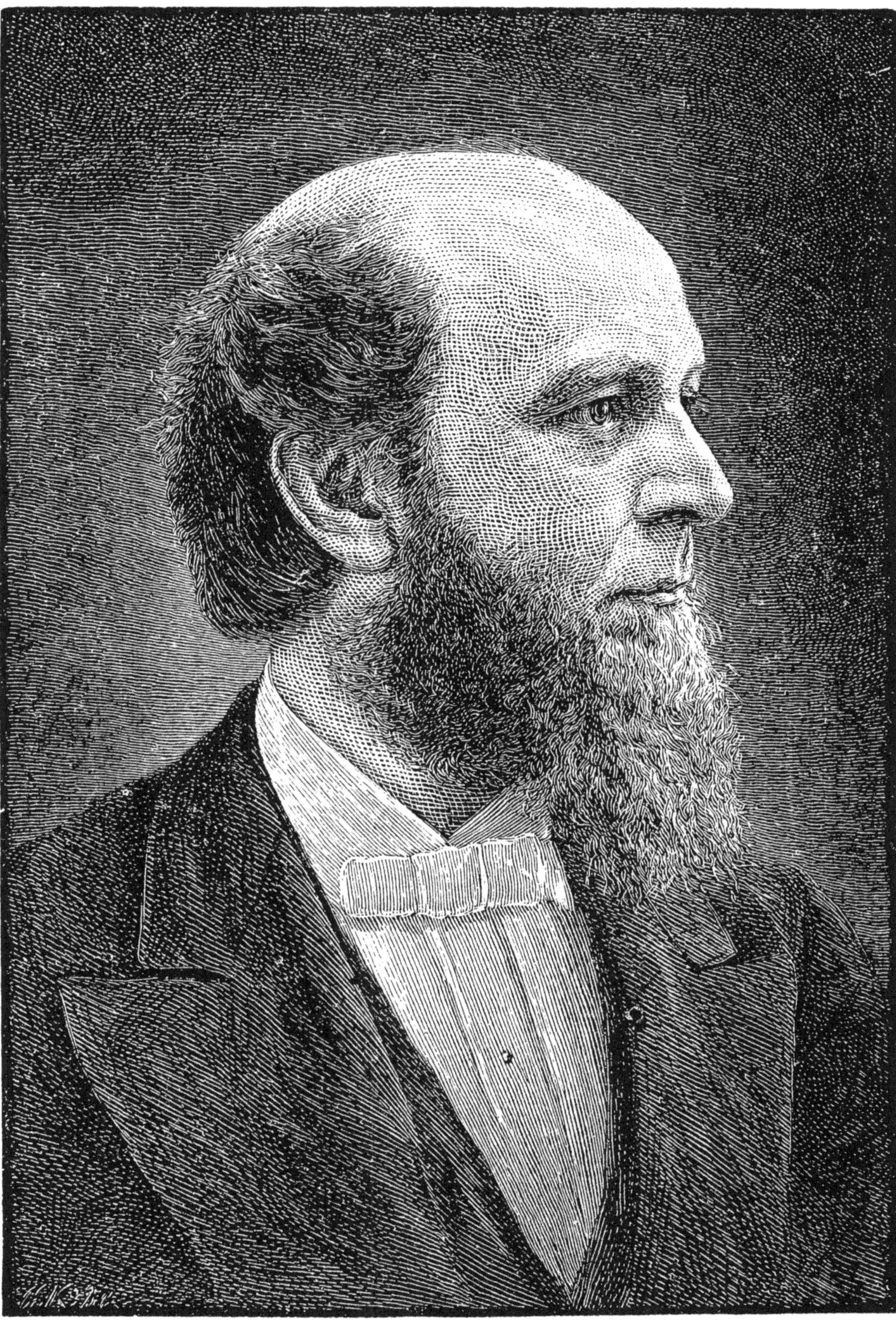

MEN

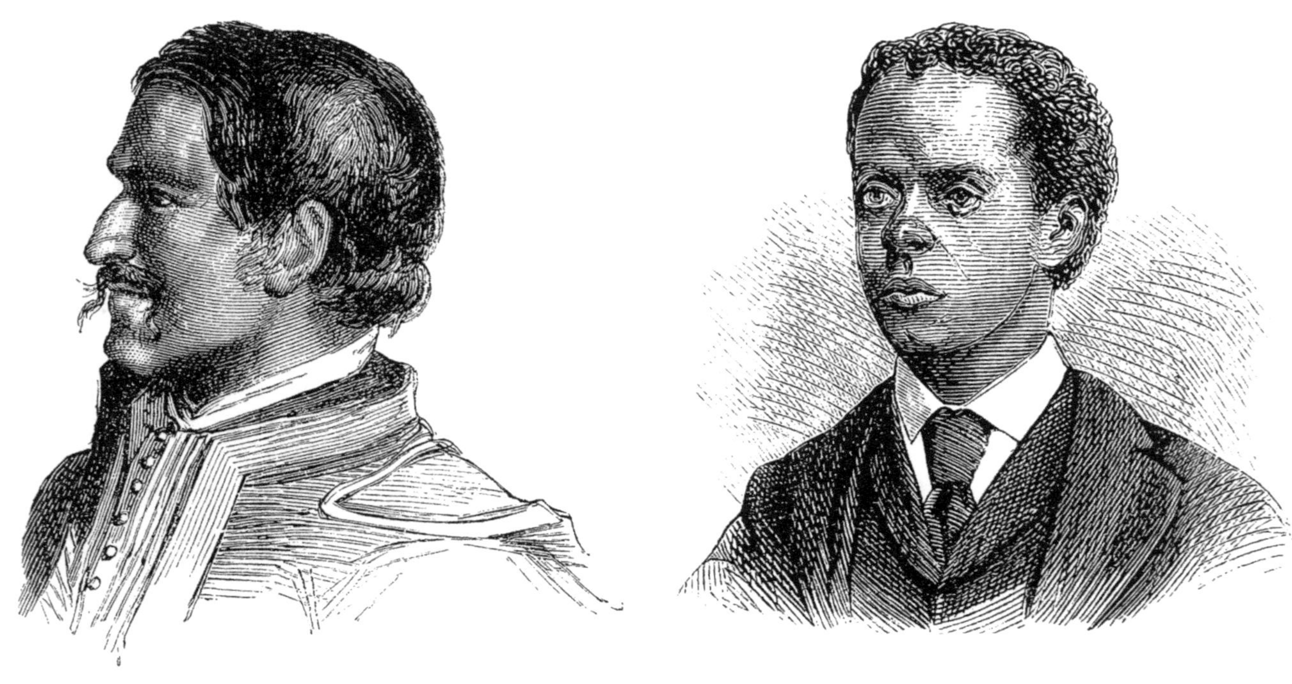

317

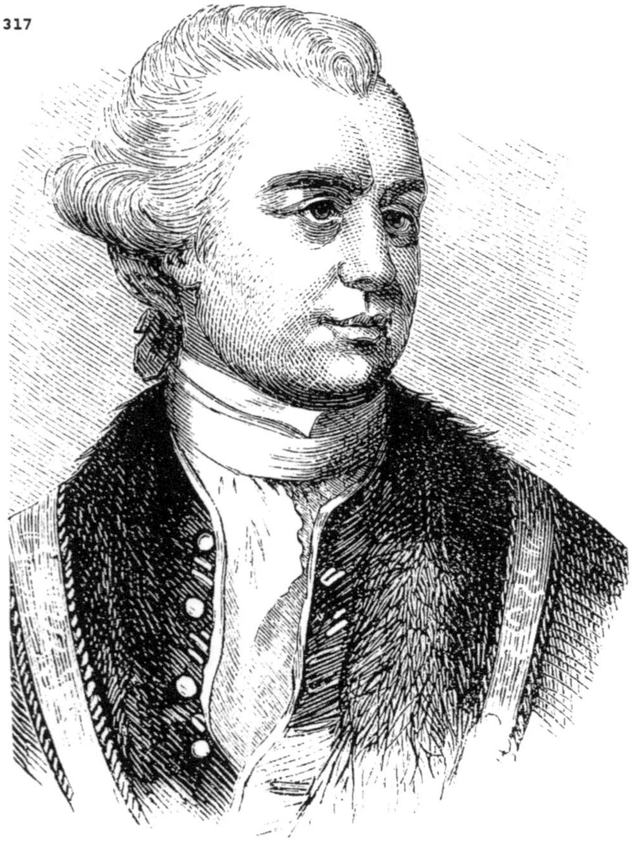

318

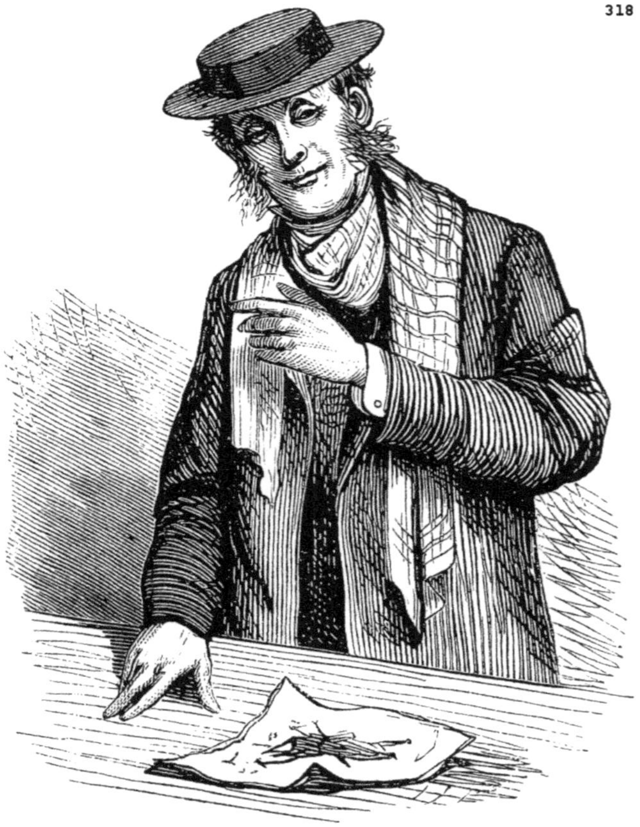

319

320

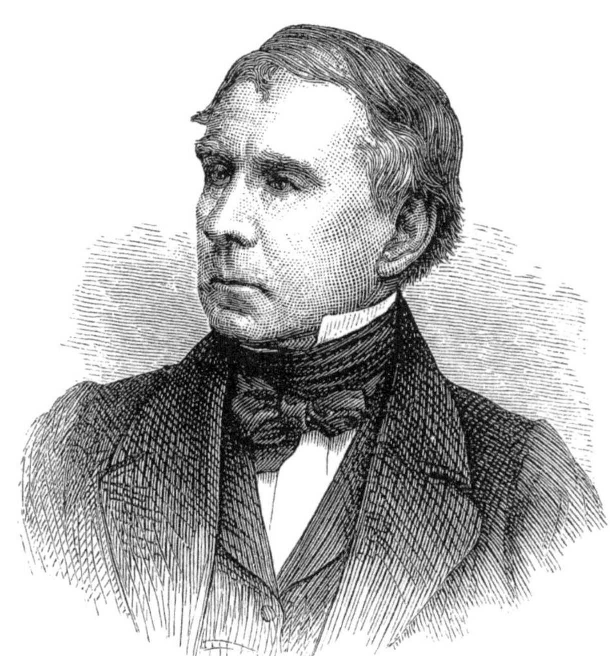

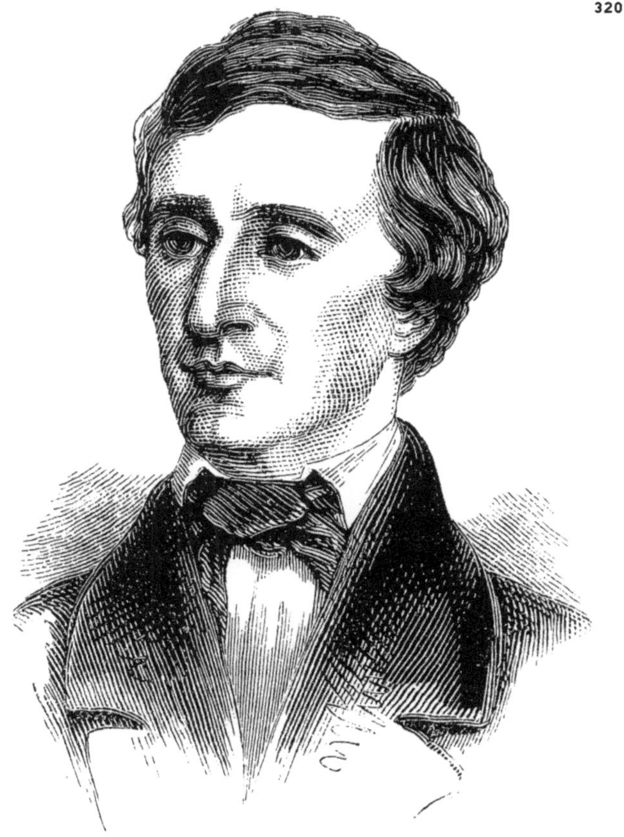

321

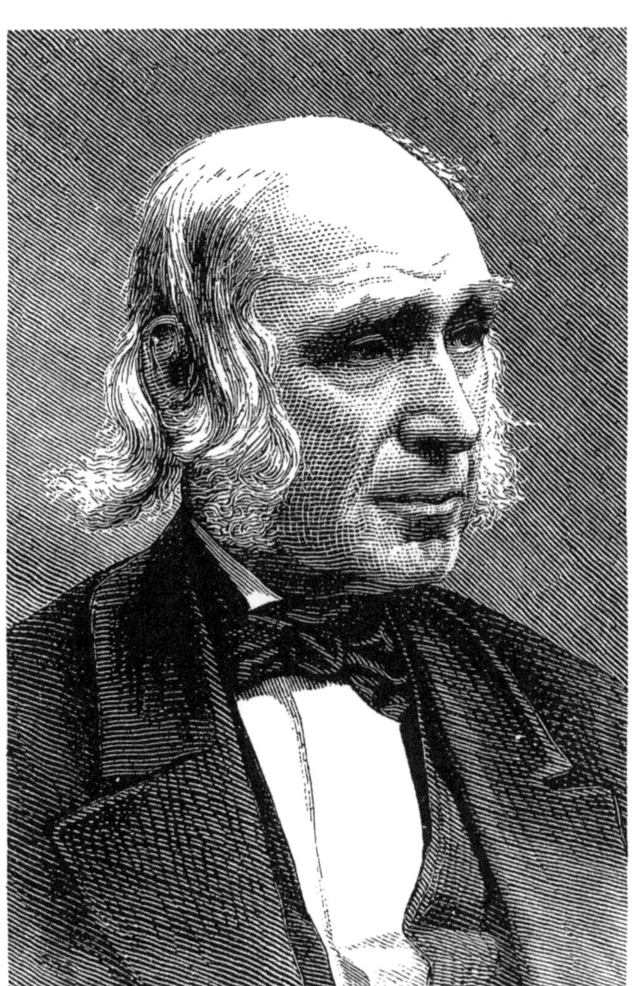

322

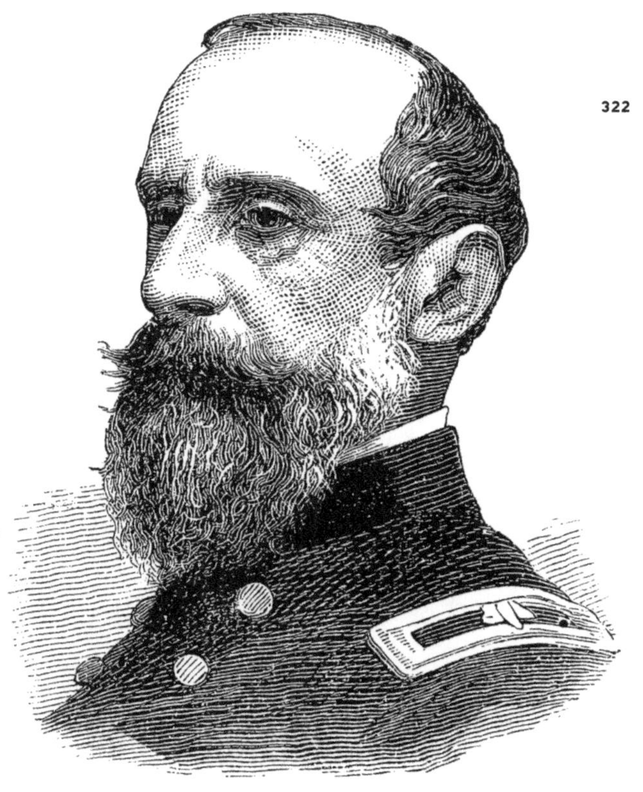

323

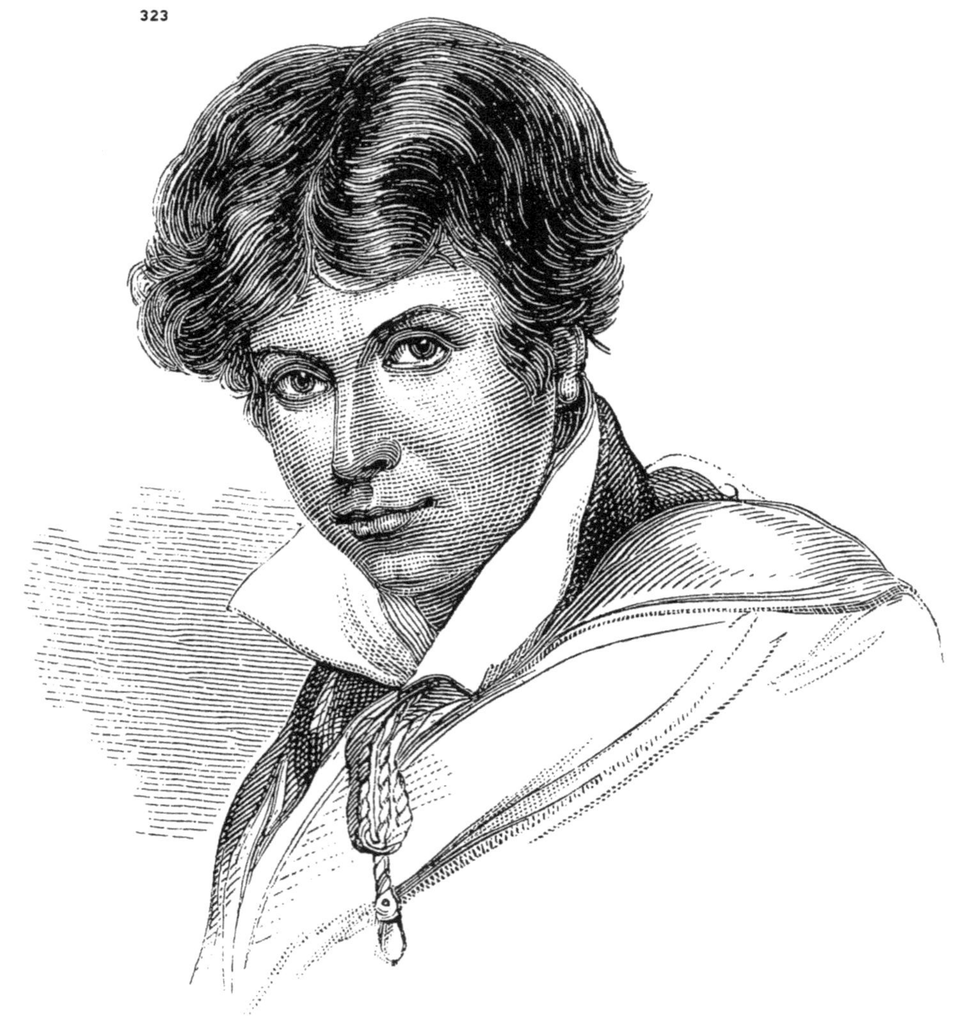

324

325

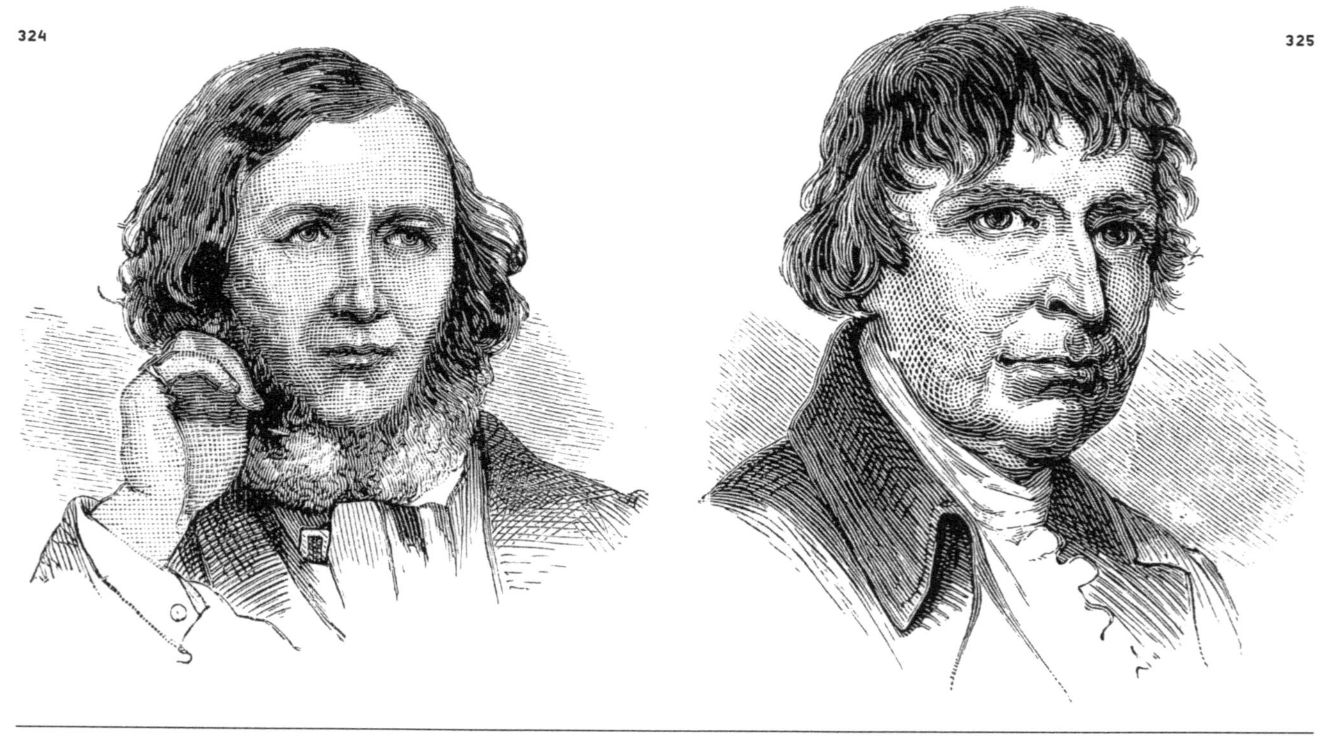

326

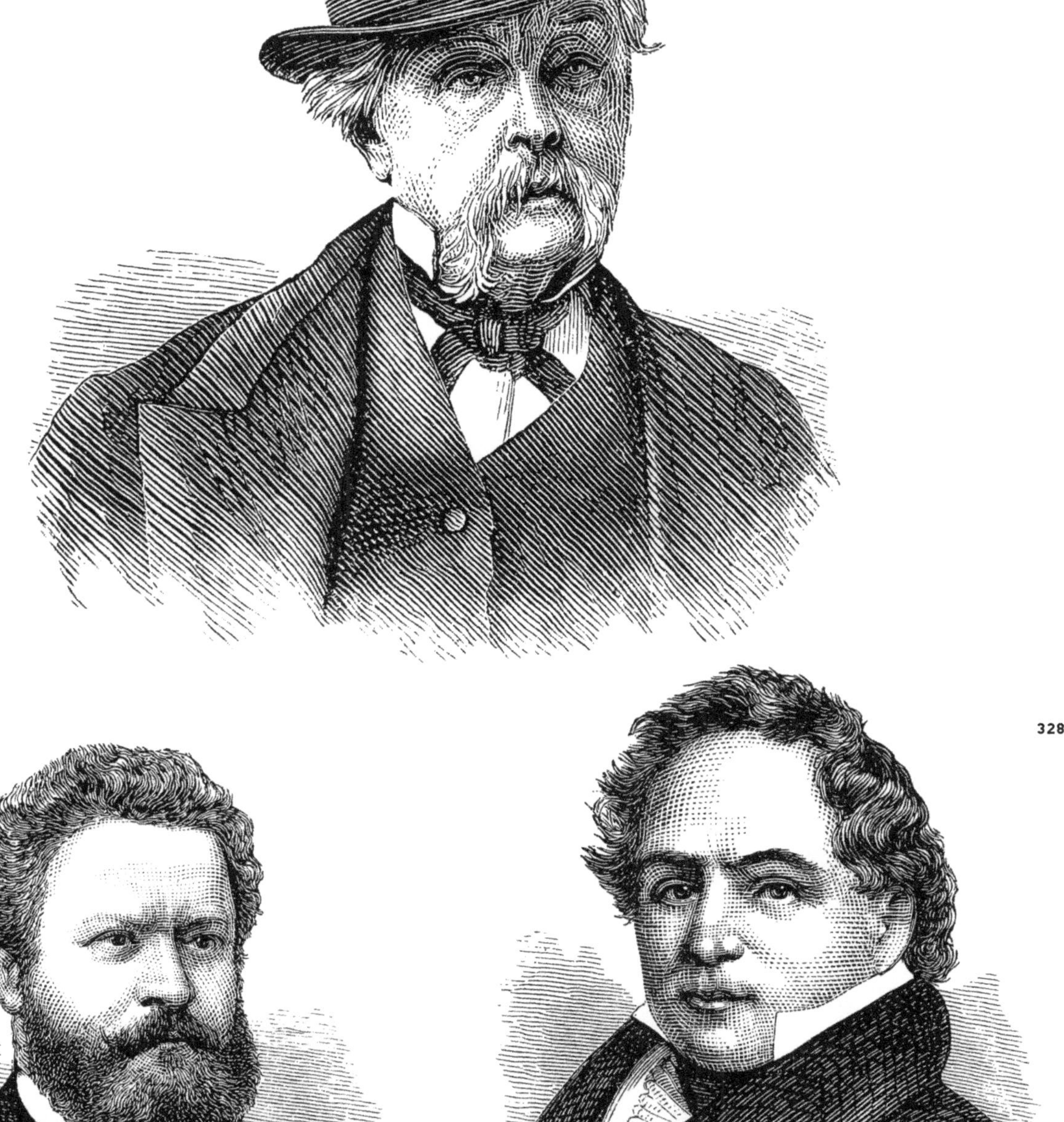

327

328

MEN

329

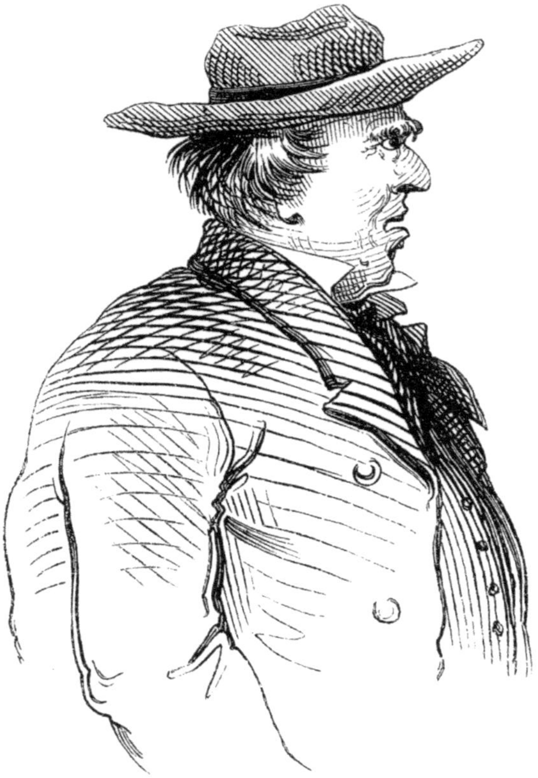

330

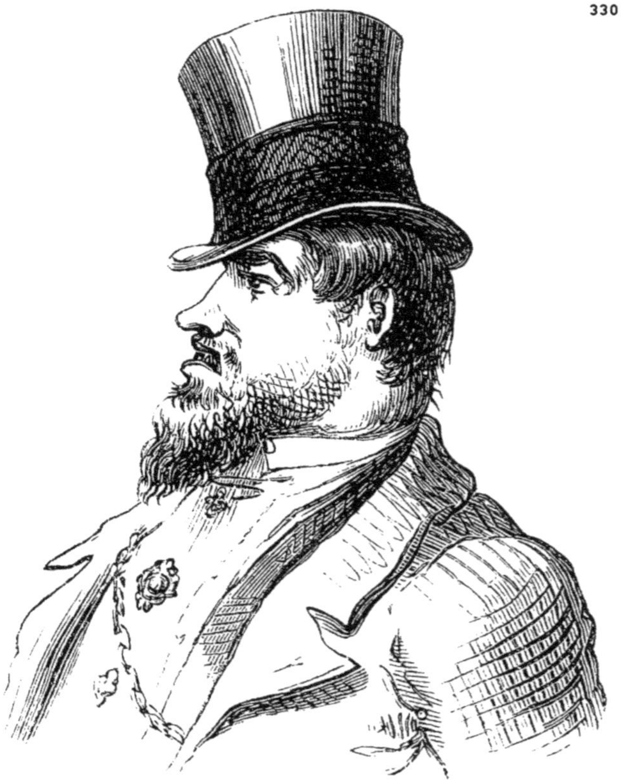

331

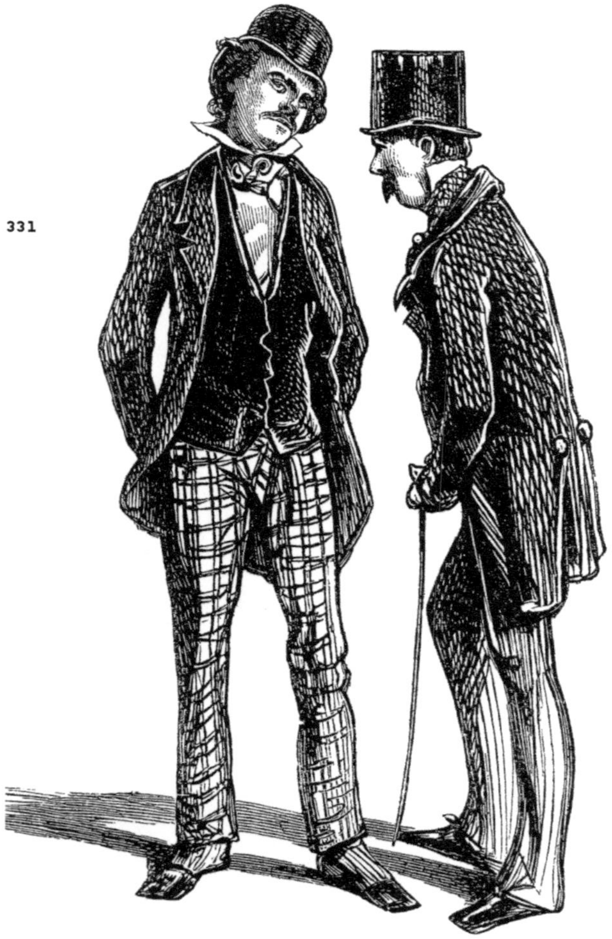

332

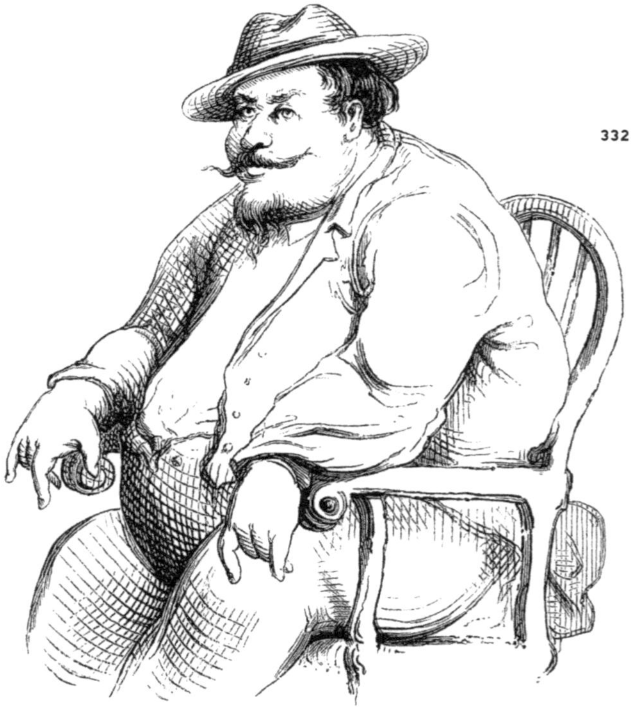

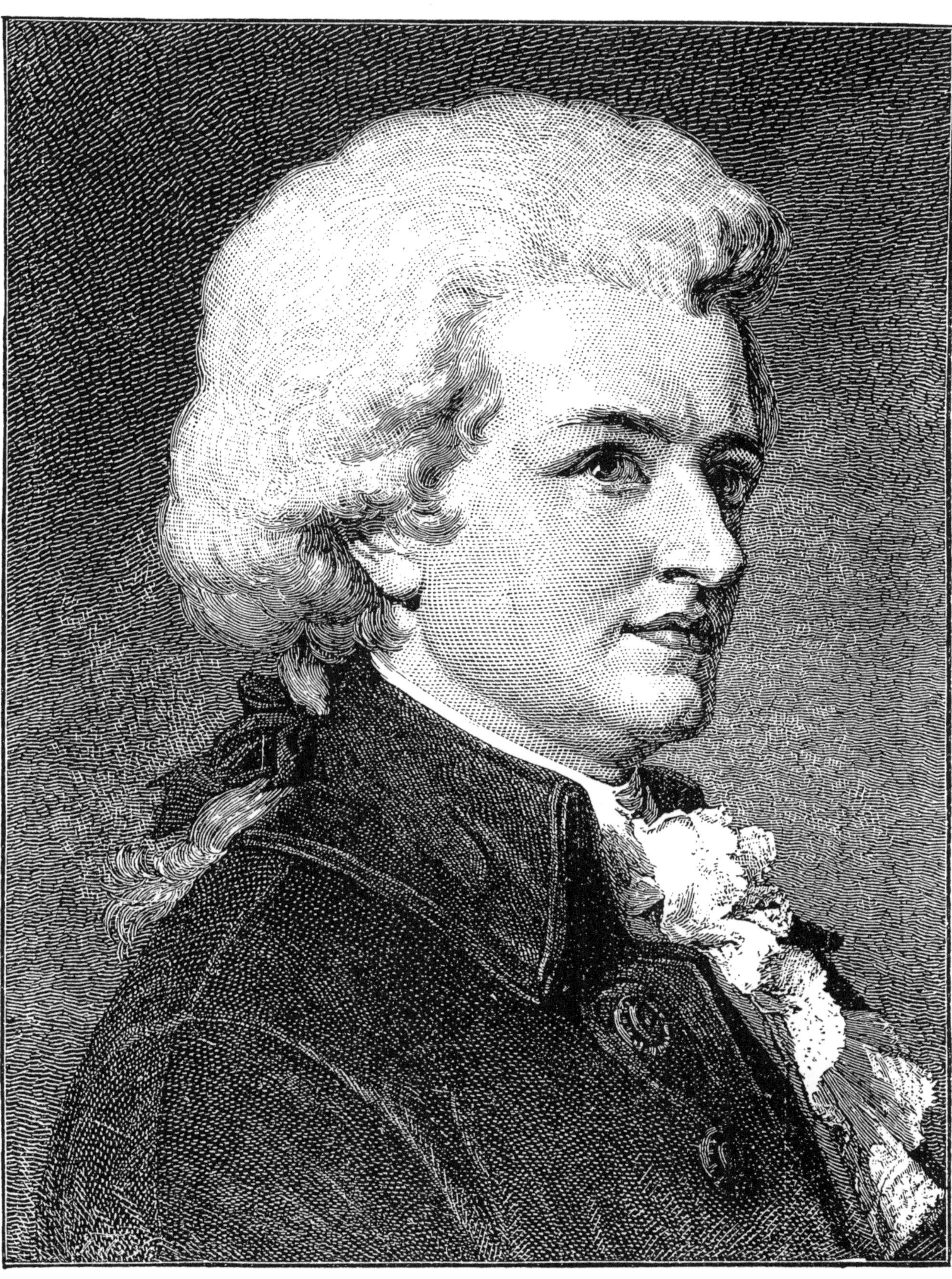

MEN

334

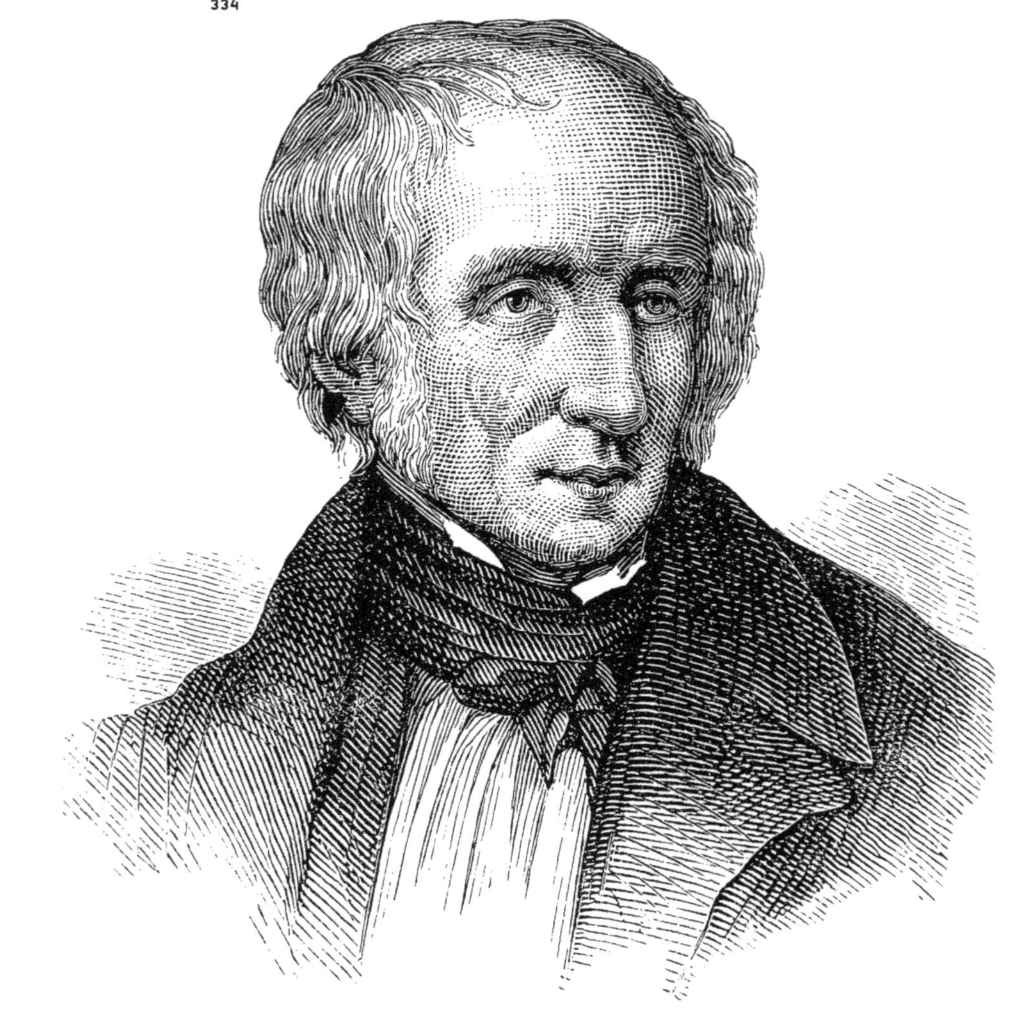

335

336

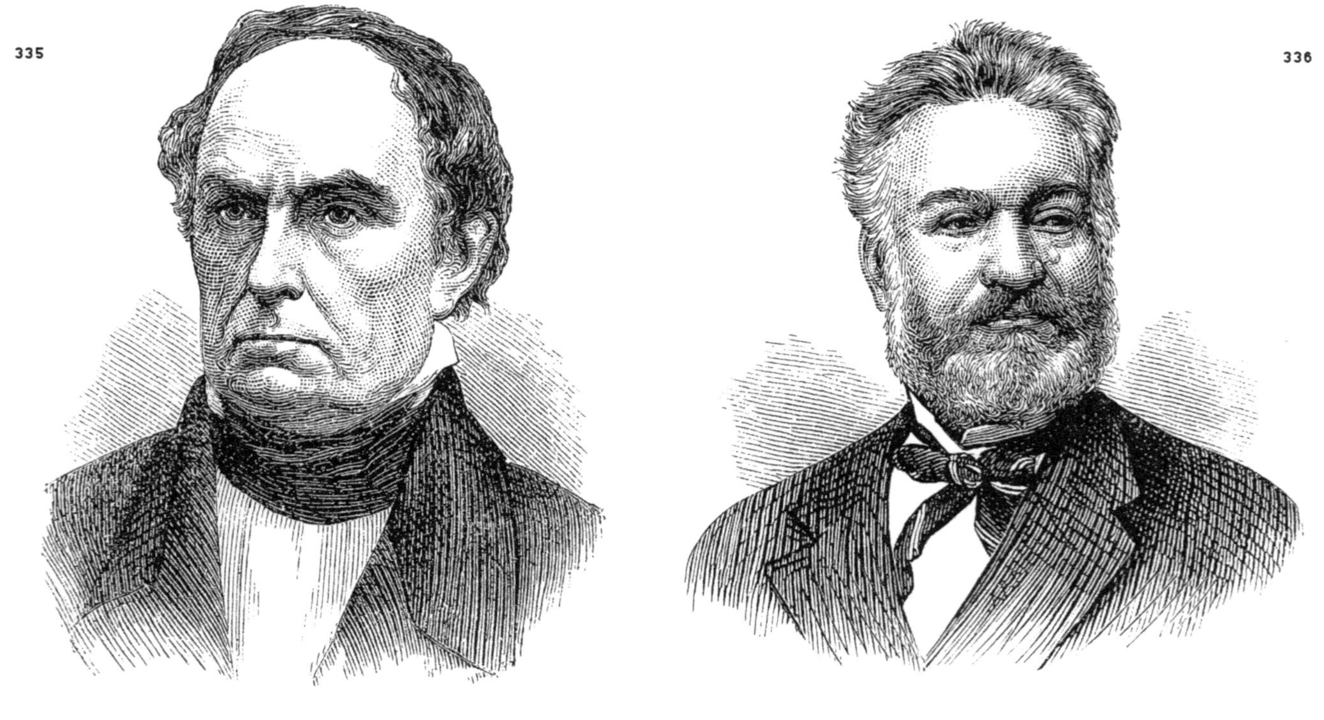

337

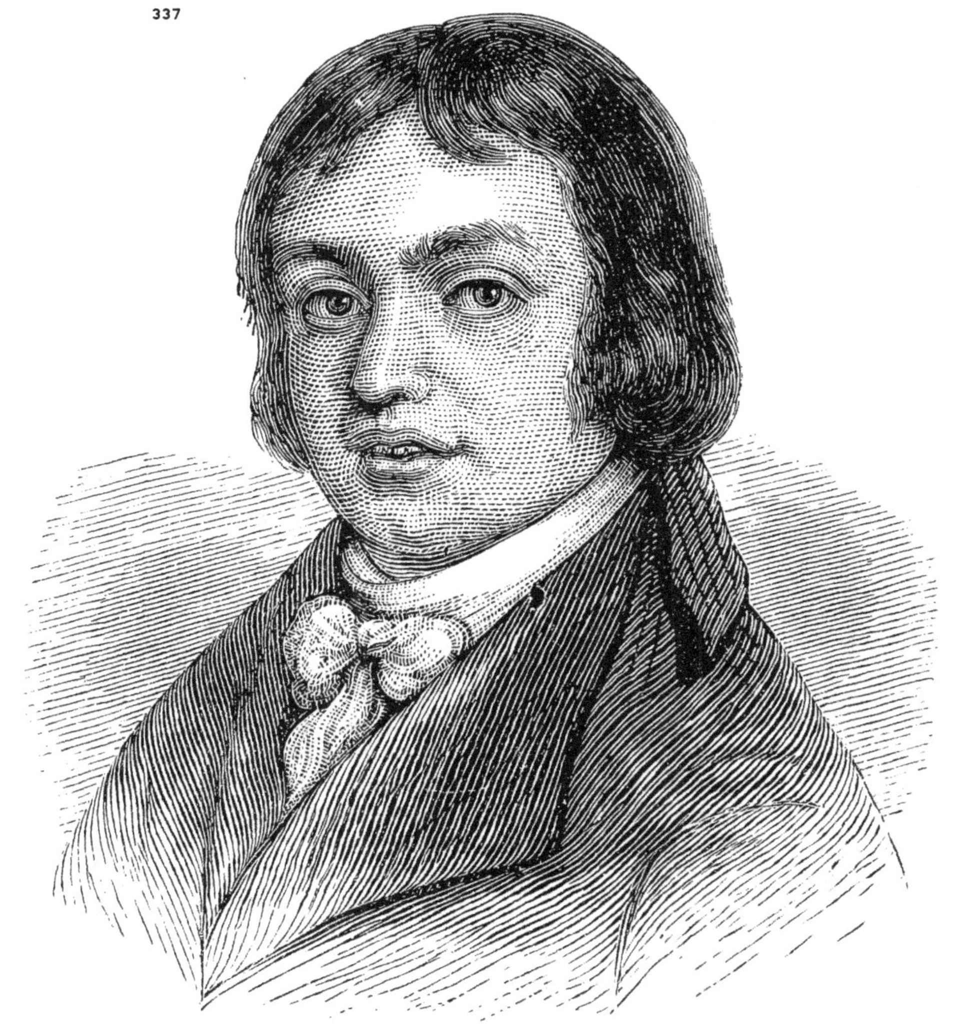

MEN

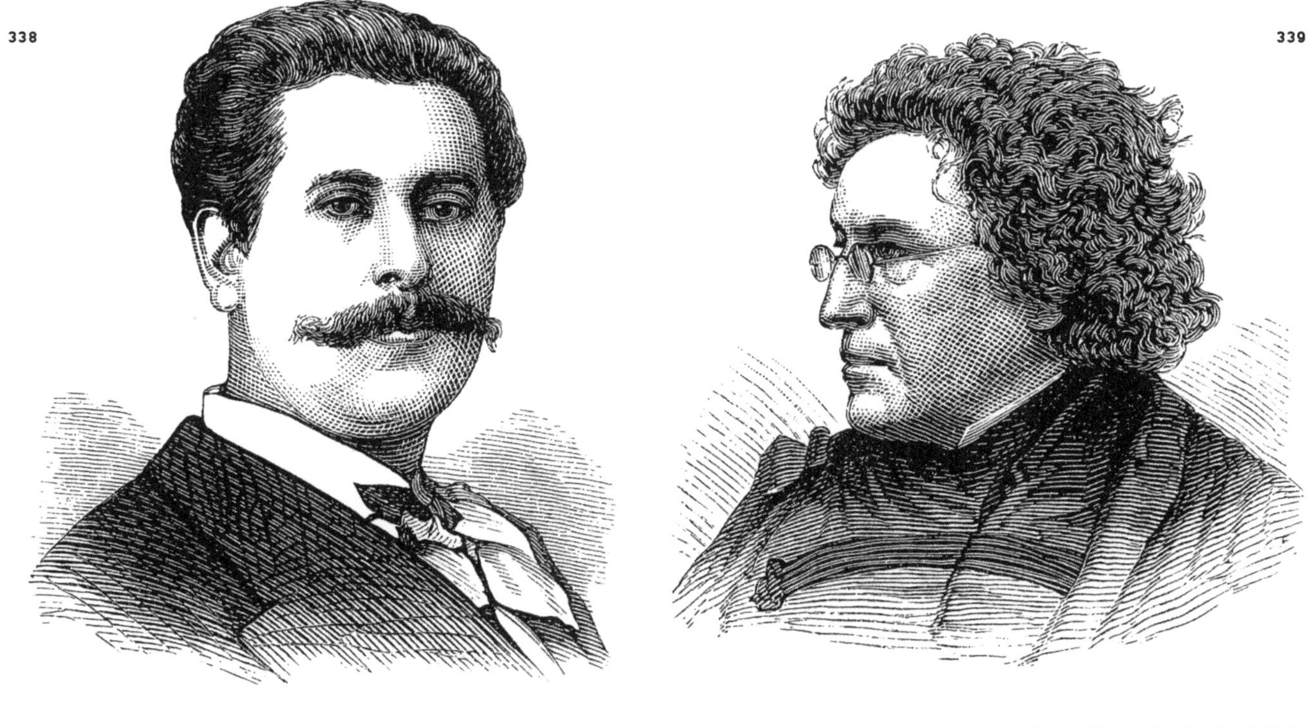

338

339

MEN

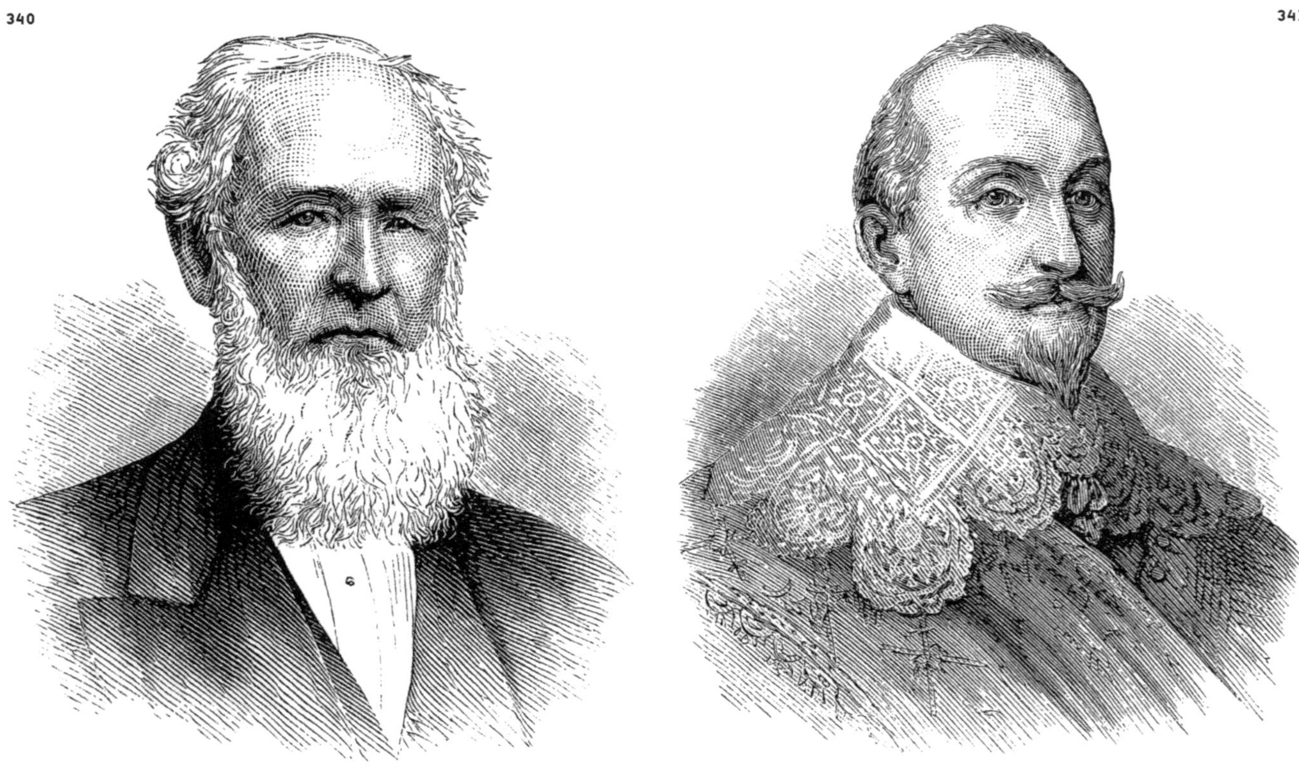

340

341

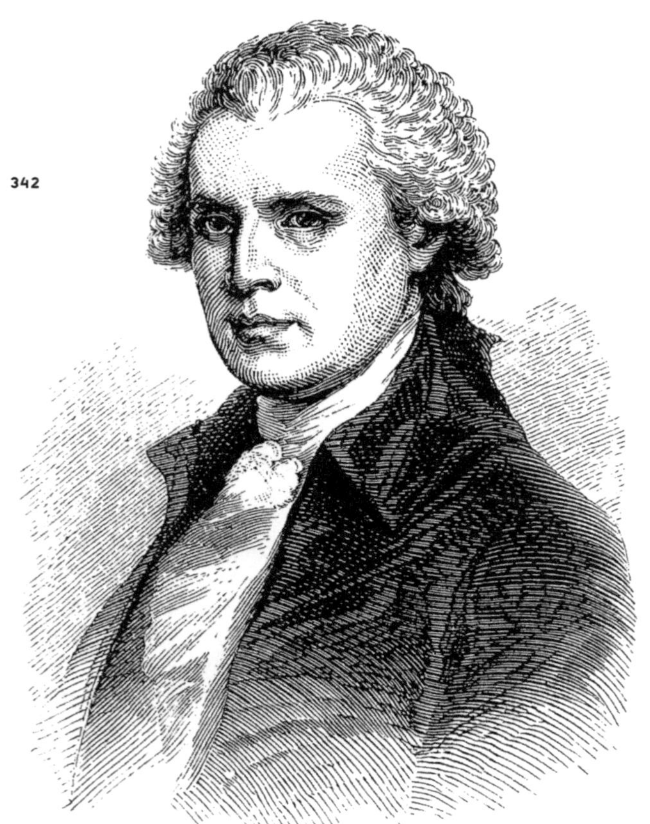

342

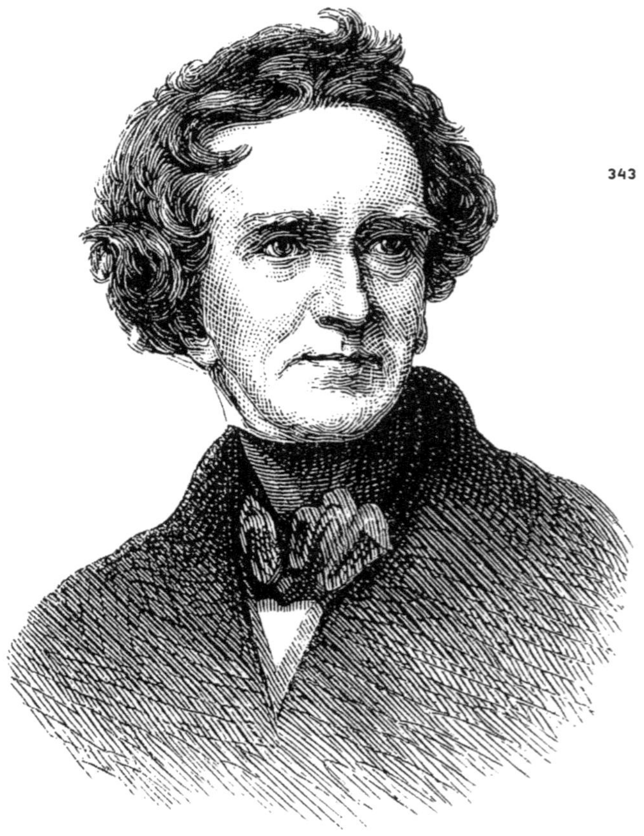

343

344

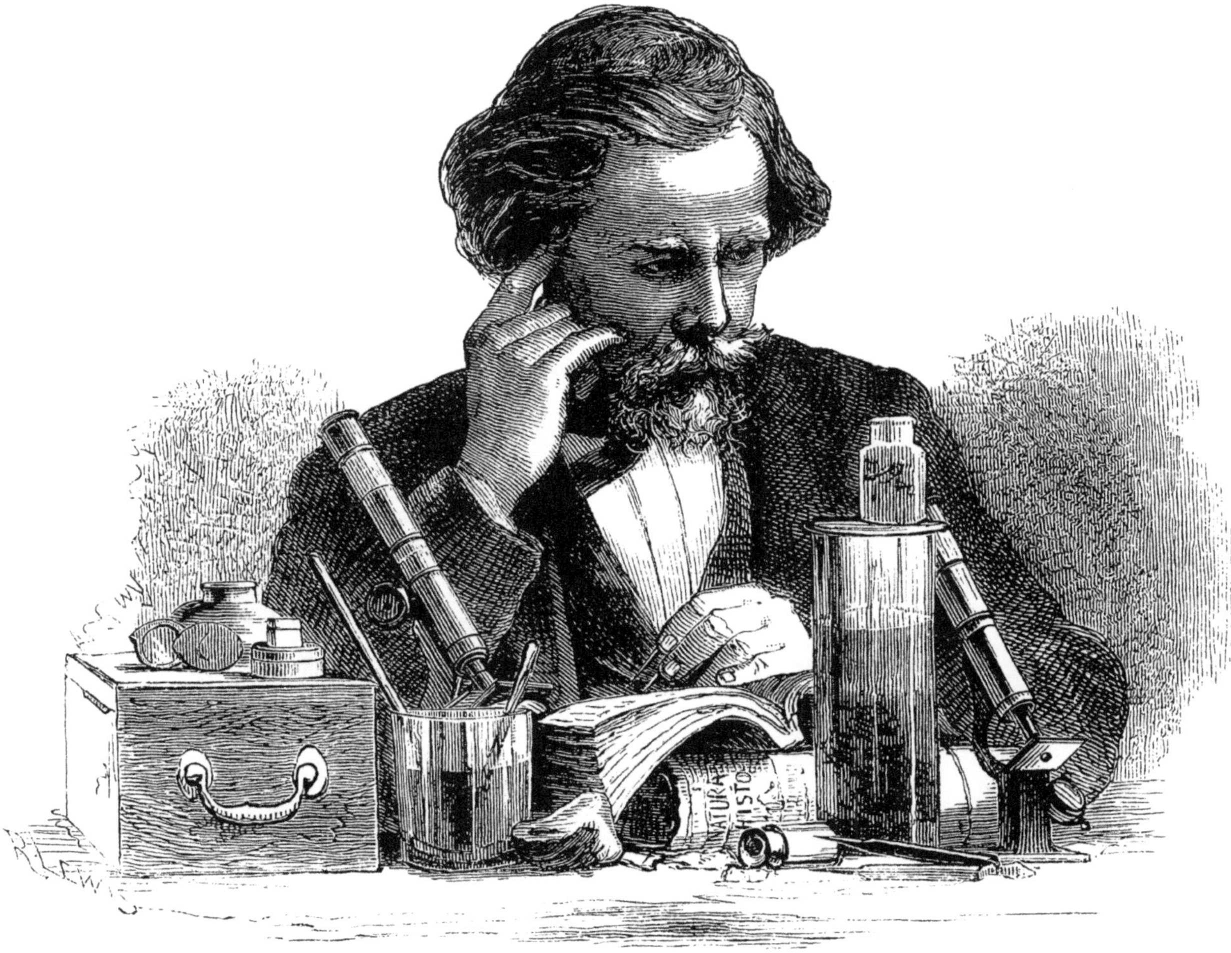

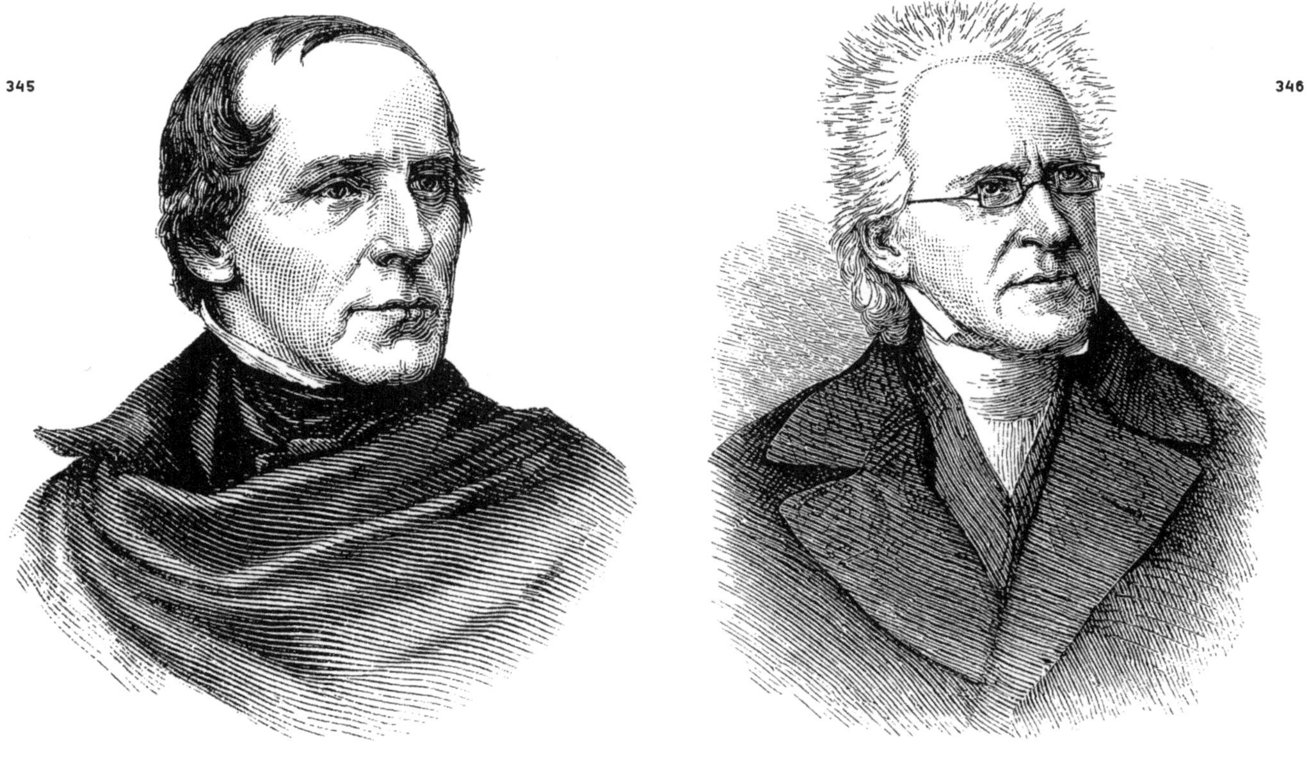

345

346

347

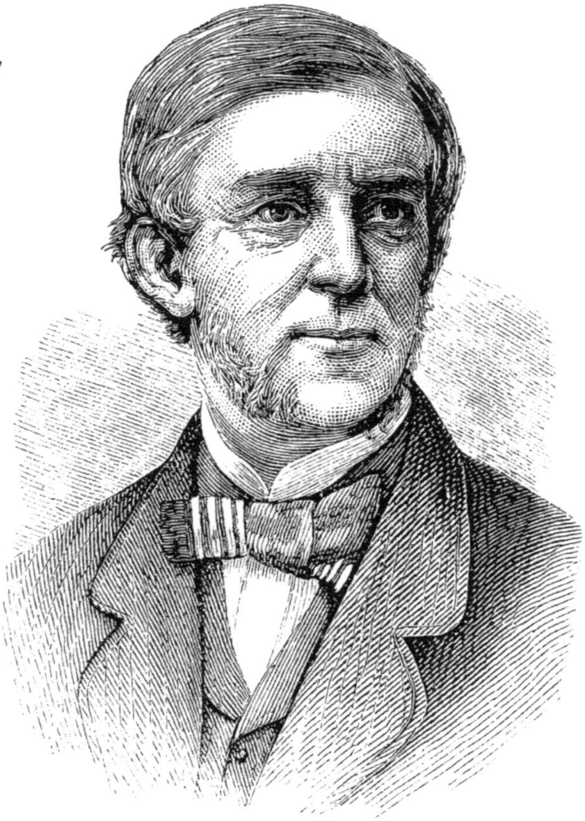

348

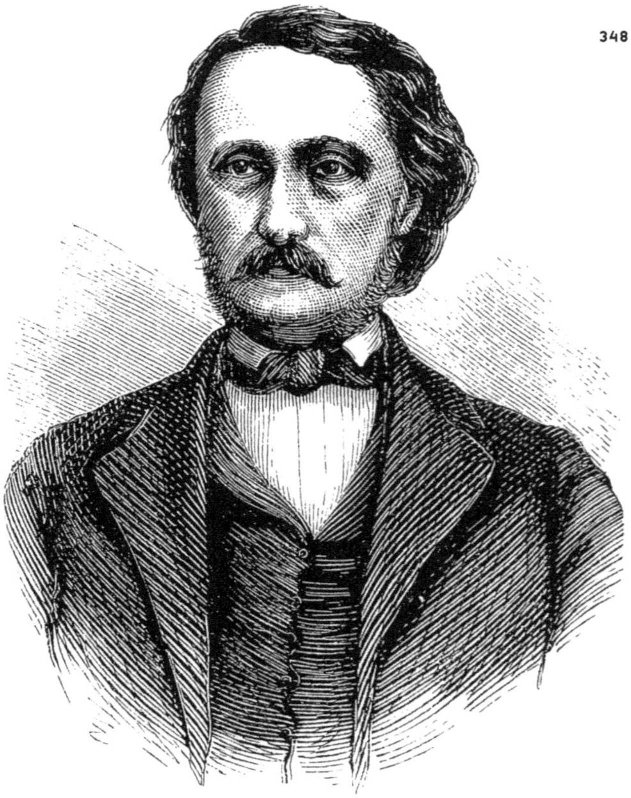

349

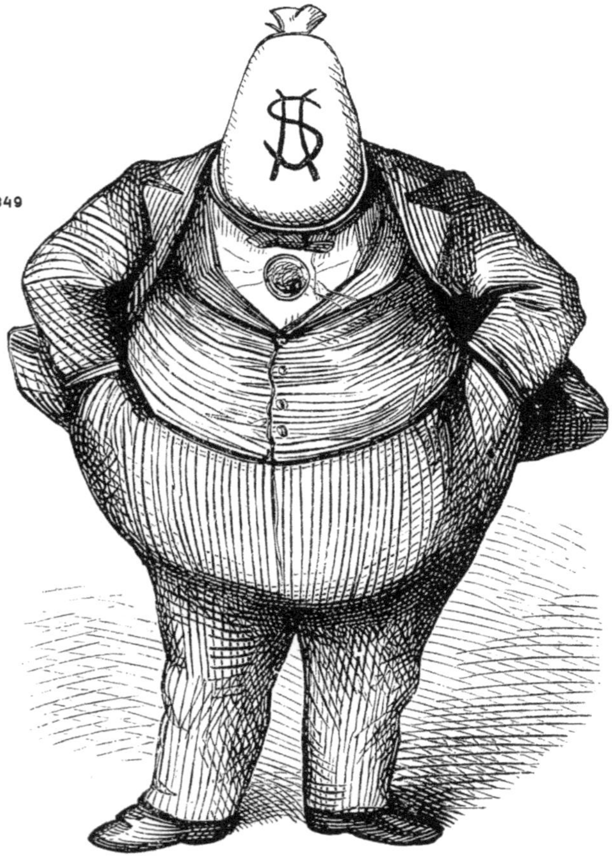

350

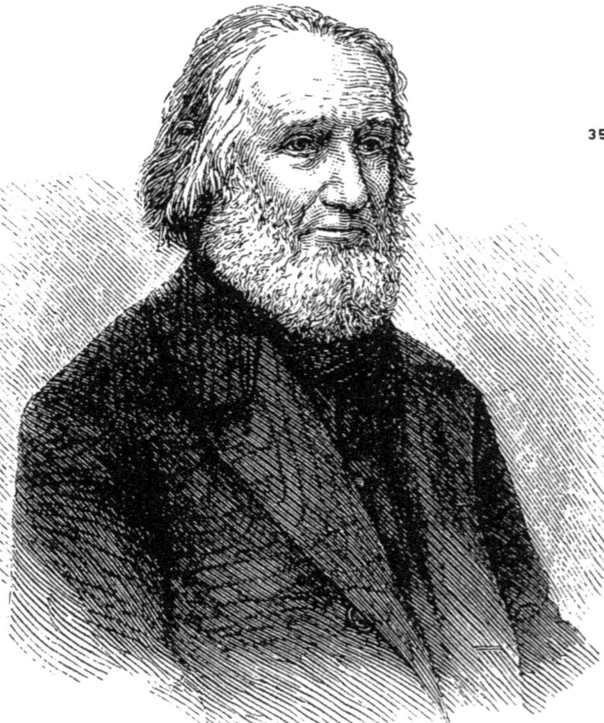

351

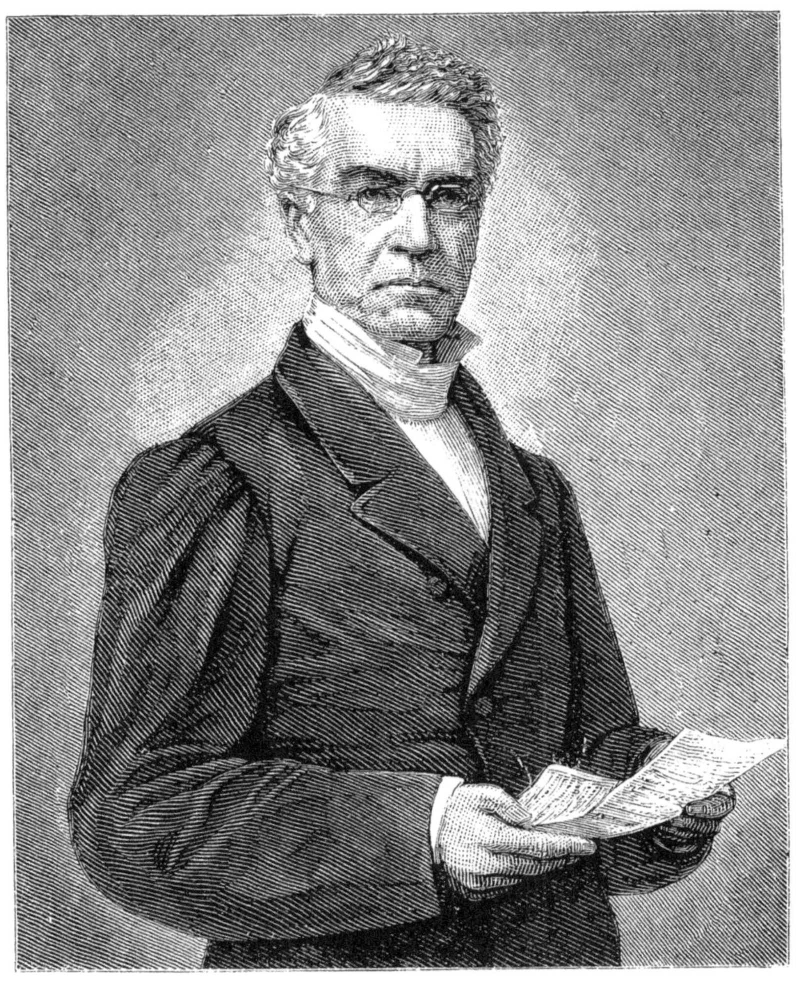

352

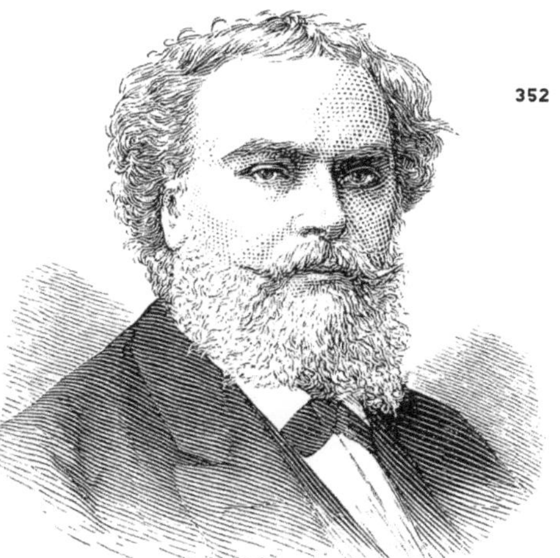

353

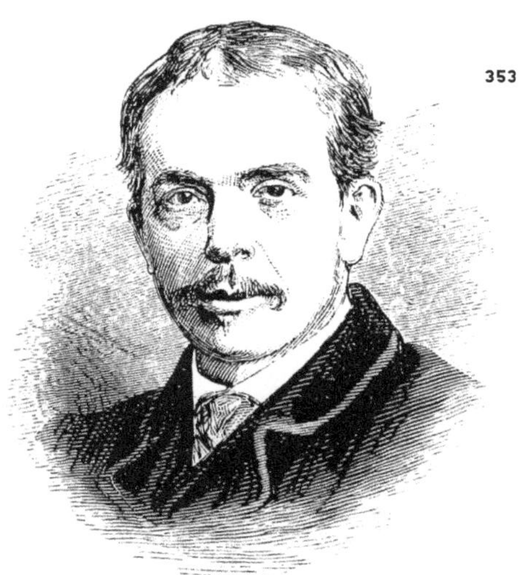

MEN

354

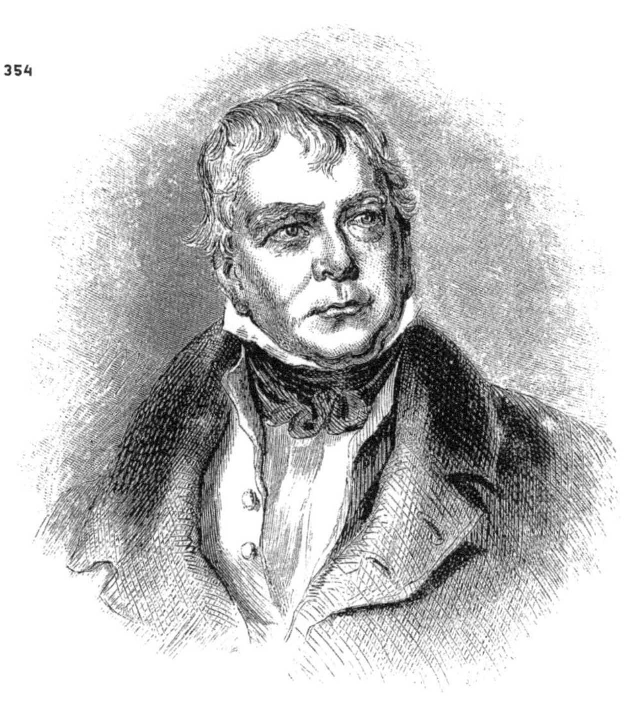

355

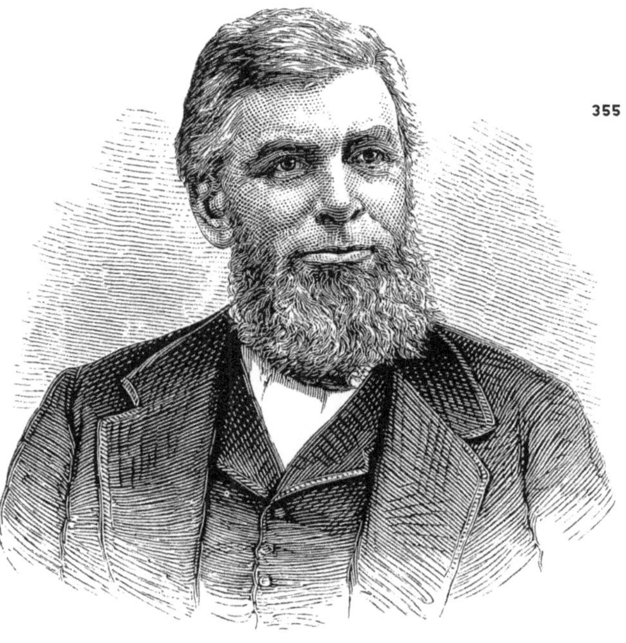

356
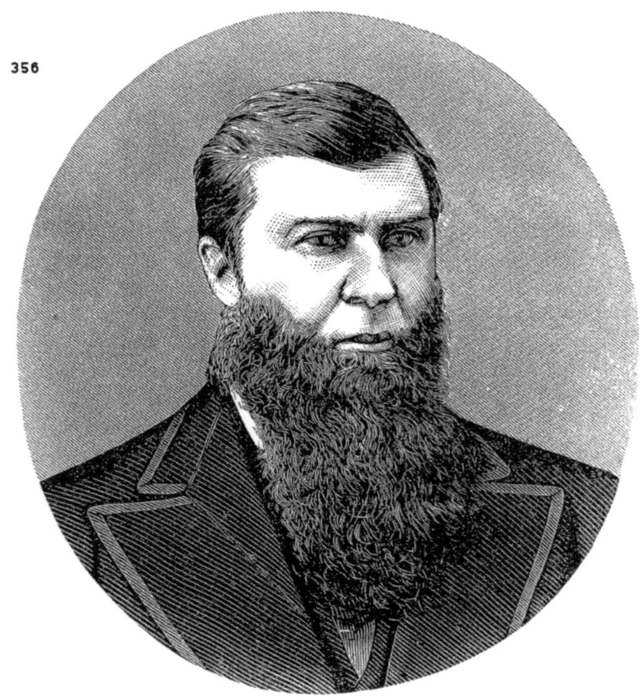

357
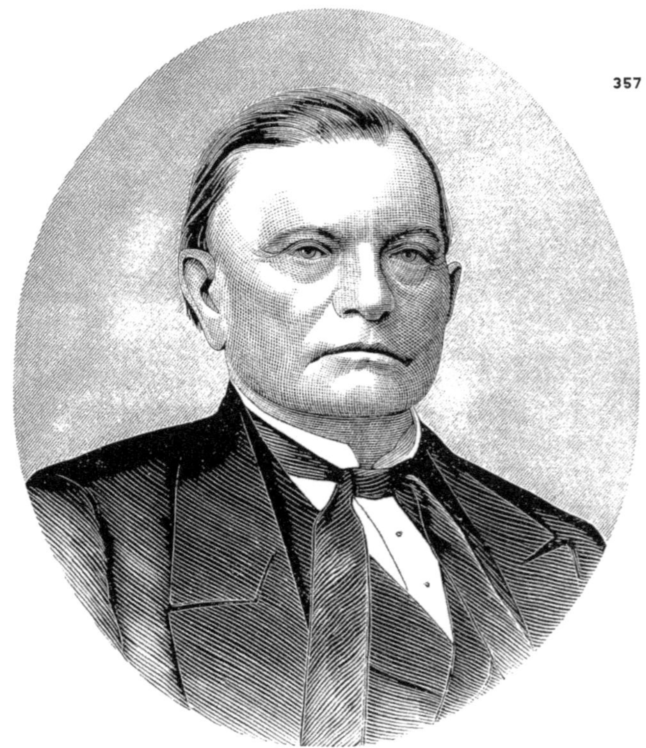

MEN

358
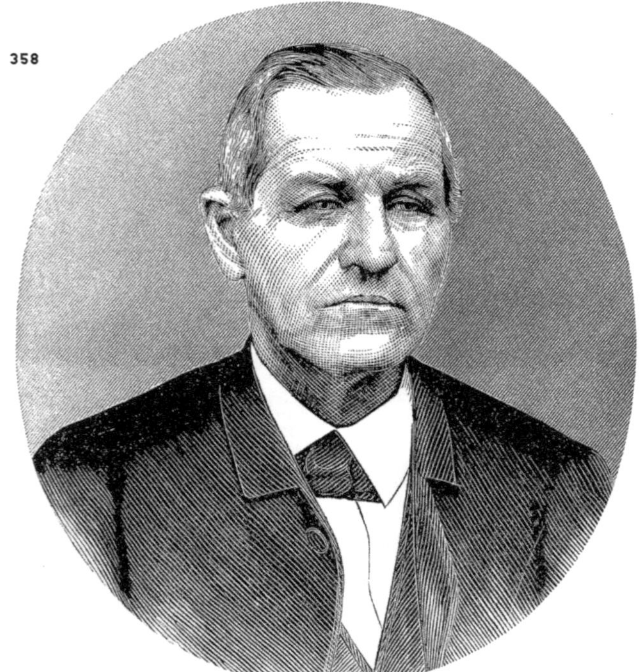

359
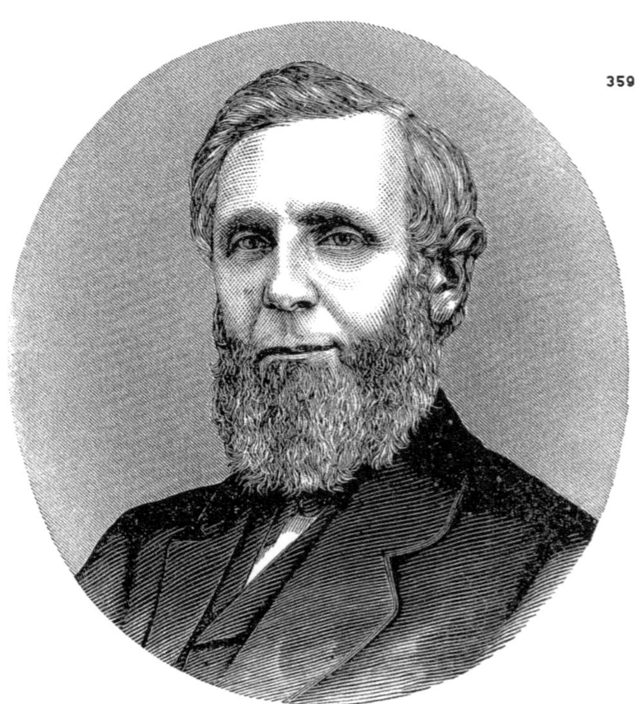

360

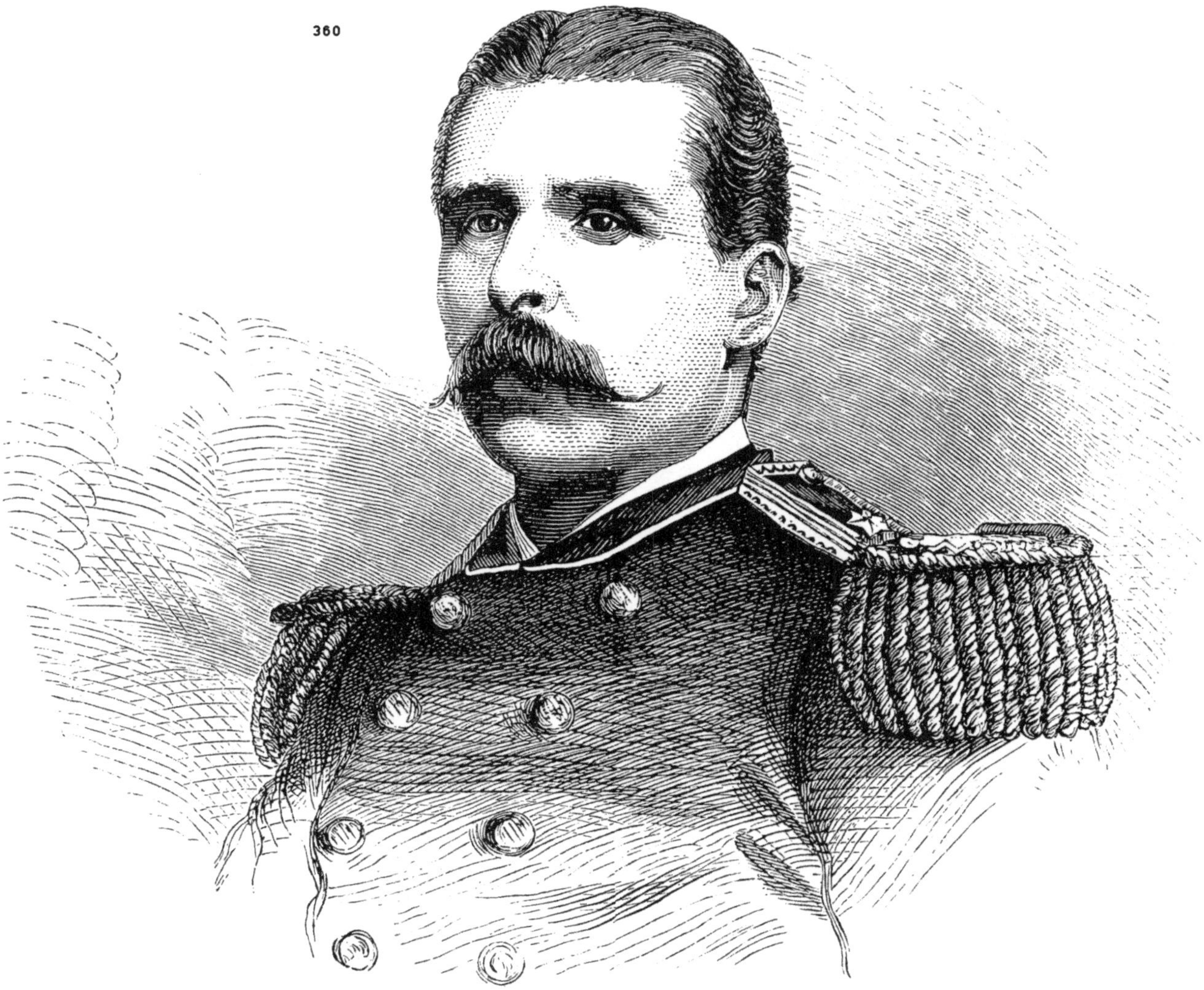

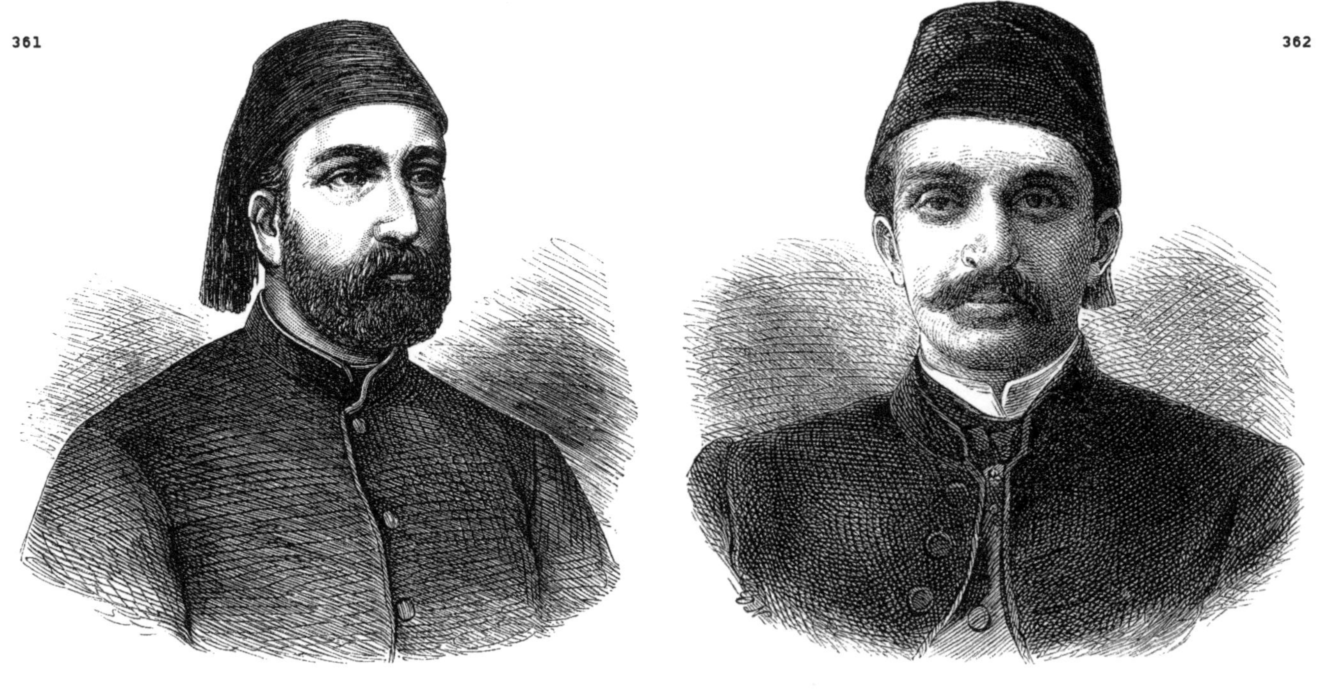

361 362

363

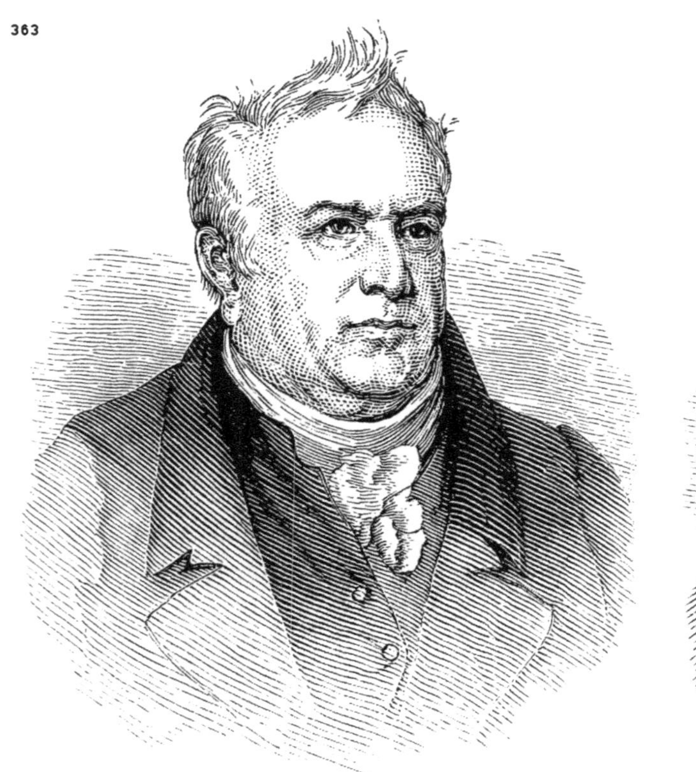

364

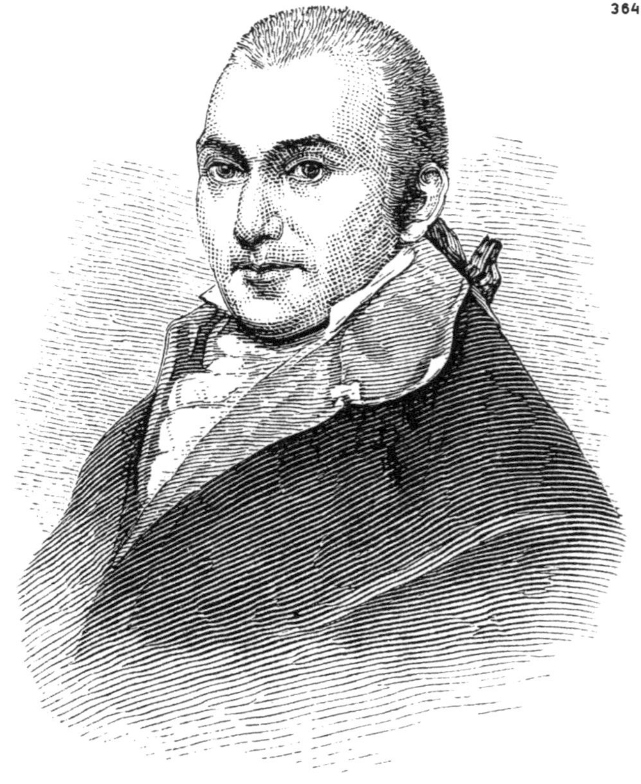

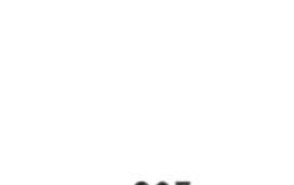

365

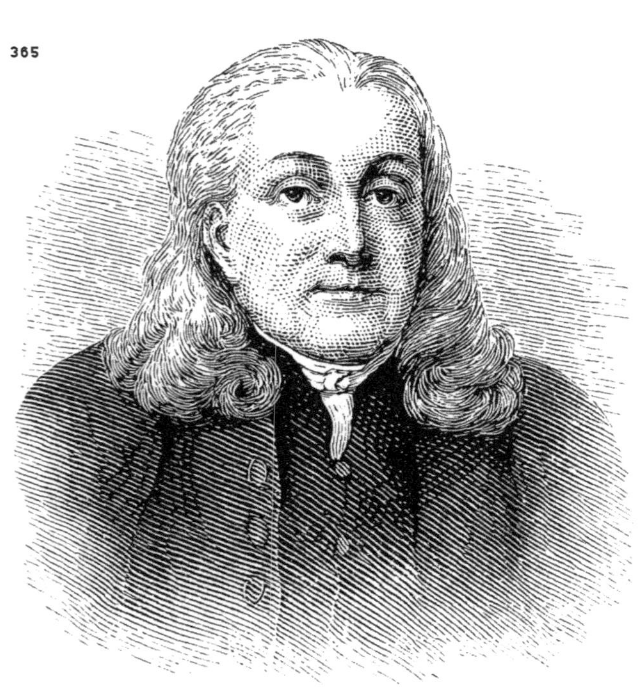

366

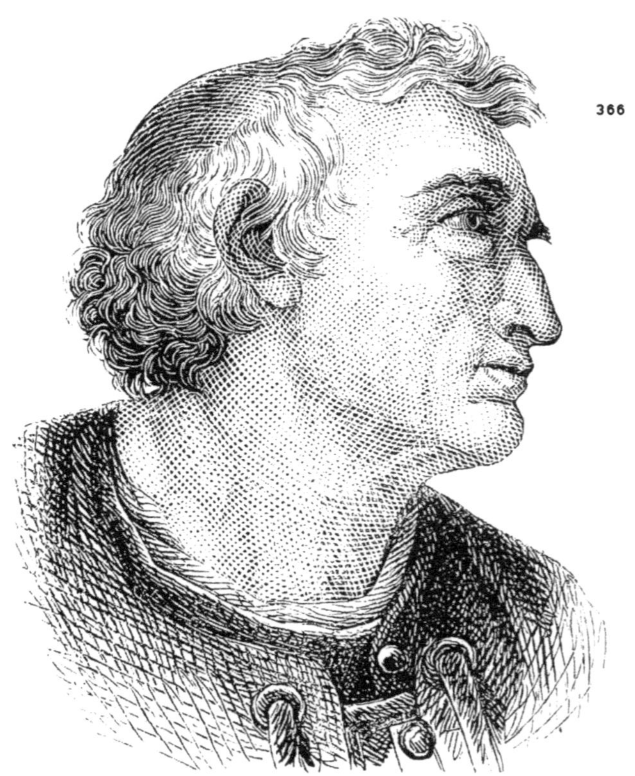

367

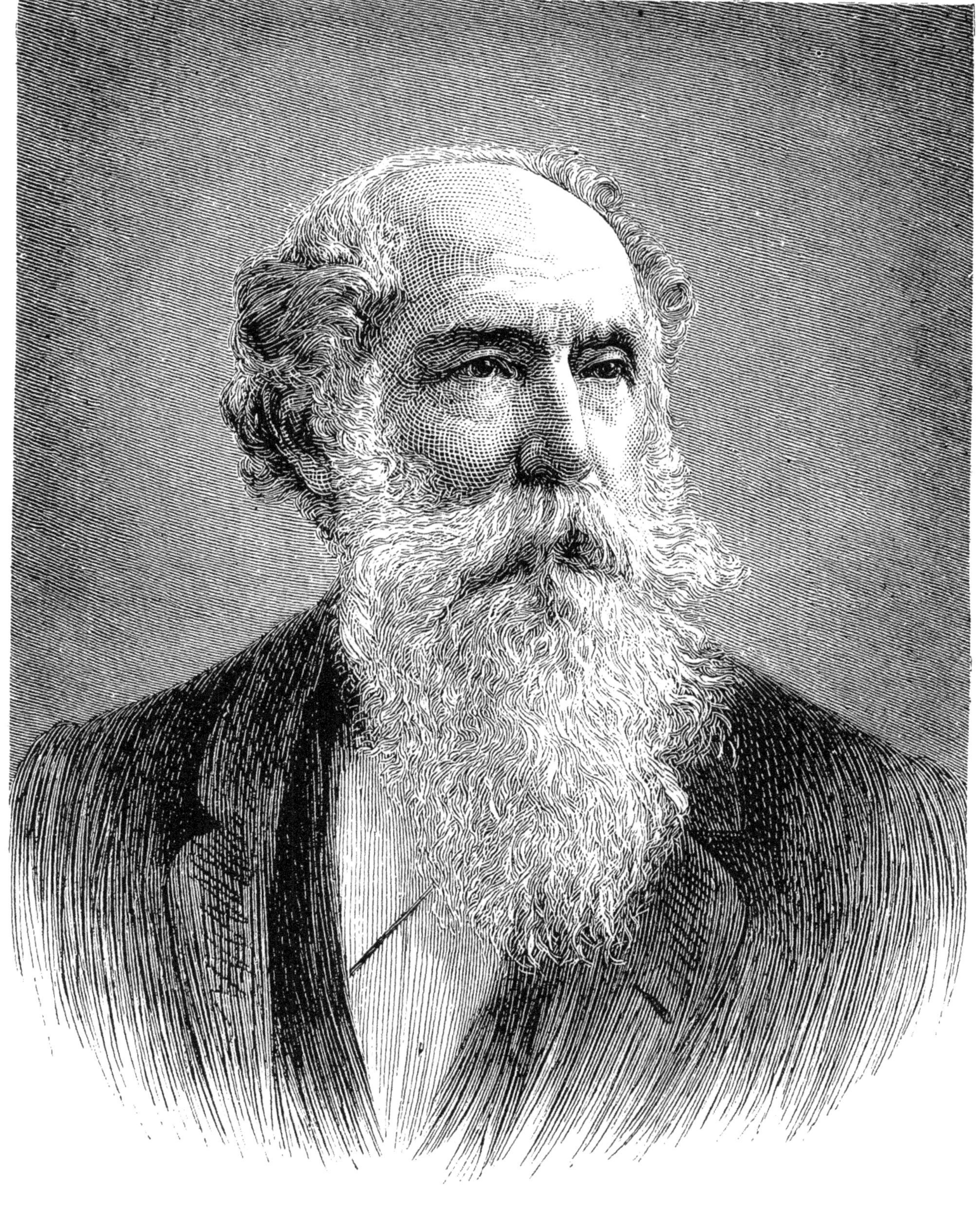

MEN

MEN

LIST OF ILLUSTRATIONS

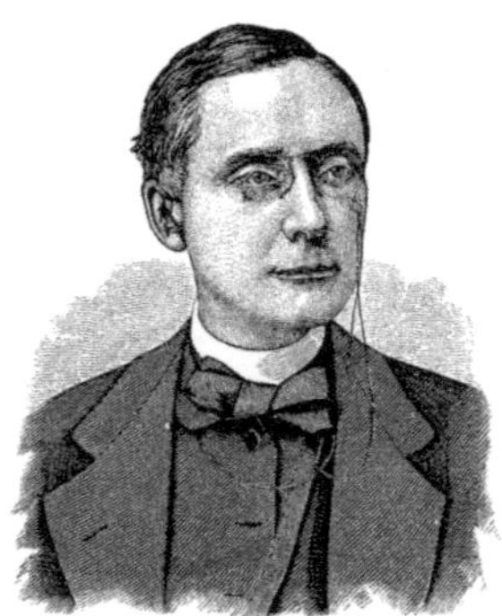

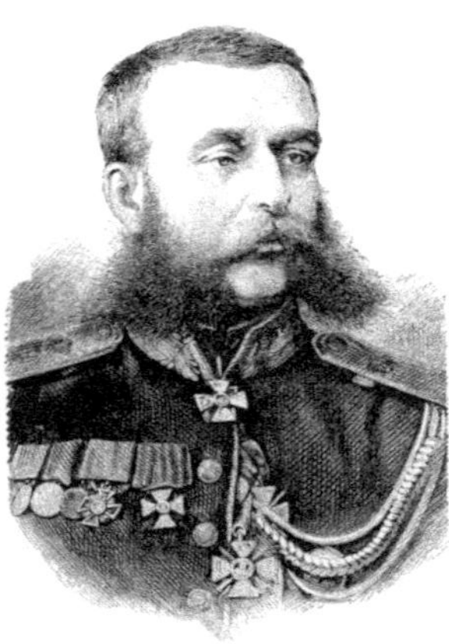

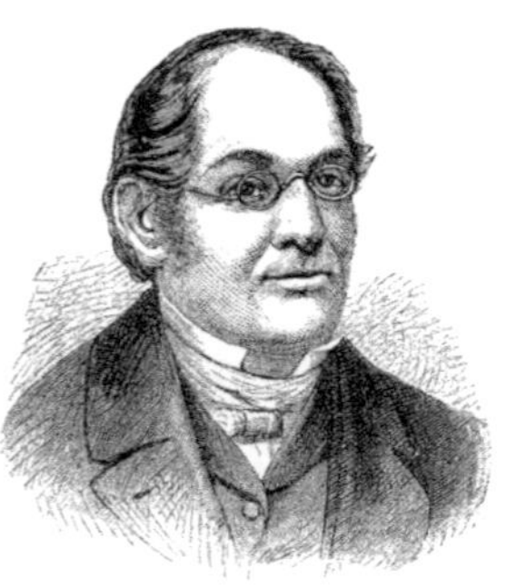

1. John Stuart Mill
2. B. Trentman
3. J.H Bass
4. Napoloeon II, 1865
5. Cyrus W. Field
6. Hon. Charles J. Folger
7. Samuel R. Wells
8. Ralph Waldo Emerson
9. Rev. R. S. Storrs
10. James Russell Lowell
11. Rev. Dr. Morgan Dix
12. Hon. Thaddeus Stevens
13. Gen Ulysses S. Grant
14. Wendell Phillips
15. Rev. Dr. E. S. Porter
16. Jacob M. Howard
17. Rev. Dr. J.A.M Chapman
18. Hon. WM. M. Evarts
19. Edward Eggleston
20. Hon. Frederick Douglas
21. Sir John A. Macdonald
22. Landgrave Thomas Smith II
23. The Most Reverend. John Travers Lewis
24. Eastman Johnson
25. F.E.Spinner
26. Elihu Burritt
27. Henry Bergh
28. Henry W. Longfellow
29. Chas A Zollinger
30. Rev. Dr. John Hall
31. Lawrence B. Stockton
32. Abdul Kerim
33. Abdulaziz, Sultan of the Ottoman Empire
34. General Alimpitch
35. Prince Gorchakov
36. Alexander heir to the Russian throne
37. Bismark
38. Achmed Mukhtar Pasha
39. Svetozar Miletić
40. Edhem Pasha
41. Benjamin Disraeli
42. Eugene Schuyler
43. Redif Pasha
44. Alexander II Czar of Russia
45. General Eduard Totleben
46. Walter Baring
47. General Melikoff
48. Hassan Pasha
49. Luka Petkovitch
50. Safet Pasha
51. General Tchernayeff
52. Gladstone
53. Native American Man Wearing Headdress
54. Grand Duke Michael
55. Hobart Pasha
56. Mahmoud Damad Pasha
57. The Emperor of Austria
58. Nicholas I, Prince of Montenegro
59. Milan, Prince of Serbia
60. Murad V
61. Prince Hasan
62. Suleiman Pasha
63. Osman Pasha
64. The Circassian Chieftain Shamil
65. Lieutenant General Radetsky
66. The Marquis of Sailsbury
67. General Gurko
68. General Skobeleff
69. Grand Duke Nicholas
70. Abdul Hamid II, Sultan of the Ottoman Empire
71. Wilhelm, German Emperor
72. Midhat Pasha
73. A Cossack man, unnamed in source material
74. Prince Charles I of Romania
75. Marquess of Bute
76. A.P Edgerton
77. Andrew Lewis
78. A barefoot Man
79. Prince Charles Maurice de Talleyrand Périgord
80. Vittorio Alfieri
81. Captain Wright
82. John Keats
83. Lucien Bonaparte, brother of Napoleon
84. A Cheese Maker
85. Alvin Adams
86. Émile de Girardin
87. A Boy from Quimperlé
88. Henry Hopkins Sibley
89. Charles Lamb
90. Ralph Waldo Emerson
91. Franklin Benjamin Sanborn
92. Charles Force Deems
93. Count Otto Von Bismark, 1865
94. Olivier Émile Ollivier, 1865
95. Bishop of Bulgaria, 1879
96. Miloš Obrenović
97. Milan Obrenović
98. Dave Mears
99. King William I, 1865
100. Ignaz Moscheles
101. Sigismond Thalberg
102. Charles Robert Leslie
103. Charles William Eliot
104. William Hazlett
105. W M Penn
106. John F Kensett
107. George M Wheeler
108. Matthew Vassar
109. Man Standing Hand in Pocket
110. James Russell Lowell
111. Louis Agassiz
112. William Dean Howells
113. Count D'Orsay
114. General Sherman, 1894
115. General Lyon, 1894
116. James Logan
117. Rev. B. M. Palmer
118. Judge E. North Cullom
119. James F. Casey, Esq
120. W. P. Harper
121. P. F. Herwig, Esq
122. Christian Roselius, Esq
123. Gen. P. G. T. Beauregard
124. WM. S. Pike Esq
125. Judge John A. Campbell
126. Capt. T. P. Leathers
127. Col. J. B. Price
128. WM. H. Bell, ESQ
129. A. S. Badger (Chief of police)
130. Dr. Warren Stone, 1874.
131. Charles Fitzenreiter
132. B. M. Turnbull
133. W.M.P. Kellogg
134. J.M.G Parker
135. I.N Marks
136. B.T Walshe
137. Col S. N. Moody
138. Captain Will McCann
139. Geo. S. Lacey, Esq
140. Hon. P. B. S. Pinchback
141. Joseph Simms, 1891
142. Henry Bergh, 1891
143. Johann Friedrich Blumenbach, 1891
144. Matthew Simpson, 1891
145. Charles Loring Elliot
146. Prince Albert
147. John M. Clayton
148. George Stephenson
149. Judah Touro
150. George Fox

151. William Cullen Byant
152. John A Andrew
153. Owen Jones
154. William Makepeace Thackeray
155. James Gordon Bennett
156. David M Stone
157. Charles A Dana
158. Oswald Ottendorfer
159. Whitelaw Reid
160. Hugh Hastings
161. Andrea Doria
162. George Jones
163. Hippolyte Adolphe Taine
164. Hans Makart
165. Francesco Petrarca
166. Dante Alighieri
167. Peter Paul Reubens
168. Franz Lenbach
169. Jean Francois Millet
170. Gabriel Max
171. Constant Troyon
172. A Trio of Men Outside
173. Man Holding Staff
174. Ludwig Knaus
175. Recling Man
176. Jean Baptiste Carpeaux
177. Man Wearing a Feathered Hat
178. Holman Hunt
179. Alexander Ramsey
180. Colonel Hankins
181. F.H. Cowen
182. Samuel Thomson
183. Arapaho Medicine Man Known as Washington For His Hat
184. Black Coal, an Arapaho Man
185. Arapaho Scout Known as Sharp Nose for his Physical Features and Scouting Ability
186. Arapaho Boy, a Son of Sharp Nose
187. George Combe
188. Sir Michael Costa
189. Prince Napoleon Jerome Bonaparte
190. Otto Goldschmidt
191. Carlos Bonaparte, father of Napoleon
192. Joseph Bonaparte, brother of Napoleon
193. Louis Bonaparte, brother of Napoleon
194. Gesturing Man
195. Joseph Barnby
196. Theo Marzails
197. Edward Lloyd
198. Napoleon IIV
199. Napoleon III
200. Jerome Bonaparte, brother of Napoleon
201. Vincenz Priessnitz
202. Franz Defregger
203. A Trio of Men
204. M. Bonnat
205. Hippolyte Adolphe Taine
206. Vicat Cole
207. Dr Judd
208. Dr Damon
209. John Ericsson
210. Benjamin Tallmadge
211. J.L Williams
212. John Campbel
213. John Hough
214. J.D Nuttman
215. Schuyler Colfax
216. Hon O Bird
217. Joseph K Edgerton
218. O.P Morton
219. P.F. Randall
220. John Lockwood
221. Thomas A Hendricks, 1875.
222. John Roch, 1875.
223. Willard Carpenter
224. Martin L Pierce
225. David Danaldson

226. Samuel Hanna
227. G.W.Robbins
228. H.A. Peed
229. Horace P Biddle
230. H. Bates
231. George W. Wood
232. W.C.Wilson
233. E.T. Cox
234. B.C. Hobbs
235. Chauncy Rose
236. Robert Brackenridge
237. Dr Joseph F Tuttle
238. WM T Ros
239. Nathaniel Hawthorne
240. Giuseppe Mazzini
241. Edgar Allan Poe
242. Alexander Hamilton Stephenson
243. Henry Wadsworth Longfellow
244. Professor Morse
245. Edward Everett
246. Charles Joseph McCurdy
247. William Augustus Muhlenberg
248. Gilbert Stuart
249. Tim Longbow
250. Col. John Trumbull
251. Garrett Allan Walker
252. Horatio Greenough
253. Christian Priest
254. Bismark
255. Hiram Powers
256. Edwin Erle Sparks
257. John Howard Raymond
258. Alexandre Dumas
259. Arsène Houssaye
260. Alexandre Dumas père
261. Prince Alexander Mikhailovich Gorchakov
262. Sir Humphry Davy
263. Jakob Ludwig Felix Mendelssohn Bartholdy
264. Louis Chetlain
265. Jean-Léon Gérôme
266. Henry Barth
267. Jean-Louis-Ernest Meissonier
268. Joshua Coffin
269. M. Léon Bonnat
270. Eugene De Kieffer, 1894
271. Walter Savage Landor
272. William G. Fargo
273. A Man Waking a Boy in a Boat
274. Thomas Faed
275. James Renforth
276. Samuel R. Curtis
277. Lord Fife and Prince Esterházy
278. Lord Londonderry and Kangaroo Cook
279. Two Men
280. Lord Yarmouth
281. Ernesto Camillo Sivori
282. Giuseppe Verdi
283. Giuseppe Mazzini
284. Niccolò Paganini
285. Erasmus Quellinus II
286. Félicien David
287. E.B. Martindale
288. Man Smoking A Cigar
289. Camillo Benso di Cavour
290. C l'anson
291. Framz Snyders
292. Ferdinand De Lesseps
293. William Ellery Channing
294. A Man Stalking a Seal
295. Francis J. Herron
296. James G. Blunt
297. Maj. Gen. Philip E. Sheridan, 1865
298. Truman Seymour
299. A Neopolitan Fisher Boy
300. Karl Theodor Von Piloty

301. Rev. Bishop Wilmer
302. Hon James Lewis
303. Dr. W. N. Mercer
304. Leigh Hunt
305. James Arnold
306. A Player Sent off the Pitch
307. John Keats
308. Laughing Man in Hat
309. Walter Brown
310. Leigh Richmond
311. Otto Von Bismark
312. Thomas Hughes
313. Man Ringing A Bell
314. John H Vincent
315. A Bosnian Man, 1879
316. Man Wearing Suit
317. John Wilkes
318. Smiling Man in Hat
319. Bryan Waller Procter (pseud. Barry Cornwall)
320. Henry David Thoreau
321. Amos Bronson Alcott
322. Charles Devens
323. Leigh Hunt
324. Robert Browning
325. Theophilus Parsons
326. James W Hale
327. Edmond About
328. Josiah R. Snelling
329. Man in Hat in Profile
330. Man in Top Hat
331. Two Men Standing
332. Man Sitting on Chair
333. Wolfgang Amadeus Mozart
334. William Wordsworth
335. Daniel Webster
336. Louis Veuillot
337. S.T Coleridge
338. Paul de Cassagnac
339. Cornelius Conway Felton
340. Henry Wells
341. Gustavus Adolphus
342. John Singleton Copley
343. Thomas Sully
344. Professor Samuel Lockwood
345. Thomas Cole
346. Rembrandt Peale
347. Oliver Wendell Holmes Jr.
348. Massimo d'Azeglio
349. A Man with a Head for Money
350. Alexander Anderson
351. John Todd
352. Alexandre Cabanel
353. George H Boughton
354. Sir Walter Scott
355. Morrison Remick "Mott" Waite
356. Jacob F. Studebaker
357. Elisha G. English
358. Charles Louder
359. A.S. Evans
360. Luigi Palma di Cesnola
361. Osman Baicha, 1879
362. Abdul Hamid, 1879
363. Oliver Wolcott
364. James Gould
365. Tapping Reeve
366. Amerigo Vespucci
367. William Wood

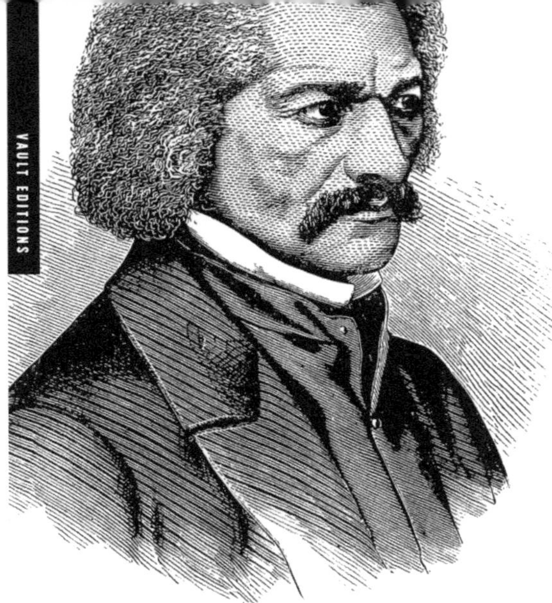

LEARN MORE

At Vault Editions, our mission is to create the world's most diverse and comprehensive collection of image archives available for artists, designers and curious minds. If you have enjoyed this book, you can find more of our titles available at vaulteditions.com.

REVIEW THIS BOOK

As a small, family-owned independent publisher, reviews help spread the word about our work. We would be incredibly grateful if you could leave an honest review of this title wherever you purchased this book.

JOIN OUR COMMUNITY

Are you a creative and curious individual? If so, you will love our community on Instagram. Every day we share bizarre and beautiful artwork ranging from 17th and 18th-century natural history and scientific illustration, to mythical beasts, ornamental designs, anatomical illustration and more. Join our community of 100K+ people today— search @vault_editions on Instagram.

DOWNLOAD YOUR FILES

STEP ONE

Enter the following web address in your web browser on a desktop computer.

www.vaulteditions.com/pages/pam

STEP TWO

Enter the following unique password to access the download page.

pam23876288sxda

STEP THREE

Follow the prompts to access your high-resolution files.

TECHNICAL ASSISTANCE

For all technical assistance, please email: info@vaulteditions.com

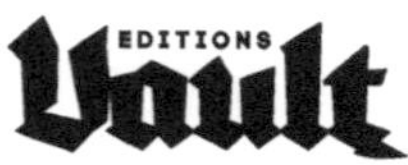

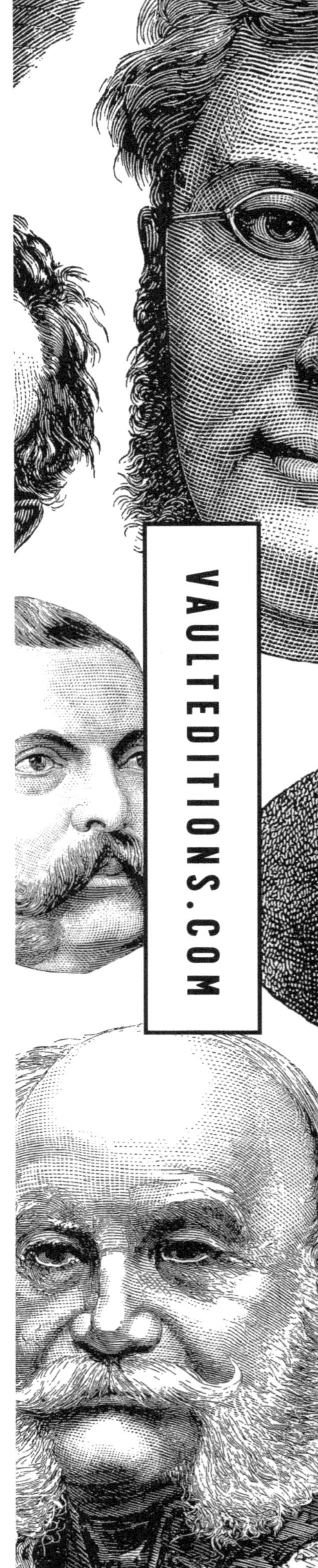